⚅ INSIGHT **C I T Y G U I D E**

BaNGKOK

Discovery
CHANNEL

APA PUBLICATIONS   **L**
Part of the Langenscheidt Publishing Group

✱ INSIGHT GUIDES
BanGKOK

Editor
Francis Dorai
Editorial Director
Brian Bell
Art Director
Klaus Geisler
Picture Editor
Hilary Genin
Cartography Editor
Zoë Goodwin
Desktop Assistant
Carol Low
Production
Kenneth Chan

Distribution

UK & Ireland
GeoCenter International Ltd
The Viables Centre, Harrow Way
Basingstoke, Hants RG22 4BJ
Fax: (44) 1256 817988

United States
Langenscheidt Publishers, Inc.
36–36 33rd Street, 4th Floor
Long Island City, NY 11106
Fax: (1) 718 784 0640

Australia
Universal Publishers
1 Waterloo Road
Macquarie Park, NSW 2113
Fax: (61) 2 9888 9074

New Zealand
Hema Maps New Zealand Ltd (HNZ)
Unit D, 24 Ra ORA Drive
East Tamaki, Auckland
Fax: (64) 9 273 6479

Worldwide
**Apa Publications GmbH & Co.
Verlag KG (Singapore branch)**
38 Joo Koon Road, Singapore 628990
Tel: (65) 6865 1600. Fax: (65) 6861 6438

Printing

Insight Print Services (Pte) Ltd
38 Joo Koon Road, Singapore 628990
Tel: (65) 6865 1600. Fax: (65) 6861 6438

©2006 Apa Publications GmbH & Co.
Verlag KG (Singapore branch)
All Rights Reserved

First Edition 1988
Fourth Edition 2005 (Reprinted 2006)

ABOUT THIS BOOK

The first Insight Guide pioneered the use of creative full-colour photography in travel guides in 1970. Since then, we have expanded our range to cater for our readers' need not only for reliable information about their chosen destination but also for a real understanding of that destination. Now, when the Internet can supply inexhaustible – but not always reliable – facts, our books marry text and pictures to provide that much more elusive quality: knowledge. To achieve this, they rely heavily on the authority of locally based writers and photographers.

How to use this book

The book is carefully structured to convey an understanding of the city:
◆ The Best of Bangkok section at the front helps you to prioritise what you want to see: top family attractions, the most interesting walks, the best markets and malls, hot bars and clubs, as well as uniquely Bangkok attractions and money-saving tips.
◆ To understand Bangkok today, you need to know both about its past as well as what makes the city tick today. The first section covers the city's history and culture in lively, authoritative essays written by specialist Bangkok-based writers.
◆ The main Places section provides a full run-down of all the attractions worth seeing. The main places of interest are coordinated by number with full-colour maps.
◆ A list of recommended restaurants is included at the end of each chapter in the Places section. The best of these are also described and plotted on the pull-out restau-

tical format. Assisting him was British-born but Bangkok-based writer and artist **Steven Pettifor**. Contemporary art and travel are subjects close to his heart, and he has written on both for local and international publications. Pettifor was responsible for revising and updating all the Places chapters and Travel Tips, plus the chapter on Cultural Arts. Bangkok-bred freelance writer **Sarah Rooney** was equally qualified to write the People and Shopping chapters, having lived in Bangkok since childhood.

Bangkok After Dark was written by **Howard Richardson**, the former editor of *Metro*, Bangkok's first (and some say best) listings magazine. Richardson also revised the Cuisine chapter and wrote all the restaurant reviews in this guide. Spas and Wellness Centres was the work of **Chami Jotisalikorn**, a Thai spa consultant who moonlights as a lifestyle and features writer. Finally, condensing Bangkok's History into a riveting read was Chiangmai-based specialist writer **Dr Andrew Forbes**.

Among the talented photographers whose images bring Bangkok to life are **Jason Lang** (whose work has been featured in *Wallpaper* and *Travel & Leisure*) and **Marcus Wilson-Smith**.

Past writers whose work remains in condensed form in this edition include: **Steve van Beek, Kanokchan Patanapichai, Joe Feinstein, Nancy Grace, Robert Halliday, Jerry Dillon, Robert Burrows, Frank Green, Neil Kelly, Gayle Miller, Priyanandana Rangsit, John Stirling** and **Kultida Wongsawatdichart**.

CONTACTING THE EDITORS

We would appreciate it if readers would alert us to errors or outdated information by writing to:

Insight Guides, P.O. Box 7910, London SE1 1WE, England. Fax: (44) 20 7403 0290. insight@apaguide.co.uk

NO part of this book may be reproduced, stored in a retrieval system or transmitted in any form or means electronic, mechanical, photocopying, recording or otherwise, without prior written permission of *Apa Publications.* Brief text quotations with use of photographs are exempted for book review purposes only. Information has been obtained from sources believed to be reliable, but its accuracy and completeness, and the opinions based thereon, are not guaranteed.

www.insightguides.com
In North America:
www.insighttravelguides.com

rant map provided with this guide.
◆ Photo features illustrate various facets of the city, from the Jim Thompson's House and the National Museum to temple architecture.
◆ Photographs throughout the book are chosen not only to illustrate geography and architecture but also to convey the different moods of the city and the pulse of its people.
◆ The Travel Tips section includes all the practical information you'll need, divided into four key sections: transport, accommodation, activities and an A–Z listing of practical tips.
◆ A detailed street atlas and index is included at the back of the book.

The contributors

This new edition was supervised by Insight's Singapore-based managing editor, **Francis Dorai**, who restructured the book into its current prac-

CONTENTS

Maps

Map Legend **241**
Street Atlas **242–52**

Travel Tips

TRANSPORT

ACCOMMODATION

ACTIVITIES

A–Z: PRACTICAL INFORMATION

LANGUAGE

FURTHER READING

THE BEST OF BANGKOK

Setting priorities, saving money, unique attractions...
here, at a glance, are our recommendations, plus some
tips and tricks even Bangkokians won't always know

BANGKOK FOR FAMILIES

These attractions are popular with children,
though not all will suit every age group.

- **Ancient City**. See Thailand in a nutshell. Replicas of its most famous sights, some full-size, others scaled down, are strewn in this large open-air park. *See page 183*.
- **Crocodile Farm & Zoo**. Families shriek as handlers wrestle with large crocodiles and stick their heads between the snapping jaws of these monstrous reptiles. *See page 184*.
- **Dream World**. Disney World it isn't but this theme park, located in Bangkok's outskirts, has sufficiently thrilling rides and rollercoasters to keep the young ones happy. *See page 159*.
- **Dusit Zoo**. This is not Asia's best zoo but it still attracts droves of Thai families on weekends. *See page 117*.
- **Rose Garden Country Resort**. Traditional dancers, Thai boxing and other folk culture and crafts are packaged and performed in a garden setting outside Bangkok. *See page 167*.
- **Samphran Elephant Ground**. Learn about the pachyderm's role in Thailand, with fun elephant rides and re-enactments of battles. *See page 168*.

ONLY IN BANGKOK

- **Canal Cruising**. Hop aboard a longtail boat and glide along canals (*khlong*) for a slice of Bangkok's past. *See page 208*.
- **Extreme Makeover**. On holiday, why not have a tummy tuck, nose-job, or even a gender reassignment? Bangkok is a world hub for medical tourism with 5-star care at bargain prices. *See page 233*.
- **Jumbo Queen**. See a charitable beauty pageant open to only weight-challenged women. *See page 168*.
- **Lady Boy Cabaret**. Is she or isn't she, a woman that is. Vegas-style shows by elaborately costumed transvestite performers. *See pages 66 and 222*.
- **Motorcycle Taxis**. Fast and furious, these waistcoat-wearing madmen weave through the city's gridlock with knee-scraping accuracy. Helmets optional, courage necessary. *See page 207*.
- **Thai Boxing**. Punishing and brutal, this ancient martial art is more than just sport, with drinking and gambling on the sidelines. *See page 227*.
- **Tuk-Tuk**. Reduced to a tourist curiosity, these noisy three-wheelers should be experienced at least once. *See page 207*.

ABOVE: Dream World bumper car ride.
TOP RIGHT: frenetic Thai boxing, or *muay thai*. **RIGHT:** tuk-tuk.

BEST WALKS

- **Banglamphu**. A district of old shophouses, grand mansions, remnants of the old city wall and a riverbank park. *See page 113*.
- **Chinatown**. This is Bangkok at its visceral

best: narrow lanes awash with local colour and mercantile bustle. *See page 121*.
- **Lumphini Park**. The city's favourite green lung buzzes to life at dawn and dusk with both exercise fiends and those content to just watch them. *See page 134*.
- **Rattanakosin**. The capital's historic heart brims with architectural grandeur. Royal palaces and devotional tributes stand tall in this old neighbourhood. *See page 81*.
- **Thonburi**. Experience the slower, calmer side of the city with its network of canals and vignettes of riverine life. *See page 99*.

LEFT: *yaksha* demon statue stands guard at Wat Phra Kaew.
ABOVE: Chatuchak – where shopping fantasies come alive.

BEST FESTIVALS AND EVENTS

- **Bangkok Film Festival**. A chance to view acclaimed local- and foreign-produced flicks and mingle with stars at the film screenings. Jan/Feb. *www.bangkokfilm.org.*
- **Chinese New Year**. Get into the action in Chinatown where loud firecrackers, boisterous lion and dragon dances and festival foods herald in the start of the new year for Bangkok's Chinese. Jan/Feb. *See page 227*.
- **King's Birthday**. Known as Thailand's Father's Day, key streets in Bangkok are magically lit up in the

colours of the national flag while fireworks pierce the night sky. 5 Dec. *See page 228*.
- **Loy Krathong**. Expect a visual treat as Bangkokians honour water spirits by lighting candles and incense and setting them afloat on tiny baskets along the city's waterways. Nov full moon day. *See page 228*.
- **Songkran**. Pack water pistols (along with a sense of humour) for a three-day soaking. The Thai Lunar New Year is the nation's largest and wettest celebration. 13–15 Apr. *See page 227*.

BEST MARKETS

- **Chatuchak Weekend Market**. The mother of all markets, pulling in nearly half a million people every weekend. An unbeatable shopping experience; it has it all and then some. *See page 158*.
- **Damnoen Saduak Floating Market**. This century-old market has become a bit of of a circus, with tourists clambering to photograph fruit-laden boats paddled by women in straw hats.

Still, it's worth seeking out. *See page 171*.
- **Pak Khlong Talad**. A 24-hour riot of colour and fragrance; this is where Bangkok gets all its floral garlands for temple offerings. *See page 124*.
- **Patpong Night Market**. Surrounded by sleaze and neon, the location is as much the attraction as the piles of counterfeit watches, bags, clothes and general tourist tat. *See page 144*.

BELOW: delicate baskets with lighted candles and incense are set afloat on Bangkok's waterways at Songkran.

BEST BARS & CLUBS

- **Bed Supperclub**. This futuristic oval pod with white-on-white furnishings is Bangkok's poseur central. Recline on beds at this restaurant-club as DJs entertain. *See pages 155 and 220.*
- **Distil**. This 64th-floor wine bar with heart-stopping views rises taller than any of the city's other fresh-faced nightspots. Part of State Tower's opulent Dome. *See page 221.*
- **Hu'u**. Chic Singapore import that defines contemporary cool with its cocktail lounge, art gallery and restaurant. Top DJs spin here. *See page 221.*
- **Mystique**. A three-floor grotto to hedonism, decked out in kitsch retro chic, complete with a large fish tank and a lounge clad in shocking purple. *See page 220.*
- **Q Bar**. Modelled after a New York lounge bar, this dark and seductive two-floored venue plays some of the hippest dance tracks. *See page 220.*
- **Tapas**. Located at Silom Soi 4's party strip, sit outside to ogle passers-by or head inside for the funkiest DJ-spun house grooves. *See page 220.*

ABOVE: Bed Supperclub, which dishes out great food and even better music, is where the city's hip hang out.

BEST SHOPPING EXPERIENCES

- **Emporium**. Cash-rich and beautiful people parade at this glitzy mall and connecting department store filled with designer brands. Good range of eateries too. *See pages 153 and 223.*
- **MBK & Siam Square**. This monster mall is just across the road from one of the city's last surviving low-rise street shopping enclaves. Pimply adolescents outnumber sensible adults here. *See pages 131 and 223.*
- **Panthip Plaza**. Tech-geeks should make a beeline for Bangkok's mecca for computer gadgetry. Stocks both legitimate hard and software as well as pirated games, software, DVDs and VCDs. *See pages 135 and 223.*
- **Suan Lum Night Bazaar**. More sanitised, but also more easily navigable (and infinitely cooler) alternative to Chatuchak. The sprawling bazaar stocks souvenirs, clothing, handicrafts, antiques and home decor. *See page 134.*
- **Thanon Khao San**. Apart from bars and cafés, this backpacker magnet is filled with cheap travel agents and internet cafés, along with hair-braiding, tattooing and body-piercing services. *See pages 113 and 223.*

RIGHT: Suan Lum Night Bazaar.
BELOW: Distil bar serves up drinks and stunning views from its 64th-floor perch at State Tower building.

BEST SPAS & MASSAGES

famous no-frills traditional massage school has blind masseuses giving vigorous rubdowns for next to nothing. *See page 93.*

- **Sareerarom Tropical Spa**. Tucked away in Sukhumvit, this spa is contemporary Asian in mood, with pampering treatments, holistic health and an organic café. *See page 70.*

LEFT AND ABOVE: yoga and a Thai herbal compress treatment at Devarana spa. **BELOW:** dancer at Silom Village.

- **Devarana**. Located at the luxury Dusit Thani hotel, ethereal Devarana is a million miles away from the frenetic city. Calming Zen mood with private treatment suites and a range of therapies that will ease away urban strain. *See page 70.*
- **The Oriental Spa**. In the historic Oriental, this atmospheric luxury spa sits in a century-old teakwood house on the banks of the Chao Phraya River. *See page 70.*
- **Wat Pho**. In the city's oldest temple, this

BEST CULTURAL DINING

- **Manohra**. A classic Thai feast aboard an antique teak rice barge. No chance of getting seasick as the barge leisurely cruises down the Chao Phraya River. *See page 228.*
- **Loy Nava**. Another wooden barge dinner cruise along the Chao Phraya river, helmed by an informed expat captain and with Thai dancing and traditional music on board. *See page 228.*

- **Sala Rim Nam**. At the Oriental's riverside restaurant, sit around low tables on cushions and feast on Thai food while watching a condensed history of Thai dance and drama. *See page 219.*
- **Ruen Thep Room**. Ignore the kitsch ambience of Silom Village and enjoy its value-for-money Thai dinner with classical dance and drama *See page 218.*

MONEY-SAVING TIPS

Bargaining for Best Deals While department stores have fixed prices, it's common to bargain at markets and at some small shops. If a shopowner offers to give the "best price", then negotiations are thrown open *(see text box on page 57)*. Remember to keep a sense of humour while bargaining.

Counterfeit Goods Even the most morally upright go weak in the knees when faced with the onslaught of quality knock-offs at Bangkok's markets, from watches and bags to clothing. If

you succumb, remember: you get what you pay for *(see text box on page 59)*.

Hit the Happy Hour Afternoon and early evening drinking isn't part of the Bangkok scene, so to draw customers many bars offer incredible happy hour deals – like cheap drinks from noon till 9pm or two-drinks-for-one promos.

Keep your Ticket Hold onto your Grand Palace/Wat Phra Kaew entry ticket as it also gets you into most of the Dusit Park sites (like Vimanmek Mansion and Abhisek Dusit Throne Hall, to name a few) for free.

No Invite, No Matter Check the daily newspapers and monthly listings magazines for upcoming social events, art openings and promo parties. The city's freeloaders always turn up for free buffets, drinks and entertainment. It's a great way to rub shoulders with the city's elite and fill up for free.

VAT Refunds Before making significant purchases, ask if the shop offers VAT refunds (7 percent) to tourists. Refunds *(see page 223)* can be claimed on single items of B2,000 or more, as long as your overall shopping exceeds B5,000. Allow time at the airport to process claims.

WHITE HOT BANGKOK

Sprawling and steamy Bangkok may have reinvented itself into an outpost of the hip, but its current guise is yet another stage in a city that is forever shifting, and always adapting to trends and outside influences

Observing the city today from the air-conditioned comfort of the elevated Skytrain, the Bangkok of the 1990s – ridden with choking smog, gridlocked traffic, perennial construction and persistent touts – recedes into distant memory. Most of the gleaming glass and steel towers are in place, the infamous traffic snarls are less pervasive thanks to the Skytrain and a gleaming new underground metro line, and the pollution is noticeably less smothering. The touts at Patpong are still around (some things don't change) and the steamy heat still socks you in the face if you visit in muggy April. But with the economy back on track and a firm focus on the future, Bangkok is fast making a name for itself as Asia's new metropolis of cool.

With hip hotels like the Metropolitan and Sukhothai and a clutch of uber-cool nightlife spots led by the white hot Bed Supperclub and modish Q Bar, Bangkok is a hot new destination of the 21st century. The dining scene, too, hasn't lagged far behind. Stylishly minimalist coffee clubs like Greyhound have become *de rigueur* with the city's fashionable set, and wait till you try Thai food within the rarefied atmosphere of Mahanaga, which mixes North African, Thai and Indian design accents to startling effects.

The dreadlocked backpacker crowd still gathers at Thanon Khao San with its hodge-podge jumble of cheap eateries and tawdry souvenir shops, and sleazy male tourists still make a beeline for the raunchy sex clubs of Patpong and Nana Plaza, but these scenes are oh so last century. With its feet set firmly in the present, Bangkok hardly qualifies as an Asian backwater. The shopping, too, has gone up a notch in the design quotient. The traditional stuff that Thai artisans are so famous for are still there – silver jewellery, tribal handicrafts, pottery and the like – but young Thai designers are fast making a name for themselves with bold and contemporary designs in clothing and fashion, accessories, furniture and home decor.

Thankfully, Bangkok hasn't become too painfully hip. Many of the traditional markers are still there: the golden spires of Buddhist temples, saffron-robed monks with arms outstretched at dawn for offerings, and the wafting smells of food hawked by streetside stalls. The shift to urban life has changed much of Bangkok's sensibilities, but it's a rare Thai who doesn't seek out *sanuk* (or fun), whether dining at a chic French restaurant or huddled around a pavement table piled with Singha beer and Thai street food. ❏

PRECEDING PAGES: the Wat Phra Kaew and Grand Palace complex all aglow at night; lotus buds for sale at Pak Khlong Talad flower market. **LEFT:** Thai boxer poised for action.

A CITY OF ANGELS

**Whatever you call it, Bangkok or Krung Thep (City of Angels),
the thriving metropolis that dominates Thailand is more
than 30 times larger than any other city in the kingdom.
Yet, just three centuries ago, it was little more than
a sleepy riverside village of wild plum trees**

Bangkok's history as a town began in the 16th century when a short canal was dug across a loop of the Chao Phraya River to cut the distance between the sea and the Siamese capital at Ayutthaya. Over the years, monsoon floods scoured the banks of the canal until it widened to become the main course of the river. On its banks rose two towns – originally trading posts along the river route to Ayutthaya 85 km (55 miles) north – Thonburi on the west and, on the east, Bangkok. At the time, Bangkok was little more than a village (*bang*) in an orchard of wild plum trees (*kok*). Hence, the town's name, Bangkok, which translates as "village of the wild plum".

Ayutthaya prospered as the capital of Siam (the name of old Thailand) for more than four centuries, but in 1767 it was captured by the Burmese after a 14-month siege. The Burmese killed, looted and set fire to the whole city, plundering Ayutthaya's many rich temples and melting down all the gold from images of the Buddha. Members of the royal family, along with some 90,000 captives and the accumulated booty, were removed to Burma.

Despite their overwhelming victory, the Burmese didn't retain control of Siam for long. A young general named Phya Taksin gathered a small band of followers during the final Burmese siege of the Thai capital. He and his comrades broke through the Burmese encirclement and escaped to the southeast coast. There, Taksin assembled an army and a

THE LONGEST PLACE NAME EVER

In 1782, King Rama I decided the name Bangkok was insufficiently noble for a royal city so he renamed it *Krungthep mahanakhon amonrattanakosin mahintra ayutthaya mahadilok popnopparat ratchathani burirom udomratchaniwet mahasathan amonpiman avatansathit sakkathattiya visnukamprasit.* In English this means: "Great City of Angels, City of Immortals, Magnificent Jewelled City of the God Indra, Seat of the King of Ayutthaya, City of Gleaming Temples, City of the King's Most Excellent Palace and Dominions, Home of Vishnu and All the Gods". Most Thais, however, refer to Bangkok by just two syllables, Krung Thep, or "City of Angels", in everyday speech.

LEFT: mural of the Grand Palace in Bangkok.
RIGHT: European impression of 17th-century Ayutthaya.

A ROYAL EXECUTION

After his abdication Taksin was executed in the traditional royal manner – with a blow to the neck by a sandalwood club concealed within a velvet bag.

navy. Only seven months after the fall of Ayutthaya, Taksin's forces returned to the capital and expelled the Burmese occupiers.

Move to Thonburi

Taksin had barely spent a night at Ayutthaya when he decided to transfer the site of his capital to Thonburi. Here he ruled until 1782. In the last years of his reign, he relied heavily on

two trusted generals, the brothers Chao Phya Chakri and Chao Phya Surasi, who were given absolute command in their military campaigns. Meanwhile at Thonburi, Taksin's personality underwent a slow metamorphosis, from strong and just to cruel and unpredictable. When a revolt broke out in 1782, Taksin abdicated and entered a monastery, but died shortly thereafter *(see text box above)*.

Start of the Chakri Dynasty

The official who engineered the revolt offered the throne to Chao Phya Chakri on his return from Cambodia. General Chakri assumed the kingship on 6 April – a date still commemorated as Chakri Day – thereby establishing the still reigning Chakri dynasty. On assuming the throne, Chakri took the name of Ramathibodi. Later known as Rama I, he ruled from 1782 until 1809. His first action as king was to transfer his capital from Thonburi to Bangkok.

Rama I was an ambitious man eager to re-establish the Thai kingdom as a dominant civilisation. He ordered the digging of a canal across a neck of land on the Bangkok side, creating an island and an inner city. Rama I envisioned this artificial island as the core of his new capital. Within its rim, he would concentrate the principal components of the Thai nation: religion, monarchy and administration.

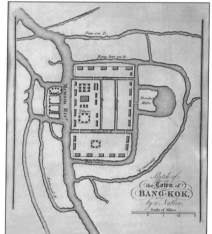

To underscore his recognition of the power of the country's principal Buddha image, he called this island Rattanakosin *(see page 81)* or the "Resting Place of the Emerald Buddha".

To dedicate the area solely to statecraft and religion, he formally requested that the Chinese living there move to an area to the southeast. This new district, Sampeng *(see page 121)*, soon sprouted thriving shops and busy streets, becoming the commercial heart of the city in what is now known as Chinatown.

Rama I then turned his attention to constructing the royal island's principal buildings. First was a home for the Emerald Buddha, the most sacred image in the realm, which, until then, had been resting in a temple in Thonburi. Two years later, in 1784, Wat Phra Kaew was completed. A palace was next on his agenda; the Grand Palace was more than a home, it contained buildings for receiving royal visitors and debating matters of state. The last building to be constructed, the Chakri Maha Prasat, was not erected until late in the 19th century. Until 1946, the Grand Palace was home to Thailand's kings. The palace grounds also contain Wat Pho, the National Museum, prestigious Thammasat University, the National Theatre, and various government offices.

Rama II and Rama III

Rama I's successors, Rama II and Rama III, completed both the consolidation of the Siamese kingdom and the revival of Ayutthaya's arts and culture. If Rama I laid the foundations of Bangkok, it was Rama II who instilled it with the spirit of the past. Best remembered as an artist, Rama II (ruled 1809–24), the second ruler of the Chakri dynasty, was responsible for building and repairing numerous Bangkok monasteries. His most famous construction was Wat Arun *(see page 101)*, the Temple of Dawn, which was later enlarged to its present height by Rama IV. He is also said to have carved the great doors of Wat Suthat, throwing away the chisels so his work could never be replicated.

Rama II reopened relations with the West, which had been suspended since the time of former King Narai, and allowed the Portuguese to open the first Western embassy in Bangkok. Rama III (ruled 1824–51) continued to open Siam's doors to foreigners. A pious Buddhist, Rama III was considered to be "austere and reactionary" by some Europeans. But he encouraged American missionaries to introduce Western medicine, such as smallpox vaccinations, to Siam.

Mongkut (Rama IV)

With the help of Hollywood, Rama IV (ruled 1851–68) became the most famous king of Siam. More commonly known as King Mongkut, he was portrayed by Yul Brynner in

The King and I as a frivolous, bald-headed despot – but nothing could have been further from the truth. He was the first Thai king to understand Western culture and technology, and his reign has been described as the bridge spanning the new and the old.

The younger brother of Rama III, King Mongkut spent 27 years as a Buddhist monk prior to his accession to the throne. This gave him a unique opportunity to roam as a commoner among the populace. He learned to read Buddhist scriptures in the Pali language; missionaries taught him Latin and English. As a monk, Mongkut delved into many subjects: history, geography and the sciences, but he

had a particular passion for astronomy. Mongkut instituted a policy of modernisation, and England was the first European country to benefit from this, when an 1855 treaty granted extraterritorial privileges, a duty of only 3 percent on imports, and permission to import Indian opium duty-free. Other Western nations followed suit with similar treaties. When Mongkut lifted the state monopoly on rice, it rapidly became Siam's leading export.

In 1863, Mongkut built Bangkok's first paved road – Thanon Charoen Krung (prosperous city) or, as it was known to foreigners, New Road. This 6-km (4-mile) long street, running from the Grand Palace southeast

FAR LEFT: Bangkok canal in the late 19th century.
LEFT: early map of Bangkok's waterways.
RIGHT: artist impression of King Mongkut (Rama IV).

along the river, was lined with shops and houses. He also introduced new technology to encourage commerce. The foreign community moved into the areas opened by the construction of New Road. They built their homes in the area where the Oriental Hotel now stands, and along Thanon Silom and Thanon Sathorn, both rural retreats at the time.

Chulalongkorn (Rama V)

Mongkut's son, Chulalongkorn (Rama V), was only 15 when he ascended the throne in 1868. The farsighted Chulalongkorn immediately revolutionised his court by ending the ancient custom of prostration, and by allowing

officials to sit on chairs during royal audiences. Chulalongkorn's reign was truly revolutionary When he assumed power, Siam had no schools, and few roads, railways, hospitals or a well-equipped military force. He brought in foreign advisors and sent his sons and other young men to be educated abroad. He also founded a palace school for children of the aristocracy, following this with other schools and vocational centres. During Chulalongkorn's reign, he abolished the last vestiges of slavery and, in 1884, introduced electric lighting. He hired Danish engineers to build an electric tram system 10 years before the one in Copenhagen was completed. He encouraged the import of automobiles about the same time they began appearing on American streets.

Chulalongkorn changed the face of Bangkok. By 1900, the city was growing rapidly eastward. In the Dusit area, he built a palace, the Vimanmek Mansion *(see page 115)* and constructed roads to link it with the Grand Palace. Other noble families followed, building elegant mansions. In the same area, he constructed Wat Benjamabophit *(see page 117)*, the last major Buddhist temple built in Bangkok.

In the area of foreign relations, however, Chulalongkorn had to compromise and give up parts of his kingdom in order to protect Siam from foreign colonisation. When France conquered Annam in 1883 and Britain annexed Upper Burma in 1886, Siam found itself sandwiched between two rival expansionist powers. Siam was forced to surrender to France its claims to Laos and western Cambodia. Similarly, certain Malay Peninsula territories were ceded to Britain in exchange for renunciation of British extraterritorial rights in Siam. By the end of Chulalongkorn's reign, Siam had given up sizeable tracts of fringe territory. But that was a small price for maintaining the country's peace and independence. Unlike its neighbours, Siam has never been under colonial rule.

BANGKOK'S PIG SHRINE

Close by Wat Ratchabophit in downtown Bangkok is an unusual shrine in the likeness of a golden pig. Dedicated to Queen Saowapha (1864–1919), the chief consort of King Chulalongkorn, the "pig shrine" is also an early monument to the women's movement in Thailand. Incidentally, Saowapha was born in the Chinese zodiacal Year of the Pig. In 1897, Queen Saowapha founded a college of midwifery in Bangkok. She also founded the Thai Red Cross Society, built schools for girls in Bangkok and in the provinces. Her court was recognised as a centre for fine arts; young girls attached to the Siamese court attained the equivalent of a university education.

Vajiravudh (Rama VI)

King Chulalongkorn's successor, his son Vajiravudh, started his reign (1910–25) with a lavish coronation. He was educated at Oxford and was thoroughly anglicised, and his Western-inspired reforms aimed at modernising Siam had a profound effect on modern Thai society.

One of the first changes that Vajiravudh

instituted was a 1913 edict which demanded that his subjects adopt surnames. In the absence of a clan or caste system, genealogy was virtually unheard of in Siam at that time. Previously, Thais had used first names, a practice that the king considered uncivilised. The law generated much initial bewilderment, especially in rural areas, and Vajiravudh personally coined patronymics for hundreds of families. To simplify his forebears' lengthy titles, he invented the Chakri dynastic name, Rama, to be followed by the proper reign number. He started with himself, as Rama VI.

As Thai standards of beauty did not conform to Western ideals of femininity, women were

autocratic and lacking in coordination. His extravagance soon emptied the funds built up by Chulalongkorn; near the end of Vajiravudh's reign, the national treasury had to meet the deficits caused by his personal expenses.

The king married late. His only daughter was born one day before he died in 1925. He was succeeded by his youngest brother, Prajadhipok, who inherited the problems created by his brother's brilliant but controversial reign.

Prajadhipok (Rama VII)

Prajadhipok's prudent economic policies, combined with the increased revenue from foreign trade, amply paid off for the kingdom.

encouraged to keep their hair long instead of having it close-cropped, and to replace their *dhoti*, or wide-legged Thai trousers, with the *panung*, a Thai-style sarong. Primary education was made compulsory throughout the kingdom; Chulalongkorn University, the first in Siam, was founded, and schools for both sexes flourished during Vajiravudh's reign.

Vajiravudh preferred individual ministerial consultations to summoning his appointed cabinet. His regime was therefore criticised as

LEFT: Chulalongkorn (Rama V) with his son Vajiravudh.
ABOVE: procession of royal barges along Chao Phraya River at Prajadhipok's (Rama VII) 1925 coronation.

In the early years of his reign, communications were improved by the advent of a wireless service, and the Don Muang Airport began to operate as an international air centre. It was also during the course of his reign that Siam saw the establishment of the Fine Arts Department, the National Library and the National Museum, institutions that continue today as important preservers of Thai culture.

The worldwide economic crisis of 1931 affected Siam's rice export and the government was forced to cut the salaries of junior personnel, and retrench officers in the armed services. Discontent brewed among army officials and bureaucrats. In 1932, a coup d'état ended absolute rule by Thai monarchs. The coup was staged by the People's Party, a military and civilian group masterminded by foreign-educated Thais. The chief ideologist was Pridi Panomyong, a young lawyer trained in France. On the military side, Capt. Luang Phibulsongkhram (Pibul) was responsible for gaining the support of important army colonels.

With only a few tanks, the 70 conspirators sparked off the "revolution" by occupying strategic areas and holding the senior princes hostage. Other army officers stood by as the public watched. At the time, Prajadhipok was in Hua Hin, a royal retreat to the south. Perceiving he had little choice and to avoid bloodshed, he agreed to accept a provisional constitution by which he continued to reign.

The power of Pibul and the army was further strengthened in October 1933 by the decisive defeat of a rebellion led by Prince Boworadet, who had been the war minister under King Prajadhipok. The king had no part in the rebellion, but had become increasingly dismayed by quarrels within the new government. He moved to England in 1934 and abdicated in 1935. Ananda Mahidol (Rama VIII), a 10-year-old half-nephew, agreed to take the throne, but remained in Switzerland to complete his schooling.

After a series of crises and an election in 1938, Pibul became prime minister. His rule,

FROM SIAM TO THAILAND

The man partly responsible for the end of Thailand's centuries-old absolute monarchy, Luang Phibulsongkhram, or Pibul, tried to instil a sense of mass nationalism in the Thais when he was elected PM in 1938. With tight control over the media and a creative propaganda department, Pibul whipped up sentiment against the Chinese. Chinese immigration was restricted, Chinese workers were barred from certain jobs, and state enterprises were set up to compete in Chinese-dominated industries. By changing the country's name from Siam to Thailand in 1939, Pibul intended to emphasise that it belonged to Thai ethnic groups and not to the Chinese.

however, grew more authoritarian. While some Thai officers favoured the model of the Japanese military regime, Pibul admired – and sought to emulate – Hitler and Mussolini. Borrowing many ideas from European fascism, he attempted to instil a sense of mass nationalism in the Thais *(see text box, left)*.

Post World War II

On 7 December 1941, the Japanese bombed Pearl Harbor and launched invasions throughout Southeast Asia. Thailand was invaded at nine points. Despite a decade of military build-up, resistance lasted less than a day. Pibul acceded to Japan's request for "passage rights", but Thailand was allowed to retain its army and political administration.

By 1944, Thailand's initial enthusiasm for its Japanese partners had evaporated. The country faced runaway inflation, food shortages, rationing and black markets. The assembly forced Pibul out from office.

Following World War II, Bangkok began to develop its economy along the lines of European countries, with new industries, firm administration and the first of many five-year plans. Bangkok began to change dramatically in response to the new prosperity. The last of the major canals were filled in to make roadways. The city began its big push to the east, as Sukhumvit and Petchburi roads changed from quiet residential areas into busy commercial thoroughfares. But it wasn't until the arrival of the American forces in the late 1960s that the city gained its present look. Large infusions of money from the US (Thailand was America's staunchest alley in the Vietnam War) resulted in a burgeoning economy, multi-storey buildings and a population that swelled in response to new jobs. The Thai military, which had steadily been gaining power in Thai politics, reached its peak of influence during these years.

In 1946, while on a visit to Thailand from school in Europe, the now adult King Ananda was found shot dead in his palace bedroom. He was succeeded by his younger brother, Bhumibol Adulyadej (Rama IX), the present monarch *(see page 27)*, who returned to Switzerland to complete law studies. He did not, however, take up active duties until the 1950s. By then, Thailand had been without a king for 20 years.

The first few years after the end of World War II were marked by a series of democratic civilian governments. In 1948, under threat of military force, Pibul assumed power once again, ushering in a period marked by strife, failed coup attempts and corruption.

In 1957, a clique of one-time protégés overthrew Pibul. The leader, General Sarit Thanarat, and two cohort generals, Thanom Kittikachorn and Prapas Charusathien, ran the government until 1973, employing martial law. All three men used their power to amass huge personal fortunes but they also deserve credit for developing Thailand. Health standards improved, the business sector expanded, construction boomed, and a middle class began to emerge, especially in Bangkok. Yet, the dictatorial trio did not anticipate that socio-economic changes would lead to new aspirations.

The October 1973 revolution

On 13 October 1973, a demonstration to protest against the military dictatorship attracted some 400,000 people to Bangkok's Democracy Monument. The following day, however, the protest turned violent and at least 100 students were shot by riot police. Discovering that their army had deserted them, the generals fled to the US.

Two elections in the mid-1970s produced civilian governments but the diverse parties could not work together for long. Political parties, labour unions and farming organisations sprang to life with very specific grievances. The middle class was originally strongly supportive of the student revolution, as were some of the upper class. But they came to fear that total chaos or a communist takeover was at hand.

The 1976 return of General Thanom, ostensibly to become a monk, sparked student protests and paramilitary counter-protests. On 6 October, police and paramilitary thugs stormed Thammasat University. Students were lynched and their bodies burned on the spot. A faction

LEFT: 1947 coronation of King Bhumibol Adulyadej.
RIGHT: rally at Bangkok's Democracy Monument.

of army officers seized power. Self-government had lasted but three years. Ironically, the civilian judge appointed to be prime minister, Thanin Kraivichien, turned out to be more brutal than any of his uniformed predecessors. Yet another military coup ousted Thanin in October 1977. For the next decade, two relatively moderate generals headed the government.

Another military coup

A former general was popularly elected in 1988, but was deposed two years later in a bloodless military coup spearheaded by General Suchinda Kraprayoon. The junta, which called itself the National Peace Keeping

ous public, mostly middle-class people, began gathering at rallies in Sanam Luang and near Democracy Monument, in Bangkok. More than 70,000 people alone met at Sanam Luang on 17 May 1992. Late in the evening, soldiers fired on unarmed demonstrators. Killings, beatings, riots and arson attacks continued sporadically for the next three days. The Thai broadcast media is controlled by the government, and so were obliged to carry out a news blackout of the events. But owners of satellite dishes, along with viewers around the world, watched the coverage of "Bloody May". The crisis ended when King Bhumibol intervened. A little later, the unrepentant Suchinda bowed

Council (NPKC) installed a businessman and ex-diplomat, Anand Panyacharun, as a caretaker premier in 1991. To their surprise, Anand exhibited an independent streak and made several important reforms in the government. In fact, he earned plaudits for running the cleanest government in memory.

As expected, the junta's new party won the most parliamentary seats in the March 1992 elections. Unexpected, however, was the public discontent when the former coup leader General Suchinda assumed the prime ministership in April 1992 without having stood for election.

With eerie echoes of the mid-1970s, professionals, lawyers, social workers and the curi-

out and left the country. The Democrat Party and other prominent Suchinda critics prevailed in the September 1992 re-elections.

Democracy prevails

Prime Minister Chuan Leekpai, considered honest but ineffectual, persisted for almost three years from 1992 to 1995, a record for a civilian government. Setting another record, he was not toppled by a coup. But by the end, Chuan had lost much of the goodwill of the pro-democracy groups that had lifted him to power.

Chuan battled constantly to keep his coalition working together. It finally disintegrated when some members of Chuan's own party were implicated in a land reform scandal. Elections in July 1995 brought an old-style politician, Banharn Silpa-archa, to the premiership. As the Thai press phrased it at the time, both Banharn and his party, Chart Thai, had a strong "reputation" for corruption. Regardless, military leaders reaffirmed that they had no plans to intervene in politics.

Economic crisis

The Thai economy, which registered phenomenal annual growth rates for over a decade to emerge as one of the famous "Tiger" economies of Southeast Asia, suddenly saw the good times come to an end. By late 1996, inflationary pressures, a widening current account deficit, and slower economic growth led to a censure motion against the 14-month-old Banharn Silpa-archa government. Elections held in November 1996 saw a coalition headed by the New Aspiration Party come to power. NAP leader Chavalit Yongchaiyudh became Thailand's 22nd Prime Minister, but many of his partners in government were the same as in the previous administration and little was done to stem the economic rot that had set in.

By February 1997, international ratings agency Moody's had downgraded Thailand's long-term credit rating. By the middle of the year, the government was forced to order the closure of 16 finance companies that were in the red. The final straw came shortly afterwards, on 2 July, when the Chavalit administration decided to drop the traditional currency peg in favour of a "managed float". This had the disastrous double effect of sending the currency down in a devaluation spiral and making the foreign debts of local corporations skyrocket.

The pressure to float the baht was partly caused by aggressive attacks by foreign hedge funds, and enormous sums from the country's foreign exchange reserves were spent in its defence. The upshot of all this was that the government had to eat humble pie and ask the International Monetary Fund for US$17 billion to help keep the country afloat. The crisis saw businesses go bankrupt and many thousands lose their jobs, due to closures or downsizing.

New constitution

Amid all this, 27 September 1998, turned out to be an important day because a censure vote on the Chavalit government was scheduled to be held an hour before the vote on the draft of a new, more open constitution. Despite fears that the new charter would not be passed, it sailed through Parliament after some acrimonious wrangling. Yet, later in the year, as the economic crisis deepened, Chavalit had to bow to pressure from the public, especially the business lobby, and step down.

This brought in a Democrat government headed by Prime Minister Chuan Leekpai. After over a year of hard work, the economy,

LEFT: the military has always featured in Thai politics.
RIGHT: traffic jams still plague Bangkok despite the opening of the Skytrain and the new subway line.

TRAFFIC WOES

The 1980s and '90s saw the vertical growth of Bangkok. Its skyline changed dramatically but along with it came congested roads and notorious traffic jams. In the early 1980s, various government officials suggested solutions to ease Bangkok's traffic problem. Eventually the ideas evaporated, mired in corruption or woefully poor cooperation between competing agencies – only to be recycled a year or two later. Thankfully, the situation has improved vastly with the construction of a complex network of elevated expressways. To ease traffic further, in 1999, Bangkok's first mass transit system, the Skytrain, started operations, and in 2004 a metro line opened.

which had bottomed out, began showing gradual signs of recovery. The process was helped along by a banking reform package in August 1998 that helped boost confidence in the country among foreign investors. The government also pushed forward business laws to help speed up corporate debt restructuring.

The Thaksin administration

By 2000, the economy seemed well on the road to recovery. In 2001, general elections saw the populist leader of the Thai Rak Thai (TRT) party, billionaire entrepreneur Thaksin Shinawatra, replace Chuan as premier – amid allegations of vote-buying and rigging.

2004, leaving some 5,395 dead (and another 2,845 people missing at time of press) has considerably boosted his popularity throughout the rest of the country.

Although criticised by many for his "CEO" style of government, reported penchant for promoting the interests of his friends and family in the government and private sectors, and unwillingness to accept criticism, Thaksin was again returned to power as prime minister in the February 2005 elections. Thaksin is hugely popular in the provinces, but much less so in the south and among the middle classes of Bangkok.

In January 2006, Thaksin faced another political crisis when the Shinawatra family

To date, Thaksin's governance has proved controversial. In the deep south, long troubled by a Malay-Muslim insurgency, Thaksin replaced army control with that of the police, antagonising the locals. On 28 April 2004, 107 Muslim militants, mainly youths, were killed in Pattani. On 25 October in the same year Muslim demonstrators were shot at in Narathiwat, and 78 others suffocated while being transported to detention centres. As a result, support for Thaksin in southern Thailand has dwindled almost to nothing.

However, Thaksin's swift and efficient response to the tragic tsunami that destroyed its southern beach resorts on 26 December

was accused of evading taxes when they sold their stake in Shin Corporation, one of Thailand's largest telecommunications companies, for US$1.9 billion. Although the accusation proved groundless in the end, thousands of protesters took to the streets in Bangkok, and the opposition asked for his resignation. In response, Thaksin announced a snap election in April 2006. Opposition parties boycotted the elections, and although Thaksin won again, he resigned as prime minister in the face of mass protests, appointing his deputy, Chidchai Wannasathit as the new premier. ❑

ABOVE: Thailand's ex-premier, Thaksin Shinawatra.

Much-loved Monarchy

Thai people take the institution of the monarchy very seriously. Ever since the first independent Thai kingdom was established more than seven centuries ago, the Thais have been ruled over by kings. It is true that, since the revolution of 1932, the monarchy has been constitutional – but the Thais continue to love and honour their royal family, and especially its father figure, King Bhumibol Adulyadej, with a consuming passion.

Thailand's first royal capital, Sukhothai, was succeeded by Ayutthaya in 1351, and then by Bangkok in 1782. Perhaps as a consequence of this continuity, the Thai people are confirmed monarchists, with the throne making up one of the three central pillars of the national polity – in Thai *chat*, *sat* and *pramahakasat* – Thai Nation, Buddhist Religion and Chakri Dynasty. It would be hard to overestimate the affection and respect Thais feel for their kings, and this applies to non-Buddhist minorities as well. In many Muslim homes, for example, it is common to find a framed print of the king hanging next to a picture of the Kaaba at Mecca in a convincing statement of both spiritual and mundane loyalty.

After the tragically early death of his brother King Ananda Mahidol (Rama VIII) in 1946, the succession passed to Thailand's present monarch, King Bhumibol Adulyadej. Born not in Thailand, but in distant Cambridge, Massachusetts, where his father Prince Mahidol Adulyadej was studying medicine at Harvard University, young Bhumibol soon proved a worthy successor to his grandfather King Chulalongkorn (Rama V). For a full six decades, often accompanied by his enduringly popular wife Queen Sirikit, he has travelled all over the kingdom, equally at home with peasants from the poor northeast or at high-tech research laboratories in the major cities. When not engaged in promoting ecological awareness or some major new agricultural work, he enjoys jazz music. An accomplished musician, he plays several instruments and has written many popular numbers. Perhaps because of this ability to reach the common man, he enjoys an extraordinary popularity shared in the past only by King Chulalongkorn.

Although a constitutional monarch, because of the affection in which he is held by Thais, King Bhumibol does play a political role, occasionally intervening when he feels politicians have got out of hand. In May 1992, when military strongman Suchinda Krapayoon seized power in a coup, the king intervened to end three days of riots and killings when soldiers fired on unarmed

demonstrators near the Democracy Monument. Suchinda was forced to resign in disgrace, and democracy was restored.

More recently King Bhumibol has made it clear on a number of occasions that he disapproves of Prime Minister Thaksin Shinawatra's executive style of government. Thaksin, generally not a man who tolerates criticism, has been obliged to listen. So great is the moral authority of the king that no politician can afford to ignore him. He is the final bulwark against oppression and authoritarianism, yet he remains a modest, even diffident man, conscious of his position as *po luang*, the "royal father" of his people. ❏

RIGHT: King Bhumibol and Queen Sirikit.

Decisive Dates

Pre-Thai Civilisation

3600–250 BC Ban Chiang culture flourishes in northeastern Thailand.

4th–8th centuries AD Influence of Mon and Khmer empires spreads into Thailand.

9th–13th centuries Thai people migrate south from Yunnan Province in China into northern Thailand.

The Sukhothai Era

1238 Khmer power wanes. Kingdom of Sukhothai founded by King Intradit.

1277–1318 Reign of Ramkamhaeng in Sukhothai. Often called Thailand's "Golden Age", the period saw the first attempts to unify the Thai people, the first use of Thai script, and flourishing of the arts.

1281 Chiang Saen kingdom founded in the north.

1296 Lanna kingdom founded at Chiang Mai. King Mengrai controls much of northern Thailand and Laos.

1318–47 King Lo Thai reigns at Sukhothai. Slow decline of Sukhothai kingdom begins.

1438 Sukhothai is now virtually deserted; power shifts to Ayutthaya to the south and along the Chao Phraya River.

The Kingdom of Ayutthaya

14th century Area around Ayutthaya settled by representatives of Chiang Saen kingdom.

1350 City of Ayutthaya is founded by Phya U-Thong, who proclaims himself Ramathibodi I. Within a few years he controls the areas belonging to the Sukhothai kingdom and the Khmer empire.

1369 Ramesuen becomes king.

1390 Ramesuen captures Chiang Mai.

1393 Ramesuen seizes Angkor, base of the Khmer empire, in Cambodia.

1448–88 Reign of King Trailok, who finally unites the Lanna (Chiang Mai) and Ayutthaya kingdoms.

1491–1529 Reign of King Ramathibodi II.

1569 Burmese seize and destroy Ayutthaya.

1584 Naresuen declares the independence of Siam.

1590 Naresuen becomes king and defeats Burmese. Ayutthaya expands rapidly at the expense of Burmese and Khmer empires and flourishes as a major city.

1605–10 Ekatotsarot reigns; begins significant economic ties with Europeans.

1610–28 Reign of King Songtham. British arrive and obtain land for a trading factory.

1628–55 Reign of Prasat Thong. Trading concessions expand and regular trade with China and Europe is established.

1656–88 Reign of King Narai. British influence expands. Reputation of Ayutthaya as a magnificent city and a remarkable royal court spreads in Europe.

1678 Constantine Phaulkon arrives at Narai's court and gains great influence; French presence expands.

1688 Narai dies, Phaulkon executed.

1733–58 Reign of King Boromakot. Ayutthaya enters a period of peace; the arts and literature flourish.

1767 Burmese King Alaungpaya captures and sacks Ayutthaya, destroying four centuries of Thai civilisation. Seven months later General Phya Taksin returns and expels the Burmese. He moves the capital from Ayutthaya to Thonburi, near Bangkok.

Beginning of Chakri Dynasty

1767 Phya Taksin crowned as King Taksin.

1779 Generals Chao Phya Chakri and Chao Phya Surasi, his brother, conquer

Chiang Mai, expel the Burmese from what is now Thailand and take control of most of the Khmer and Lao kingdoms. The statue of the Emerald Buddha is brought from Vientiane, Laos, to Thonburi.

1782 Taksin is deposed and executed, and Chao Phya Chakri is offered the throne, founding the Chakri dynasty and assuming the name Ramathibodi (later Rama I). Capital is moved across the river to what is now known as Bangkok. Under Rama I, the Siamese kingdom consolidates and expands its strength. Rama I revives Thai art, religion, and culture. Work begins on the Grand Palace and Wat Phra Kaew in Bangkok.

1809–24 Reign of Rama II; best known for construction of Wat Arun and many other temples and monasteries. Rama II reopens relations with the West, suspended since the time of Narai.

1824–51 Reign of Rama III, who continues open-door policy with foreigners. Encourages American missionaries to introduce Western medicine to Siam.

1851 King Mongkut (Rama IV) ascends the throne. He is the first Thai king to understand Western culture and technology.

1868 Chulalongkorn (Rama V) ascends the throne, reigning for the next four decades. Schools, infrastructure, military and government modernised. Slavery is abolished.

1910–25 Reign of Vajiravudh (Rama VI), Oxford-educated and Westernised, he made Thai people adopt surnames. Schools for both sexes flourished during his reign.

1925–35 Reign of Prajadhipok (Rama VII). Economic pressures from the Great Depression rouse discontent among Thais.

Modern Thailand

1932 A coup ends the absolute monarchy and ushers in a constitutional monarchy.

1939 Siam's name is officially changed to Thailand, "Land of the Free".

1941 Japan invades Thailand with the acquiescence of the military government.

1946 King Ananda is killed by gunman; Bhumibol Adulyadej (Rama IX) ascends throne.

1973–91 Bloody clashes between the army and students bring down the military government; political and economic blunders bring down the subsequent civilian government three years later. Various military-backed and civilian governments come and go for the next 20 years.

1992 Another clash between military forces and civilian demonstrators results in the military leaving government to civilian politicians. Thailand begins five years of unprecedented economic growth.

1996 King Bhumibol celebrates his golden jubilee of 50 years on the throne.

1997 Thailand's economy begins a free-

fall as the baht loses half of its value. Start of the Asian economic crisis.

1998 Thailand follows guidelines established by the IMF to resuscitate its economy.

1999–2000 The Thai economy shows signs of recovery.

2001 Populist leader Thaksin Shinawatra is elected as prime minister.

2004 Attacks in the largely Muslim-dominated south. Tsunami hits southern Thailand and causes widespread devastation.

2005 Thaksin is elected for a second term as prime minister in February.

2006 Opposition parties boycott snap elections; Thaksin resigns as premier. ❑

LEFT: Buddha image at Wat Phra Si Sanphet in Ayutthaya. **RIGHT:** guards at Bangkok's Grand Palace march at a parade.

PEOPLE

Bangkok residents are identified by the glittering "hi-so" set, wealthy Chinese, tiny pockets of Muslim-Thais and Indians, Western expats as well as illegal migrants from Burma and Cambodia. Despite the disparities, a strong sense of the community is the common denominator

The quintessential Bangkokian appears in many guises. Sitting behind the darkened windows of a chauffeur-driven Mercedes is the high-society lady on her way to a VIP gala function. Hurrying up the steps of the Skytrain station is the young and smartly dressed office manager, late for a meeting. Slicing up a watermelon on his cart in front of a towering office block is the fruit vendor busy with the lunchtime crowds. Bangkok is a city of contrasts – between wealth and poverty, east and west, the old and the new. The city's inhabitants dwell on all sides of these delineations, with many creatively straddling more than one divide.

City on the move

Bangkok is forever shifting, always adapting to Western trends and outside influences. The cityscape is in a constant state of renewal, with old wooden buildings frequently demolished to make way for modern office and shopping complexes. For the most part, Bangkokians are creatures of this environment, enthusiastically embracing all things new. Trends spread through the city like wildfire, from the recent craze for fitness gyms to Starbucks copy-cat cáfes. This perennial change is oiled by the generally accepting Thai nature *(see text box)* and the Buddhist concept of non-attachment.

Though the capital's official population hovers around six million, the large number of migrant workers bring most estimates closer to 10 million. Bangkok's biggest growth spurt

COOL HEARTS

The essential ingredient to surviving the stresses of daily life in the bustling, traffic-clogged streets of Bangkok is the Thai concept of *jai yen* (literally, cool heart). *Jai yen* is about taking obstacles in your stride. It is the antithesis of out-of-control tempers and sudden anger. This very Thai concept ensures that an oasis of calm exists inside every Bangkokian; differences of opinion rarely escalate to fistfights and misunderstandings are countered with a smile. The accompanying phrase that answers to all of life's vicissitudes is *mai pen rai*, or "never mind". Make use of both these concepts and Bangkok will seem a little less difficult.

PRECEDING PAGES: worshippers at a Chinatown temple.
LEFT AND RIGHT: faces of modern Bangkok.

took place during the economic boom from the 1980s to mid-'90s, when the Bangkok dream became a reality for many. As glass-and-chrome condos rose into the sky, Western fast-food outlets flooded the streets, along with glitzy nightclubs and swanky restaurants.

When the economic crash in 1997 brought the city to a stand-still, Bangkokians simply did what they always do: adapt. The city saw a return to all things Thai, as local wisdom rose up to heal the scars of fast-paced globalisation. Historically, rather than fight outside influences, Thailand has always welcomed it, choosing compromise over conflict. While there are those who deride Bangkok as not representing the

"real" Thailand, the city stubbornly retains a sense of Thai-ness. Beneath the yellow arches of McDonald's you'll find women threading fragrant jasmine garlands. Next to every modern skyscraper is an old shrine where the spirits of the land are still propitiated each day.

Sanuk means fun

The city is infused with the Bangkokian's search for *sanuk*, a Thai word meaning fun. The quantity and quality of *sanuk*, whether in work or play, determines if something is worth pursuing. Checking out anything new – the latest movie, a recently-opened restaurant or shopping mall – is a sure-fire *sanuk* activity. Gatherings of friends always have high *sanuk* value, whether it's an evening beneath the gaudy chandeliers of a karaoke club, or huddled around a tin table on the pavement quaffing whisky.

Doing anything alone is generally considered *mai sanuk* (not fun). Thailand's culture and society have traditionally been centred on agriculture, an activity that nurtures a sense of community. The shift to urban life has changed much of the countryside's ways, but it is a rare Thai who does not enjoy getting together with friends. Most are puzzled by Westerners who dine or holiday alone, as they do not understand the occasional need for solitude. The *sanuk* quota of any given event can usually be gauged by the number of people involved: the general rule being "the more, the merrier". It is a rule which also explains the Bangkokian's love of the mobile phone – more than half of the city's inhabitants own one – with which they need never feel alone.

ROYAL PEDIGREE DOG

Another inhabitant of the city is the ubiquitous Bangkok street dog. Attempts to quell their numbers through sterilisation programmes have, so far, proved unsuccessful. Known as *maa phan thaang* (literally, "dog of a thousand paths", referring to the multitude of different breeds that have gone into its pedigree), the Bangkok stray was given elevated status in recent years when King Bhumibol published *The Story of Tongdaeng*, a Thai-and-English-language biography of the street-side mongrel that he brought to stay in the royal palace.

The rags-to-riches tale of Tongdaeng has captivated Bangkokians. You have to put your name on a long waiting-list to get a much-coveted Tongdaeng T shirt. There is even a recipe book to commemorate Tongdaeng's nine puppies, each named after a famous Thai dessert. The king is fond of weaving moral messages into simple stories and, in this book, the various anecdotes of Tongdaeng's life expound on the values of intelligence, manners, loyalty and gratefulness – Tongdaeng always sits silently by His Majesty's feet with her paws neatly crossed in the traditional Thai manner of respect. By highlighting the merits of a stray dog, many believe the king is sending out a message that class, rank and money are not the most important things in life.

Hi-So and Lo-So

Bangkok society is fiercely hierarchical. At the top of the pyramid are the "hi-so", a Thai slang abbreviation for high society. The phrase and its counterpart, "lo-so" (for low society), are used to boost or deride a person's standing: "She's *very* hi-so.", or, "Oh no, he's too lo-so." The city's hi-so tribe is not limited only to aristocratic Thai families; the boom of the 1980s and early '90s created a significant *nouveau riche* class; being hi-so is as much about glamour and wealth as it is about pedigree. The hi-so are pictured in the society pages of newspapers and magazines (like the English-language *Thailand Tatler*), with the women

bias in Thailand or racial conflicts like those found in neighbouring countries. While some estimates state that a quarter of Bangkok's population is Chinese, it is now hard to differentiate between Chinese and Thais as most second and third generation immigrants are Thai citizens and no longer speak Chinese.

All over the city are billboards advertising the *moo bahn*, or housing estates, that litter the outskirts of Bangkok. Depicting Western-style houses complete with two children and a dog playing in the garden, they appeal to Bangkok's burgeoning middle-classes. Residing on cheaper land at the city's edge means a long daily commute to work.

sporting big hair and big jewels. Hi-so life is a seemingly endless whirl of lunches, cocktail parties and shopping.

Many members of the hi-so are Sino-Thai. The Chinese knack for entrepreneurial know-how has ensured that much of Bangkok's wealth is controlled by Sino-Thai families. Chinese traders have lived in the Bangkok area since the 18th century, and have been assimilated, to a remarkable degree, into the life of their adopted land. Chinese and Thais have intermarried freely and there is no anti-Chinese

Mixed races and migrants

A curious Bangkok phenomenon of recent years is the rise of the *luuk kreung*, literally "half child". *Luk kreung* are mixed-race children, mostly with one Thai and one Caucasian parent. The *luk kreung* "look" is astoundingly popular with Bangkokians and many Bangkok celebrities are *luuk kreung* TV presenters, pop stars, soap opera actors and actresses, or models. The *luk kreung* epitomises Bangkok's hybrid culture: Thai, but also a little bit Western. It is a blend that infuses everything from the mix-and-match style of pop music to the city's creative takes on fusion cuisine.

Of the less lauded minorities in the city,

LEFT: Buddhism is a way of life for many Thais.
ABOVE: Skytrain guard; trendy Thai teens.

Indians make up the second largest group after the Chinese. There are around a million Muslim Thai-Malays who are fairly well-integrated into Thai society, if somewhat discriminated against, especially in the wake of recent political turmoil in the Muslim provinces of the deep South. There are also significant groups of expatriates living in Bangkok, working mostly for international companies. Among them are some 25,000 Westerners, known as *farang* or foreigner in Thai, and around 50,000 Japanese, whose "Little Tokyo" is centred around Sukhumvit Soi 33/1.

Less integrated with Bangkok society are the illegal immigrants fleeing poverty in

Cambodia and Burma (Myanmar). They provide the city with low-cost labour and are forced into the jobs no one else wants; on construction sites, refuse collection and in factories and brothels. Of the estimated one million migrant workers in Thailand, 800,000 are from Burma.

Rising above and beyond all these social divisions is the king and the Thai royal family. Even to cultured urbanites, His Majesty King Bhumibol *(see page 27)* is still the much-loved and revered figurehead of the nation. Portraits of the king and queen hang in almost every office, shop and restaurant. At cinemas, the audience stands while the national anthem is played before each film. In many ways, the king acts as a moral arbiter for all Bangkokians; while the city races helter-skelter towards all that is new, the monarch stands as a symbol of Thai tradition and old-world values *(see also text box page 34).*

Bangkok as a village

The most neglected Bangkokians are the city's poorest. Inner-city slums, such as the infamous one at Klong Toey, are home to hundreds of thousands of destitute people. Slum-life is fuelled by *yaa baa* (the Thai word for amphetamines means, literally, "crazy medicine") and desperation forces many people into crime and prostitution. Many are migrants escaping rural poverty in the dry plains of Isaan in northeastern Thailand. Though the Bangkok dream has yet to filter into their lives, the city would surely collapse without them. Manpower from the northeast provides the city with a crucial task-force of taxi and tuk-tuk drivers, construction workers, cleaners and security guards. Many find work in the streets as roving vendors or rubbish-collectors.

Living away from the air-conditioned world of shopping malls and nightclubs, these rural migrants bring a touch of the village to the capital. Add this to the fact that most Bangokians are only a generation or two removed from the paddy field and one could conclude that Bangkok – for all its dynamism and flair – is really just a big village disguised as a city.

Proof comes in the form of one of the most popular radio stations, Ruam Duay Chuay Kan, or "Let's Get Together and Help Each Other". The radio station is broadcast live, 24-hours-a-day, and its concept is simple: a person calls in with a problem and the presenters muster all the forces of good in the city to solve it. Bureaucratic tangles are untied, lost relatives are reunited and even Bangkok's steaming gridlock can be moved when drivers hear that a screaming woman in labour is trying to get to hospital. The radio show emphasises the familiar sense of community inherent in village life. Through it, Bangkokians can share practical advice, help out in times of trouble and, of course, stick their noses into other people's businesses. Most of all, though, the station is proof that the big bad city has a heart of gold. ❑

LEFT: an immigrant labourer in Thailand.

Sin City Bangkok

Bangkok's reputation as a "city of sin" is sadly well deserved. Though prostitution is technically illegal, sex is openly for sale in the capital's many girlie bars, brothels and massage parlours. It is an accepted and common practice for Thai men to patronise prostitutes or have a *mia noi*, literally "little wife" or mistress on the side. Ask any Thai woman and she will tell you with a rueful shake of her head that all Thai men are *chao choo*, or adulterers.

While Thai men tend to patronise more discreet brothels or, at the higher end, plush member-only clubs, foreign tourists are catered for at the loud and brash red-light districts of Patpong and Nana Entertainment Plaza *(see pages 144 and 152).* Sex tourism began with the Vietnam War when thousands of American troops took their R&R in Bangkok, or at the nearby beach resort of Pattaya (now a veritable Patpong-on-the-Sea). Due to the city's legal laxity towards the sex trade, bars and brothels multiplied and, by the 1980s, Bangkok had become one large, lascivious playground with plane-loads of men on sex tours being flown in from Japan, the Middle East, Europe and the US.

Most of Bangkok's sex-workers come from the poverty-wracked region of northeast Thailand, or Isaan. As the Thai economy increasingly turned towards export industries, rural incomes based on small-scale agriculture were diminished and the bright lights and bad ways of the big city beckoned. Sadly, women working in the capital's red-light districts often have the consent of their families, and in fact regularly send money home each month. The pay is infinitely better than working in a factory – the only other option for an uneducated country girl. Many sex-workers hang on to the Cinderella dream that they will be rescued by a client; indeed, more than a few cross-cultural marriages have had their beginnings in a Bangkok brothel.

NGOs working in Thailand no longer focus their primary efforts on extricating women from prostitution. They have found that few in the business are motivated to get out; the money is just too good. Organisations such as Empower instead educate bar girls about the dangers of HIV, and teach them English so that they are less likely to be exploited by their clients.

The other end of the sex trade is infinitely more grim. Young women and girls are trafficked from neighbouring Laos, Burma and Cambodia. Lured by promises of factory jobs or waitress work, they unwittingly sell themselves into locked-up brothels in the capital. There, they must work under inhu-

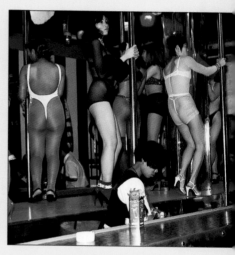

man conditions until they have earned back the price the brothel-owner paid for them.

All this insalubrious activity has had a trickle down on Bangkok society. In the past few years there has been a backlash against the loose sexual morals on display among Bangkok teenagers. Under pressure from teachers and concerned parents, the Thai government launched a Social Order Campaign *(see page 63)* to keep underage Thais away from Bangkok's seedy nightlife. With random drug raids, earlier closing times and frequent ID checks, the campaign has been largely successful and is surprisingly popular with the average Bangkokian. ❏

RIGHT: bartop dancers in Patpong.

RELIGION

Buddhism is central to the lives of most Thais, as shown by the many rituals and practices that are part of daily life. Yet a strong thread of animism and superstition persists, as evidenced by the presence of tiny "spirit houses" in the compounds of hotels, homes and offices

Buddhism – a philosophy, rather than a religion – has played a profound role in shaping the Thai character, particularly in the way in which people react to events. The Buddhist concept of the impermanence of life and possessions, and of the necessity to avoid extremes of emotion or behaviour, has done much to create the relaxed, carefree charm that is one of the most appealing characteristics of the Thai people.

Theravada Buddhism

Most of the Thai population are supporters of Theravada Buddhism, which is also the main Buddhist form practised in neighbouring countries like Laos, Cambodia, Burma (Myanmar), as well as Sri Lanka. Nevertheless, even a casual visitor to temples in these countries will quickly see differences between them. As they have done with most outside influences – Khmer temple decorations and Chinese food, for instance – the Thais have evolved a Buddhism of their own cast over the centuries.

Theravada Buddhism is a mixture of Buddhist, Hindu and animistic beliefs, and, as the oldest of all Buddhist faiths, it is the only one to trace its origins directly back to the teachings of the Gautama Buddha in the 6th century BC. The central doctrines are based on the temporary nature of life and the imperfections of all forms of beings.

With the help of a complicated system of rules, each Thai, whether lay person or monk,

LEFT: Buddha images in Leng Noi Yee temple.
RIGHT: young novice monks.

tries to achieve spiritual merit in the present life so that it will favourably influence their next life – thus permitting an existence that will be characterised by less suffering and ultimately lead to *nirvana*, or enlightenment. To this end, almost all the religious activities that a traveller will experience in Thailand have to do with merit-making. A man who spends some part of his life as a monk will earn merit by living in accordance with the strict rules governing monastic life. So, too, a person who supports the monks on a daily basis by donating food, or who visits a temple to pray for a sick person, gains merit.

The Buddha image in front of which the

prayers are offered provides only a formal background for these activities. Neither the statue, nor the Buddha himself, is worshipped.

Mahayana Buddhism

In addition to Theravada Buddhism, there is Mahayana Buddhism that is practised by those of Chinese descent. Visitors are likely to spot

Mahayana temples in Bangkok's Chinatown. Mahayana literally means "Greater Vehicle"; the defining belief, according to this doctrine is that those who have attained nirvana return to help others reach the same state. The various Buddhist sects and practices that predominate in China, Tibet, Taiwan, Japan, Korea and Vietnam are classified as Mahayana.

Chinese Buddhism, at least that practised in Thailand, primarily consists of incense, lucky charms, and heaps of other folk practices. The visitor entering a *sanjao,* or inner shrine, of such a temple will have a chance to shake sticks out of a canister, from which a fortune can be told. At funerals, paper money

and doll-size cardboard houses (complete with paper Mercedes Benz cars) are burned to assist the deceased in his or her next life.

Temple life

Most of Thailand's 300,000 monks or so live in *wat* (temples), practising and teaching the rules of human conduct laid down by the Buddha. There are literally hundreds of Buddhist temples in the cities and suburbs, usually sited in serene pockets of densely packed neighbourhoods and serving as hubs for the spiritual and social life of the community.

The term *wat* defines a large, walled compound made up of several buildings, including a *bot* or hall where new monks are ordained, and one or more *viharn* where sermons are delivered. It may also contain a belltower, a *ho trai* (library), and *guti,* or monk meditation cells, as well as a domed edifice, called *chedi* in Thailand, or *prang* in Cambodia, and *stupa* or *pagoda* in other countries. *Chedi* contain the ashes or relics of wealthy donors, emulating the Buddha whose ashes and relics were placed by his instruction in a mound of earth.

Tradition requires that every Buddhist male enter the monkhood for a brief period before marriage, and companies customarily grant paid leave for male employees wishing to do so. The entry of a young man into monkhood is seen as repayment to parents for his upbringing, and for bestowing special merit on them, particularly his mother. Unlike other Buddhist countries, women cannot be ordained in Thailand. It is thus popularly believed that a son, as a monk, can earn merit for his mother and other female relatives.

For all its spartan life, however, a Buddhist *wat* in Thailand is by no means isolated from the real world. In addition to the schools that are attached to most *wat* (for centuries, the only schools were those run by monks), the *wat* has traditionally been the centre of social and communal life in the villages. Monks serve as herbal doctors, psychological counsellors and arbitrators of disputes. They also play an important part in daily life, such as blessing a new building, or at birthdays and funerals.

Spirits and amulets

When Buddhism started in what is now Thailand in the early years, it promised a better life for farmers. But as it provided little assistance with the unfathomable tragedies of daily life, and certainly no answer to the questions of the supernatural, the people continued to worship their old deities and spirits to fill in what they saw as gaps in Buddhism.

The variety of *phi* (spirits) in Thailand is legendary. A seductive female *phi*, believed to reside in a banana plant, is said to torment young men who come near it. Another bothersome one takes possession of her victims and forces them to remove their clothes in public. (For some reason, the most destructive spirits seem to be female.)

To counteract the spirits and potential dangers in life, protective spells are cast and kept in small amulets *(see pages 92 and 111)* mostly worn around the neck. Curiously, the amulets are not bought, but rather rented on an indefinite lease from "landlords", often monks considered to possess magic powers. Some monasteries have been turned into highly profitable factories for the production of amulets. There are amulets that offer protection against accidents while travelling or against bullet and knife wounds; some even boost sexual attraction. All this has no more to do with Buddhism than the protective blue-patterned tattoos sported by some rural Thais to ward off evil.

Spirit houses

No building in Thailand, not even the humblest wooden hut, will be seen today without a "spirit house", or at least a house altar. In ordinary residences, the small doll-like house may resemble a Thai dwelling; in hotels and offices, it is usually an elaborately decorated mini-temple. In either case, these spirit houses serve as the abodes of the resident spirits. As it is within their power either to favour or plague the human inhabitants of the actual house or building, the spirit house is regularly adorned with placative offerings of food, fresh flowers and incense sticks. If any calamity or ill luck befalls the members of the compound, it may be necessary to call in an expert to consult the spirit to determine what is wrong.

One of the most famous spirit houses in Bangkok is the Erawan Shrine, at the inter-section of Ratchadamri and Ploenchit roads *(see page 132)*. This shrine, honouring the Hindu god Brahma, was erected by the owners during the construction of the original Erawan hotel in the 1950s, after several workers were injured in mysterious accidents. The shrine soon acquired a widespread reputation for bringing good fortune to outsiders as well.

A less well-known shrine sits in the compound of Bangkok's Lai Nert Park Hotel. Its offerings consist entirely of phalluses, ranging from small to gargantuan, sculpted from wood, wax, stone or cement, and with fidelity to real life. They are left by women hoping to conceive a child, or who unable to do so. ❑

BRAHMAN BELIEFS

Many of the Thais' non-Buddhist beliefs are Brahman in origin, and even today Brahman priests officiate at major ceremonies. The Thai wedding ceremony is almost entirely Brahman, as are many funeral rites. The rites of statecraft pertaining to the royal family are presided over by Brahman priests. One of the most popular of these, the Ploughing Ceremony (Raek Na), takes place each May in Bangkok. To signal the start of the rice-planting season, sacred oxen are offered a selection of grains. Astrologers watch the events carefully, as the grains the oxen choose will determine the amount of rainfall to come, and the success or failure of the crops in the year ahead.

LEFT: making a request at Erawan Shrine.
RIGHT: garlanded flower offerings at Erawan.

TEMPLE ART AND ARCHITECTURE

The temple *(wat)* plays a vital role in every community, large and small; for many visitors Thailand's temples are the country's most enduring sights

A typical Thai *wat* (or temple) has two enclosing walls that divide it from the secular world. The monks' quarters are situated between the outer and inner walls. In larger temples the inner walls may be lined with Buddha images and serve as cloisters for meditation. This part of the temple is called *buddhavasa* or *phutthawat*. Inside the inner walls is the *bot* or *ubosot* (ordination hall) surrounded by eight stone tablets and set on consecrated ground. This is the most sacred part of the temple and only monks can enter it. The *bot* contains a Buddha image, but it is the *viharn* (sermon hall) that contains the principal Buddha images. Also in the inner courtyard are the bell-shaped *chedi* (relic chambers), which contain the relics of pious or distinguished people. *Salas* (pavilions) can be found all around the temple; the largest of these areas is the *sala kan prian* (study hall), used for saying afternoon prayers. Apart from Buddha images, various mythological creatres *(see page 86)* are found within the temple compound.

ABOVE: a double gallery enclosing the *bot* of Wat Pho houses 394 seat bronze Buddha images. These were brought from Sukothai and Ayutthaya during the reign of Rama I, and are of assorted periods and style The base of the main image contains the ashes of Rama I.

BELOW: gilded *chofa* (bird-like decorations), intricately carved gables, and green and ochre coloured tiles are common features of Thai temple roofs.

ABOVE: temple exteriors are often very ornate, such as that of the Bot of the Emerald Buddha at Wat Phra Kaew. Gold tiles, glass mosaic, lacquer and mother-of-pearl are some of the materials used.

BELOW: Thai temple murals are created on a background that has been prepared and dried before the artist paints on it using coloured pigments mixed with glue. Often featured on the interior of temple walls, such murals depict the classic subjects of Thai painting, including tales from the *Jataka* (Buddha's birth and previous lives) and other Buddhist themes, and also vignettes of local life. During the reign of Rama III (1824–51), mural painting reached its peak, with artists not only following the principles of traditional Thai art, but also introducing new elements, like Western perspective. The mural below, from Wat Suthat in Bangkok, is an example of the late 18th-century art style (better known as the Rattanakosin Period).

BELOW: the gleaming Phra Si Rattana Chedi at Wat Phra Kaew is bell-shaped with a ringed spire and a three-tiered base, a feature of Sri Lankan reliquary towers. Close-up inspection will reveal a surface made up of thousands of tiny gold mosaic pieces.

BELOW: these towering *chedi* at Wat Pho sit on square bases and have graceful and elegant proportions, remininscent of the Lanna-style architecture of north Thailand. Decorated with coloured tiles, the *chedi* are memorials to the first four Chakri kings.

BELOW: Wat Arun features five rounded *prang* – reflecting Cambodian-Khmer influence – encrusted with thousands of broken porcelain pieces. These porcelain shards were leftover ballast from Chinese ships which visited Bangkok in its early days.

THE CREATIVE ARTS

While Thailand's traditional dance-dramas are an entrenched part of its performing arts scene, its young indie movie industry, cutting-edge contemporary theatre and dance, and modern artists and sculptors are fast gaining international attention

Like most of Southeast Asia, some of the symbols and aesthetics of Thailand's culture are perhaps most keenly appreciated by people outside the country. In the realm of performing arts for instance, Thai dance drama is recognised as among the world's most dazzling and stylistically challenging.

Many visitors to Thailand do try and seek out some form of traditional artistry to enforce their perceptions of Thailand as an exotic land rich in cultural heritage. Many, however, miss out on Thailand's contemporary art scene, which is fast gaining recognition in international circles. So by all means, take in a traditional dance-drama or admire the faded beauty of a temple mural, but be sure to spend some time at the capital's modern art galleries, experience contemporary cutting-edge theatre or watch an indie movie directed by one of Thailand's imaginative young directors.

Thai dance-drama

The origins of traditional Thai theatrical arts are entwined with court ceremony and religious ritual, some of which can still be seen today in Bangkok's Erawan Shrine *(see page 132)* or at the Lak Muang *(see page 88),* where performers are hired to dance as a means of thanksgiving to the spirit gods. Both drama and dance are inseparable as the dancer's hands and body express the emotions that the silent lips do not, with the storyline and lyrics provided by a singer and chorus on the side of the stage.

LEFT: Thai *lakhon* dancers in traditional costume.
RIGHT: Thai dancer at Erawan Shrine.

A *phipat* orchestra *(see page 47)* creates not only the atmosphere, but also an emotive force.

It is thought that the movements of dance-drama originated in *nang yai* (shadow puppet) performances of the 16th and 17th centuries. Huge buffalo hides were cut into the shapes of characters from the *Ramakien*. Against a torch-lit translucent screen, puppeteers manipulated puppets, using their silhouettes to tell complex tales of good and evil. As they moved the figures across the screen, the puppeteers danced the emotions they wanted the stiff figures to convey. These movements gradually evolved into an independent theatrical art.

The most identifiable form of dance-drama

is the *khon*, historically performed by a large troupe of male dancers wearing beautifully crafted masks. Originally staged for the royal court, these days a condensed version of several episodes from the *Ramakien* – based on the Hindu epic *Ramayana* – is adapted into a short medley of palatable scenes for tourist dinner shows *(see page 218)*. The entire *Ramakien* would take 720 hours to perform. The colourful masks depict beasts and demons from the epic tale, with each performer trained to portray the particular character of each creature through gestures and actions.

The most graceful dance is the *lakhon*. There are two forms: the *lakhon nai* ("inside"

lakhon), once performed only inside the palace walls by women, and the *lakhon nawk* ("outside" *lakhon*), performed beyond the palace by both sexes. Garbed in costumes as elaborate as their movements, the performers glide slowly about the stage, their stylised movements conveying the plot. *Lakhon*'s rich repertoire includes scenes from the *Ramakien*, and tales like *Inao*, with its romantic storylines.

There have always been two cultures in Thailand: palace and village. The village arts are often parodies of the palace arts, but more burlesque, with pratfalls and bawdy humour. *Likay* is the village form of *lakhon*, played out against gaudy backdrops to an audience that walks in and out of the performance at will, eating and talking, regardless of what happens to the performers on stage.

Puppet theatre

Traditional puppet theatre has also lost most of its Bangkok audiences to television. One troupe struggling to survive is the Joe Louis Theatre at the Suan Lum Night Bazaar, which stages a *hun lakhon lek* puppet show nightly *(see also pages 67, 135 and 218)*. Visually mesmerising and based on *khon* masked dance drama, the performance requires three puppeteers who manipulate sticks attached to the marionettes to bring them to life. This endangered art form was revived by Sakorn Yangkeawsot, who goes by the moniker Joe Louis.

Updating the *hun lakhon lek* theatre by allowing freer movement and more detailed costuming, and also by incorporating contemporary themes based on social issues and modern

---

THAI CLASSICAL MUSIC

To the uninitiated, classical Thai music sounds like a jarring and ear-piercing mishmash of contrasting tones without any pattern. The key is to listen to it as one would jazz, picking out one instrument and following it, switching to another as the mood moves one. Thai music is set to a scale of seven full steps, with a lilting and steady rhythm. Each instrument plays the same melody, but in its own way and seemingly without regard to how others are playing it. Seldom does an instrument rise in solo; it is always being challenged and cajoled by the other instruments of the orchestra.

A classical *phipat* orchestra is made up of a single reed instrument, the oboe-like *phinai*, and a variety of percussion instruments. The pitch favours the treble, with the pace set by the *ching*, a tiny cymbal, aided by the drums beaten with the fingers. The melody is played by two types of *ranad*, a bamboo-bar xylophone, and two sets of *gong wong*, tuned gongs arranged in a semicircle around the player.

Another type of orchestra employs two violins, the *saw-oo* and the *saw-duang*, usually heard accompanying a Thai dance-drama. A variation of the *phiphat* orchestra performs at a Thai boxing *(muay thai)* match to spur the sinewy combatants to action.

speech, Joe Louis has been successful in reviving this art form without diluting its origins.

Modern theatre and dance

Sadly, this is one area where modern innovation has been stifled, compounded by language barriers (for international appreciation) and budget limitations. The recent closure of the Bangkok Playhouse, one of the capital's few contemporary theatres, is yet another nail in the coffin.

The only venue left that stages and produces quality modern productions is Patravadi Theatre in Thonburi. The open-air venue is run by Patravadi Mechudhon, whose adaptations of classic Thai tales meld traditional local dance

2005 theatre season a new work called *Eclipse* premiered, presenting a visual feast of Thai drummers and dancers, based on a tale of Buddhist suffering during an eclipse of the moon. Patravadi Theatre also hosts the annual Bangkok Fringe Festival, which presents a varied programme of dance, drama and music.

Classical literature

Thais have always placed a heavy emphasis on oral tradition. Unfortunately, most of the country's classical written literature was destroyed when the Burmese sacked Ayutthaya in 1767. At the heart of Thai literature is the *Ramakien*, the Thai version of the Indian *Ramayana*. The

and theatre with modern Western styling. Some of its works fuse elements of Asian dance forms like Japanese *butoh* and Indonesian *wayang kulit*. Patravadi Theatre *(see also pages 66 and 218)* stages its acclaimed shows, some of which have toured overseas, on Saturday and Sunday nights June–February.

Its past shows have included the landmark *Sahatsadecha* in 1997, which artfully blends Thai *khon* with *nang yai*. The show was so successful that it went on to perform at the Biennale de la Danse, in Lyon, France. In its

LEFT: Joe Louis puppeteers. **ABOVE:** a scene from *Eclipse*, and Patravadi Theatre's dancers in rehearsal.

enduring story has found a home in the literature, dance and drama of many Asian countries. Familiarity with the *Ramakien* enables one to comprehend a variety of dramatic forms, its significance for the Thai monarchy, and its role as a model for exemplary behaviour.

The *Jataka* tales are also of Indian origin, telling of Buddha's reincarnations prior to enlightenment, though some are probably based on tales that existed before the Buddha lived. The first tales were translated from Pali script to Thai in the late 15th century. They have generated many other popular and classic stories, such as *Phra Aphaimani*, written by Sunthorn Phu, the 18th-century poet laureate.

Modern literature

It wasn't until the 1920s that Thai novels were published, with themes mainly touching on social or political issues. In the 1950s, however, censorship became so heavy and writers so harshly persecuted that quality fiction practically disappeared for 20 years. Thai writers since the 1980s have enjoyed a measure of political freedom. While they remain social critics, there are efforts to write fiction of literary merit. Many landmark Thai books were translated into English in the early 1990s. The late prime minister and cultural advocate Kukrit Pramoj's *Many Lives* for instance gives a good introduction to the Buddhist way of thinking. His *Four Reigns* is a fictional yet accurate account of court life in the 19th and 20th centuries. Also of note are Kampoon Boontawee's *Children of Isan* and Botan's *Letters from Thailand*.

The highlight of the literary calendar is the SEA Write awards, held every August/September. The 2002 Thai winner, young blood Prabda Yoon, stirred things up with the old establishment by penning works that connect to Thai youth.

Expatriate writers like Jake Needham and Christopher Moore bring a Western perspective to life in the kingdom, though the majority of such scribes feel compelled to wallow in the seedier aspects of the capital's nightlife, with somewhat predictable storylines.

BUDDHA IMAGES

The focal point of the *bot* and *viharn* (ordination and sermon halls) of a Thai temple is the Buddha image. The image is not considered a representation of the Buddha, but is meant to serve as a reminder of his teachings. Buddha images cast in bronze, or carved in wood or stone, constitute the bulk of classic Thai sculpture. Buddha images epitomise the zenith of sculpting and employ some of the finest artistry (and some of the highest prices) of any arts. Superb examples of bas-relief sandstone carving can be seen around the base of the *bot* of Bangkok's Wat Pho (*see page 92*). Delicately executed, the dozens of panels depict scenes from the *Ramakien*.

Traditional art

The inner walls of the *bot* (ordination halls) and *viharn* (sermon halls) in Thai temples are traditionally covered with murals. In the days before public education, the temple was the principal repository of knowledge for the common person. Monks were the teachers, and the interior walls of the temples were illustrated lectures. The principal themes are the life of Buddha, with the back wall generally depicting the *Maravijaya*, in which all earthly temptations are united to break the meditating Buddha's will and prevent his achieving nirvana.

The murals at Buddhaisawan Chapel in Bangkok's National Museum are among the finest examples of Thai painting. Others include the murals at Wat Suthat and the 19th-century paintings at Wat Bowonniwet. Although restored several times with less than perfect accuracy, the *Ramakien* murals in the walls surrounding Wat Phra Kaew include wonderful scenes of village and palace life.

Traditional art is also executed in the form of lacquer and gold paintings found on the shutters of most Thai temples. The best examples of lacquer painting can be found on the walls of the Lacquer Pavilion at Suan Pakkad Palace. Equally stunning are the intricate mother-of-pearl work by Thai artisans.

Contemporary art

At the turn of the 20th century, King Chulalongkorn commissioned several European artists to embark on art projects in Bangkok, a trend the government continued in 1923 when they hired Italian sculptor Corrado Feroci. The Florentine artist proved catalytic in the development of modern Thai art right through the 1960s; locals even gave him the adopted name of Silpa Bhirasri. He is attributed as being the forefather of modern art in Thailand, and established the country's first School of Fine Arts, which later became Silpakorn University.

Spirituality and Buddhism have been, and still are, major precepts in contemporary art – whether created by neo-traditionalist painters like Thawan Duchanee and Chalermchai Kositpipat, whose late 20th-century paintings reinvigorate traditional perceptions of Thai identity, or the meditative installations in the 1990s by the late Montien Boonma. Rising artist Sakarin Krue-on uses spiritual metaphors as his basis, appropriating traditional imagery to question the blind adoption of Western trends.

Aside from the spiritual, the 1997 economic collapse fuelled many local artists to question the effects of globalisation on the Thai populace. Rebellious artist Vasan Sitthiket blurs his art with faux political campaigning to highlight his contempt for national policies, while conceptual photographer Manit Sriwanichpoom ridicules the Thai urbanite's consumerist compulsions with his satirical *Pink Man* series.

FAR LEFT: a Thai woodcarver. **LEFT:** mother-of-pearl inlay on door at Wat Ratchabophith. **RIGHT:** modern art work by Sakarin Krue-on entitled *White Party*.

Cinema

Like most places in the world, Hollywood blockbusters dominate the cinemas. Of late however, a few talented Thai directors have been receiving acclaim for their works on the international film circuit. Leading the charge is the new wave director Apichatpong Weerasethakul, whose 2002 film *Blissfully Yours* was awarded the *Prix un certain regard* at the Cannes Film Festival, followed by the atmospheric 2004 film *Tropical Malady* (*Sud Pralad*), which also picked up a special prize at Cannes. Apichatpong's 2004 collaboration with Thai-American artist Michael Shaowansai on the hilariously campy *Adventures of Iron Pussy* –

about a cross-dressing superhero – is proof that Thai cinema is engaging and provocative to both domestic and international audiences.

Another name to watch out for is Jira Malikul, whose directing debut *Mekhong Full Moon Party* delves into one of Thailand's oldest and most endearing myths – the *naga* serpent.

Unfortunately, many such films don't get the airing they should in local cinemas. Still, Bangkok now has an indie cinema (House on RCA), and the Lido in Siam Square provides imaginative programming. Additionally, there are countless film festivals, including three versions of the Bangkok Film Festival, plus short film, animation, EU and British festivals. ❏

CUISINE

Thai cuisine is not just about tongue-numbing, tear-inducing spices. Distinct regional, ethnic-migrant and Thai-fusion styles of cooking combine to create a fabulous variety of choice and complex (yes, sometimes even bland) flavours to appeal to the serious gourmand

Thai food is expanding faster globally than any other cuisine, and it's easy to see why. Less a dining experience than a sensory attack, it's one of the few cuisines in the world capable of drawing people to a country purely on its own merits.

It's the explosive spiciness of Thai food that initially overwhelms, but what's most impressive is the extraordinary complex balance of flavours that lie underneath. And contrary to what most people think, it's not all blatantly spicy; most Thai meals will include a sampling of less aggressive dishes, some subtly flavoured with only garlic and herbs.

The variation of foods and cooking styles is immense as each of Thailand's four regions have distinct cuisines of their own. The northeast is influenced by Laos, the south by Malaysia and Indonesia, the central area by the cuisine of the Royal Thai kitchens of the capital (the one people are most familiar with), and the north by Burma and Yunnan. All types are available in Bangkok, and often at street stalls and markets serving the city's migrant communities. As usual, the busiest spots have the best food.

But Bangkok offers far more than Thai food. It's fast emerging as an international culinary hot spot with options that include Brazilian, Greek, Italian, Spanish and even a hip Michelin-starred French restaurant. Adding excitement is a clutch of new wave fusion restaurants that are boldly experimenting with Thai and Western ingredients and methods of preparation.

LEFT: chillies, limes, ginger, galangal and fresh herbs are the usual suspects. **RIGHT:** a typical Thai lunch.

How to eat Thai food

Most Thai meals have dishes placed in the middle of the table to be shared by all; the larger the group the more dishes you can try. Dish out a heap of rice onto your plate together with small portions of various dishes at the side (it's polite to take only a little at a time). Eat with a fork and spoon, using the fork in the left hand to push food onto the spoon. Chopsticks are only for Chinese and noodle dishes.

Rice is the staple; in the past it sustained workers throughout the day with just small portions of chilli, curry or sauce added for flavour. Even now, rural Thais eat large helpings of rice with just morsels of dried or salted

FIERY THAI CHILLIES

The small but very fiery Thai chillis *(prik)* comes in red or green forms but both pack a potent punch. When sliced and served in fish *sauce (nam pla)* as a condiment, it's called *prik nam pla.*

fish. Thankfully, jasmine-scented Thai rice is one of the most delicious in Asia.

Condiments on the table usually include dried, ground red chilli, sliced chilli with vinegar, sliced chilli with *nam pla* (fish sauce), and white sugar. These are mainly used to add extra flavour to noodle dishes. Many visitors are surprised to find that the peanut sauce condiment

used in many Thai restaurants in Western countries is of Malaysian or Indonesian origin; in Thailand it's only used as a dip for satay.

Northern cuisine

This is the mildest of Thai foods. Northerners generally eat *khao nio* (sticky rice), kneading it into a ball to dip into sauces and curries such as the Burmese *kaeng hanglay*, a sweet and tamarind-sour pork dish. *Khao soi* is also found in Burma, but is possibly of Chinese origin. Usually made with chicken, it has fresh egg noodles swimming in a mild coconut curry, with crispy noodles sprinkled on top.

Other northern Thai specialities include

sausages, such as the spicy pork *sai oua* (roasted over a coconut husk fire to impart aroma and flavour) and *naem* (fermented raw pork and pork skin seasoned with garlic and chilli). *Laab* is a salad dish of minced pork, chicken, beef, or fish served with mint leaves and raw vegetables to cool the spices. It's also common in the northeast.

Dipping sauces include *nam prik ong* (minced pork, mild chillies, tomatoes, garlic and shrimp paste) and the potent northern classic, *nam prik noom* (grilled chillies, onions and garlic). Both are eaten with the popular snack called *khaep moo* (crispy pork rind).

Northeastern cuisine

Northeastern (Isaan) food is simple, generally spicy, and eaten with mounds of sticky rice kept in bamboo baskets. Hot dishes include the legendary *som tam* (shredded green papaya, garlic, chillies, lime juice, and variations of tomatoes, dried shrimp, preserved crab and fermented fish) and a version of *laab*, which is spicier and sourer than its northern sister.

But perhaps the most popular Isaan food is not hot at all. *Gai yang* is chicken grilled in a marinade of peppercorns, garlic, fish sauce, coriander and palm sugar, and served with both hot and sweet dipping sauces.

Southern cuisine

The south – notable for Thailand's hottest dishes – also has gentler specialties such as *khao yam*, an innocuous salad of rice, vegetables, pounded dried fish and a southern fish sauce called *budu*. Slightly spicier are *phad sataw*, a stir-fry usually with pork or shrimp, and *sataw*, a large lima bean look-alike with a strong flavour and aroma. *Khao moke gai* is roasted chicken with turmeric-seasoned yellow rice – like an Indian *biryani*, often sprinkled with crispy fried onions.

Hot dishes include *kaeng tai plaa*. Fishermen who needed food that would last for days at sea are said to have created it by blending the fermented stomachs of fish with chillies, bamboo shoots and vegetables together with an intensely hot sauce. Even hotter is *kaeng leuang* (yellow curry), a variant of the central Thai

LEFT: chilli is a common ingredient in Thai cuisine.
RIGHT: Thai dishes at Sala Rim Naam restaurant.

kaeng som, with fish, green papaya and bamboo shoots or palm hearts in an explosive sauce.

Central cuisine

Central cuisine, which has been influenced by the royal palaces *(see text box below)*, includes many of the dishes made internationally famous at Thai restaurants abroad. It's notable for the use of coconut milk and garnishes such as grapes, which mellow the chilli heat and add a little sweetness. It's still fiery, though, so take care. Trademark dishes include *tom kha gai*, a soup of chicken, coconut milk and galangal, the celebrated hot and sour shrimp soup *tom yum goong*, and *kaeng khio waan* (green curry), with chicken or beef, basil leaves and pea-sized green aubergines. Stir-fries and noodle dishes are everywhere, due to the large Chinese presence in the central region.

Common dishes to try

Kaeng is usually translated as curry, but it covers a broad range, from thin soups to near-dry dishes like the northern *kaeng ho*. Many *kaeng* are made with coconut cream, like the spicy red curry (*kaeng pet*) and *kaeng mussaman*, a rich, sweetish dish of Persian origin with meat, potatoes and onions. *Kaeng* without coconut milk include "jungle curries", which are very spicy.

Fish and seafood have largely featured in

ORIGINS OF ROYAL THAI CUISINE

The so-called Royal Thai cuisine has hugely influenced the food of the Central Plains, with dishes such as green curry and the hot and sour shrimp soup. The great-grandson of King Rama IV, MR Sorut Visuddhi, is co-owner of Thanying, a royal Thai restaurant that serves the recipes of his mother, Princess Sulap-Walleng Visuddhi. He explains: "In the palace it was considered bad manners to perspire at the table or to eat foods that had strong smells. So we would use coconut milk to cut down on these tastes. This had a big influence on Central cooking."

The Grand Palace had many residences where each princess cooked what was called *ahaan chawang* (food

for the palace people). These recipes spread through the wealthy classes via palace finishing schools and publications such as *Mae Krua Hua Baak*, the country's first cookbook, written by Thanpuying Pliang Pasonakorn, a descendent of King Rama II.

Later, when the royal families moved out of the palaces, the kitchen hands they hired learnt the recipes and started cooking them for their own families. "Royal Thai" restaurants began to open from the 1980s, but few remain today. The intricate fruit and vegetable carving you will see at fine Thai restaurants – like the Sala Rim Naam at the Oriental hotel – is also a legacy of Royal Thai cuisine.

Thai cooking since ancient times. *Haw mok talay* is mixed seafood in a curried coconut custard and steamed in a banana-leaf cup or coconut shell. Other delicious choices to try are *poo pat pong karee* (steamed chunks of crab in an egg-thickened curry sauce with crunchy spring onion) and *hoi malaeng poo op maw din* (mussels in their shells, steamed in a clay pot with lime juice and aromatic herbs).

Meat – usually chicken, pork or beef – is cooked in all manner of styles, such as pork fried with garlic and black pepper (*muu thawd kratiam prik Thai*) or the sweet and sour *muu pad prio waan*, probably of Portuguese origin, brought to Thailand by Chinese immigrants.

THAI CHINESE CUISINE

Many ethnic Chinese in Thailand still speak the Teochew dialect of their southern Chinese ancestry, and most Chinese restaurants serve Teochew or Cantonese food. Especially famous are goose feet cooked in soy sauce, Peking duck, a wide variety of steamed and fried fish dishes, and the bite-sized lunchtime snacks called *dim sum*. Poultry, pork, seafood and mushrooms are ubiquitous items along with noodles or rice, while piping-hot Chinese tea is an integral part of every meal. Chinatown is awash with dining options although it has surprisingly few actual restaurants. Most people choose to eat at streetstalls or in tiny shophouse cafés.

Neua pad nam man hoi is a mild, delicate dish of beef fried with oyster sauce, spring onions and mushrooms. The popular and very spicy *pat pet pat bai kaprao* dishes include meat stir-fried with chillies, garlic, onions and holy basil (*bai kaprao*). Main ingredients to note are: chicken (*gai*), pork (*muu*), beef (*neua*), duck (*ped*), seafood (*talay*) and shrimp (*goong*).

Noodles and rice

Noodles – a Chinese import – have a place in Thai restaurants. The ubiquitous street-side noodle shop sells two types: *kuay tiaw*, made from rice flour, and *ba mee*, from wheat flour. Both can be ordered broad (*sen yai*), narrow (*sen lek*) or very narrow (*sen mee*), and with broth (*sai naam*) or without (*haeng*).

Common dishes are *kuay tiaw raad naa* (rice noodles flash-fried and topped with sliced meat and greens in a thick, mild sauce) and *paad thai* (narrow pan-fried rice noodles with egg, dried and fresh shrimp, spring onions, tofu, crushed peanuts and beansprouts). In *mee krawp*, the rice noodles are fried crispy, tossed in sweet-and-sour sauce and topped with sliced chillies, pickled garlic and slivers of orange rind.

Many lunchtime rice dishes are of Chinese origin. They include *khao man gai* (chicken with rice cooked in chicken broth); *khao moo daeng* (with Chinese red pork); and *khao kaa moo* (with stewed pork leg and greens). At night and in the early morning, two soup-like rice dishes are favoured. *Khao tom* comes in the water it was boiled in (with additions such as garlic-fried pork, salted egg or pickled ginger) and the close relative *joke*, which is porridge-like rice seasoned with minced pork, coriander and slivers of fresh ginger. Crispy *pathongko* (fried dough) pieces float on top.

Thai desserts

In Bangkok, *khanom* (desserts) come in bewildering variety, from light concoctions with crushed ice and syrup, to custards, ice creams and little cakes, and an entire category based on egg yolks cooked in flower-scented syrups.

The heavier Thai confections are rarely eaten after a big meal. After-meal desserts, served in small bowls, are generally light and elegant. *Kluay buat chee* has banana slices in sweetened and salted warm coconut cream.

Kluay kaek uses bananas sliced lengthwise, dipped in coconut cream and rice flour, and deep-fried until crisp. Another favourite is *taap tim krawp* (water chestnut pieces covered in red-dyed tapioca flour and served in coconut cream and crushed ice), and *sangkhaya ma-praoawn*, a coconut cream custard steamed in a young coconut or a small pumpkin.

Many desserts are startlingly inventive – you may finish a rich pudding before realising that its tantalising flavour comes from crisp fried onions. Look out for market vendors who sell "roof-tile cookies" (*khanom beuang*), crispy shells filled with strands of egg yolk cooked in syrup with shredded coconut, sweet and spicy

blends, such as Thai-style spaghetti with anchovies and chilli, served at modern cafés like Greyhound (several branches in the city).

Other modern Thai restaurants, like Mahanaga for instance, use non-traditional ingredients like lamb and salmon, and plate their essentially Thai dishes Western style. When international Thai restaurant chain The Blue Elephant opened a Bangkok branch in 2002 it introduced several fusion items, including salmon *laab,* and foie gras with tamarind. Many international restaurants – notably Jester's and Bed Supperclub – also incorporate Thai flavours like lemongrass and galangal into their broader East-West menus.

dried shrimp, coriander and coconut cream. But, if you sample nothing else in Thailand, don't miss the heavenly *khao niao ma-muand* (mango with sticky rice and coconut cream). Unfortunately, it's only available seasonally.

Thai fusion cuisine

There have been foreign influences in Thai food for centuries (even chilli, which is another Portuguese import), but recent years have seen the growth of a dedicated style of Thai-fusion dishes. It often takes the form of Italian-Thai

Refreshments

With meals Thais drink locally brewed beers such as Singha, Kloster and the stronger Beer Chang. Foreign brands brewed on licence include Heineken. The middle-class obsession with French wines is waning, and there is now a decent selection available from the New World. Among the working classes, the rice whisky brands Maekhong and Saeng Thip are popular, usually served as a "set" with ice, soda and lime. Note: fresh fruit and ice drinks will often get a splash of syrup (and salt) unless you request otherwise.   ❏

LEFT: spicy chicken and noodle soup. **ABOVE:** dining with altitude at roof-top Sirocco restaurant.

● *Restaurant recommendations are listed at the end of each chapter in the Places section.*

SHOPPING

You'll need to brush up your bargaining skills and fill up your pockets with baht before boarding Bangkok's Skytrain. It links the city's main shopping areas, packed with glitzy malls selling genuine designer goods and raucous street markets peddling fake versions

Bangkok is one of the shopping capitals of the world. It's a city where you can sniff out an antique treasure under the sweltering awnings of an outdoor market or pick up the latest Hermès handbag from a luxury marble-clad shopping mall. If you know where to look for it, just about anything is available – from Siamese pottery and traditional hand-woven silks to cutting-edge home furnishings and funky streetwear. The city caters to both spendthrifts and penny pinchers, with shops open seven days a week. The best shopping areas are conveniently connected by Bangkok's elevated Skytrain. You can glide above the traffic in air-conditioned comfort from Emporium, a glitzy shopping mall offering brands like Prada, Versace and Chanel to the rough and ready Chatuchak Weekend Market, where thousands of stalls sell everything from hilltribe jackets to quirky home accessories.

The main shopping areas converge around Thanon Rama I and Thanon Ploenchit and are linked by the Skywalk – a covered walkway beneath the Skytrain tracks – which connects the Chidlom, Siam Square and National Stadium Skytrain stations. This means you can walk from mall to mall without ever touching terra firma. Just a stone's throw from Siam Square, a warren of market stalls and shops catering to a trendy teenage clientele, is the high-end Siam Discovery Centre, as well as Mahboonkrong (MBK), a multi-storey bargain-hunter's heaven. Nearby is the recently opened

THE ART OF BARGAINING

First, don't start bargaining unless you really want to buy. Stage One involves asking the price of the item. Stage Two opens the process with a request from you to lower the price. The seller will then lower the original price, thereby signalling he (or she) is open to offers. Stage Three is when you offer your first price, which is always too low. From there the volley of bargaining begins until the final price is agreed upon. Experienced hands say you should always walk away from the seller when you've offered your best shot, hoping you will be called back with the lowest price. This doesn't always happen though, so be prepared to go back and eat humble pie.

LEFT: dazzling colours in a Thai silk shop.
RIGHT: bargaining is an essential skill in Thailand.

Siam Paragon which is marketing itself as Bangkok's ultimate shopping experience. At the other end of the Skywalk is luxury shopping at Gaysorn Plaza and Erawan Bangkok, which boasts funky fashion from the likes of Galliano and Yamomoto. Also in this area is Central Chidlom, one of the city's oldest and best-loved department stores.

The best times to shop

Bangkok hosts a number of seasonal sales which offer unique items, such as the twice-yearly prison sale of wooden furniture made by Thai prisoners. Check the local English-language newspaper listing sections for details.

Northern silversmiths pound out bowls coated with an extract of tamarind to enhance their sheen. Teakwood is carved into practical items such as breadboards and salad bowls, as well as more decorative trivets and statues of mythical gods, angels and elephants. Bronze statues of classical drama figures like the recumbent deer from the *Ramakien* make elegant decorations. Brassware, like the large noodle cabinets which street vendors sling on bamboo poles, can double up as small side tables. Natural fibre woven into placemats, laundry baskets and handbags also make great buys.

Thai craftsmen excel at lacquerware, the art of overlaying wooden or bamboo items with

Also worth attending are the annual export sales events such as Made in Thailand and Bangkok International Gifts & Houseware (BIG). Every June–July and December–January, major department stores and malls take part in the Thailand Grand Sales, though many also offer a five-percent tourist discount year round – simply show your passport at the point of purchase. Alternatively, you can claim the seven percent VAT discount at the airport *(see page 223)*.

Traditional Thai products

Thailand is famous the world over for the fine quality of its traditional handicrafts, and there is an extraordinary variety on offer.

glossy black lacquer, then painting scenes in gold leaf on this black "canvas". Bowls and trays are the main items sold. One of Thailand's lesser-known arts is nielloware, which involves applying an amalgam of black metal onto etched portions of silver or, to a lesser extent, gold. Thai craftsmen are also supremely skilled at setting oyster shells aglow in black lacquer backgrounds to create scenes of enchanting beauty.

Thais have been crafting pots for over 5,000 years with great skill. While original antiques

ABOVE: wooden carving of a scene from the *Ramakien*.
RIGHT: trendy retail shop in downtown Bangkok.

are rarities, most ceramics are still thrown along the same shapes and designs of their age-old counterparts. Among the most well-known are Sangkhaloke ceramic plates from the ancient Sukhothai with their distinctive twin fish design. Celadon is a beautiful stoneware with a light jade green or dark-brown glaze, and is used to make dinnerware, lamps and statuary. *Bencharong* originated in China and was later developed by Thai artists. Its name describes its look: *bencha* is Sanskrit for five, and *rong* means colour. The five colours of *bencharong* – red, blue, yellow, green and white – appear on delicate porcelain bowls, containers, ashtrays and decorative items. Popular blue-and-white porcelain, which also originated in China, has been produced extensively in Thailand for centuries.

Thai handicrafts are found in shops and markets all over the city, and some of the more specialist shops are worth seeking out. If pressed for time, head for Nayarana Phand in Thanon Ratchadamri, a one-stop shop for all things Thai.

Antiques

Thai and Burmese antiques are among the finest in Asia, but the real thing is hard to find these days. For the tenacious and well-informed though, treasures can still be unearthed. The centre of the city's antiques trade is located in River City, a sprawling array of shops selling genuine antiques as well as look-a-like *objets d'art*. Note: the Fine Arts Department maintains strict control over the export of religious antiques; dealers are usually able to clear buyers' purchases by obtaining export permits and shipping them abroad.

Textiles and tailoring

The glamour of Thai silk was first recognised in the late 1940s by American entrepreneur Jim Thompson. He promoted it abroad where it quickly gained wide acceptance for its bumpy texture and shimmering iridescence. Today, silk has become a major Thai industry. While the Jim Thompson shop offers an excellent range of coloured silks and ready-made products, bargains can also be gleaned from the lesser-known Jim Thompson Factory Outlet.

Also worth buying is *mudmee*, a northeastern silk characterised by subtle zigzagging lines and in more sombre hues such as dark blue, maroon and deep yellow. Dazzling embroidery

COUNTERFEIT CITY

Bangkok has long had an unfortunate reputation for the quality of its fakes, from Louis Vuitton handbags to pirated copies of the latest Hollywood movie. For a fraction of the price of the real thing you can buy reproductions of Rolex, Cartier or Tag Heuer watches. Bear in mind that some reproductions are better than others – a dud "Rolex" may stop running a few weeks after purchase. Clothes are a safer bet. Popular knock-offs include Nike, Hilfiger, Armani, DKNY and Ralph Lauren. The quality can vary tremendously, so inspect each garment carefully.

With increasing pressure from international companies, the Thai government is attempting to crack down on counterfeit goods. Though the trade is fairly open, sporadic government raids mean that watches, DVDs or audio CDs are sometimes sold more surreptitiously. The covers of pirated DVDs, for instance, are displayed in albums at street-side stalls; once buyers have made their choices, vendors will disappear to a hidden stash nearby and minutes later return with the merchandise.

Fake goods can be found almost anywhere in Bangkok's markets and shopping malls, but they proliferate mainly around the Thanon Silom and Patpong night markets, as well as the stalls that spring up along Thanon Sukhumvit (Soi 5 to Soi 11) each evening.

can be found in the modern-day versions of *teen chok* – a method with which women of the ancient Lanna kingdom in the north of Thailand symbolically wove their family histories into their sarongs. The country's northern hilltribes each have their own distinctive patchwork and embroidery designs, mainly in bright blues, magentas and yellows. At the Mae Fah Luang shop in Siam Discovery Centre, a royal initiative to promote the livelihood of Thai villagers through traditional means, you can purchase hand-woven silks and cottons in lengths, or ready-made into cushion covers and clothes.

Using local and imported fabrics, Bangkok's excellent tailors can whip up perfectly-fitted

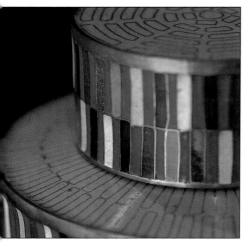

three-piece suits for men as well as elegant dresses with appliqué and beadwork for women. Choose designs from catalogues, conjure up your own creations or have your old favourites copied. If using your own material, rummage at Bangkok's famous fabric market on Sampeng Lane in Chinatown. Though some shops offer a 24-hour service, it's always best to return for at least one fitting to ensure an accurate cut.

Gems and jewellery

Thailand mines its own rubies and sapphires from the eastern coast city of Chantaburi, and also acts as a conduit for stones from Burma and Cambodia. Globally, Thailand is a major

player in the international jewellery market, and Bangkok is home to the world's leading cutters of coloured gems. Rubies range from pale to deep-red (including the famous "pigeon's blood" red); sapphires come in blue, green and yellow, as well as in the form most associated with Thailand – the star sapphire. Thai jewellers can turn gold, white-gold, silver and platinum into delicate jewellery settings and are able to produce both traditional and modern designs.

Be careful when shopping for gems and jewellery; on streets and in some small shops, the stones may not be of the quality and weight advertised. The Tourism Authority of Thailand has joined hands with gem-trading organisations to provide quality control through the Jewel Fest Club – look for the ruby-ring logo on shopfronts.

Cutting-edge Thai

Thai craftsmanship and creativity extends far beyond the realm of the traditional, and Bangkok is fast becoming a hub for cutting-edge design. Keep an eye out for some of Thailand's up-and-coming homegrown fashion labels such as the flamboyant offerings from Fly Now and Jaspal, or the more understated designs from Greyhound. Thai designers are also making waves in the area of home decor. Propaganda (at Siam Discovery Centre and Emporium) produces innovative accessories, while Cocoon (Gaysorn Plaza) offers a line of chi-chi throws and incense holders. Thai cosmetics-makers such as Harnn are also reinventing natural Thai beauty products like jasmine rice soap and tamarind facial scrubs, and packaging them in elegant rattan baskets.

Even the shopping experience is being repackaged; if you get bored of the city's seemingly limitless supply of department stores and malls, sample more eclectic boutique shops like It's Happened to Be a Closet (Siam Square) where customers are encouraged to mix-and-match vintage dress designs with homeware products and accessories. At Inspired by Inner Complexity (Sukhumvit 31) relax in the tearoom before heading to the loft for funky fashions by hip local designers. ❑

● *See also Travel Tips (pages 222–226) for more information on shopping and addresses of shops.*

LEFT: jewellery box embedded with coloured stone.

Bangkok Bazaar

In many ways, Bangkok is one vast market. Shops spill out onto pavements, goods are hawked off tarpaulin sheets, and there are makeshift vendors' stalls on virtually every street. Indeed, a trip to the *talad*, or market, is an essential part of the Bangkok experience. The city's markets provide a tantalising assault on the senses, as well as the wallet, with smells, sights and sounds galore. At markets bargaining is *de rigueur*, and is considered part of the fun of shopping. Bangkok has a market for just about every hour of the day or night, and every neighbourhood has one, if not two, of these memorable outdoor shopping emporiums.

The ultimate Bangkok bazaar is the **Chatuchak Weekend Market** *(see page 158)* affectionately dubbed "JJ" due to the alternative Thai spelling, Jatujak. Some 15,000 stalls offer a mind-boggling variety of goods. There's a pet section selling pedigree pooches as well as Siamese fighting cockerels. The antiques and crafts section has a wonderful selection of hill-tribe fabrics and accessories, and also traditional handicrafts. Chatuchak caters to the most eclectic of tastes and you will find antique jewellery, funky lamps, old Thai movie posters, hand-made paper, and more.

There are numerous markets tucked around the shopping malls and department stores of central Bangkok. The **Pratunam Market** *(page 135)* rivals Chatuchak for its selection of clothing. At midday the stalls at **Soi La Lai Sap** (literally "lane which melts your money away") sell shoes, handbags and myriad accessories. **Thanon Khao San** *(page 113)* is lined with stalls offering backpacker requisites such as silver jewellery, hand-painted cards and second-hand books.

For market-lovers, Bangkok's **Chinatown** *(see page 121)* is a must. **Pahurat Market** sells all things Indian, from saris to henna dyes. Innumerable fabric shops line narrow **Sampeng Lane**. For a real flavour of Chinatown, wander the length of **Soi Itsaranuphap**, which slices through the area like a knife

through a layer cake, passing spice shops, a fish market and stores selling religious paraphernalia. Also in Chinatown is the so-called "thieves market" known as **Nakhon Kasem** *(page 125)* where residents in the past would go to look for items burgled from their homes; these days it sells more prosaic car parts. More authentic is **Faichai**, or Flashlight Market, held on Saturday evenings along the labyrinth of streets around Central Hospital near Chinatown. It sells a variety of goods and bric-a-brac.

Damnoen Saduak, the famous floating market selling vegetables and fruit *(page 171)* on the outskirts of Bangkok, has lost

much of its authenticity and is now staged purely as a tourist attraction. For fresh produce markets with local flavour take an early morning trip to **Talad Kao** *(page 125)* in Chinatown. For nighttime shopping, head to **Suan Lum Night Bazaar** *(page 134)*. With nearly 4,000 stalls selling handicrafts, clothes and furniture, it's a smaller version of Chatuchak without the midday heat and crowds. Other evening markets, like those along **Thanon Silom** and **Patpong** *(page 144)*, as well as the stalls along **Thanon Sukhumvit** (roughly Soi 5 to Soi 11) are a treasure-trove of counterfeit goods and souvenirs, and are open until midnight. ❑

RIGHT: colourful Chatuchak market stall.

BANGKOK AFTER DARK

Bangkok by night isn't all unbridled sleaze, bump-and-grind bars and boozy cruising. There are lots of hip dance clubs and cool bars, plus a thriving live jazz and indie music scene. Less well known are its highbrow classical and modern dance and theatre events

Many visitors' expectations of Bangkok nightlife extend no further than the much-hyped up Patpong go-go bar scene, but this cosmopolitan city has plenty of options for entertainment once the sun goes down. The Thai craving for *sanuk* (fun) has in recent years seen booms in microbreweries and bars offering everything from Cuban cigars and art on the walls to clubs specialising in music as diverse as jazz, Latin, hip hop, house and mind-numbing techno, often all on the same street. In addition, there is traditional dance, theatre, opera, classical music, indie films and evening sports aplenty. Bangkok really comes alive under the cover of darkness, and never before has it offered so much choice to the nighttime reveller.

Nightlife zones

That's the good news. The bad is that the Bangkok nightlife scene has taken a hit since 2001 when the government introduced a Social Order Campaign with confusing Nightlife Zoning laws and draconian policing of entertainment venues. Bent on clamping rampant drug abuse and under-age drinking, the government has designated three nightlife zones: Thanon Silom, Thanon Ratchadaphisek and Royal City Avenue (RCA), where venues with valid dance licences can stay open until 2am. The rest must close at 1am. Of the three, the only zone found in downtown Bangkok is Silom, which means the acclaimed nightlife

LEFT: the night comes alive at infamous Patpong.
RIGHT: coffee shop at Chatuchak Market.

spots found along Thanon Sukhumvit – like Q Bar, Bed Supperclub and Mystique – all close painfully early at 1am.

The Silom zone includes the famous Patpong red light district and night market as well as numerous pubs and restaurants, but little in the way of dance clubs outside Soi 2 and Soi 4. Thanon Ratchadaphisek has been the traditional stomping ground of huge clubs and even larger massage parlours, visited mainly by Thais and Asian tourists, but recently, a clutch of smaller new bars are attracting young Thais. Of the three zones, it's RCA – long maligned as a tortuous teen hangout – that has the most scope to develop into a mature club scene. The signs are evident that it's at last responding, with venues like Astra, Code and the revamped Route 66, offering varied international music styles and brand-name DJs.

Thanks to the party-pooping Social Order Campaign, be prepared for the occasional police raid when revellers are urine-tested for drugs. During such raids, the police may ask foreigners to show their passports. Many clubs, including Bed Supperclub, Q Bar and Mystique, won't let you in without one. To get around the miserably early closing time, do as what most Thais are forced to do: start your evening early, say by 10.30pm, so there is ample time to wind down by the time the clubs close.

The club scene

Bangkok's club scene has steadily improved of late, with even luxury hotels getting into the act. Internationally hailed DJs such as Claude Challe have appeared at the Conrad Bangkok's 87, The Metropolitan hotel's Met Bar, and Zuk Bar at the venerable Sukhothai hotel. Dance music has evolved from ear-bashing techno to include hip hop, deep house, jungle, Indian vibes, and countless variations led by the cutting-edge dance clubs like Bed Supperclub and Q Bar (both Sukhumvit Soi 11) and Mystique (Sukhumvit Soi 31), all of which draw multinational crowds. All these spots regularly import international DJ acts like Cash Money

THAI ROCK AND COUNTRY

Three types of music dominate Thai-style rock and country clubs. The rock-format *plaeng puer cheewit* (Songs For Life), is played in countless Bangkok clubs notable for their kitschy decor of cowboy hats, buffalo horns and Confederate flags from the US Civil War. The music has its roots in the record collections of American GIs stationed in Thailand during the Vietnam War, and the lyrics developed as protest songs during Thailand's student uprisings of the early 1970s. The most famous practitioner of this music form is Ad Carabao, who still plays gigs with his band Carabao.

Luk thung (Child of the Rice Fields), as the name

suggests, is Thai country music and mainly appeals to the working class. Its lyrics recount "real life" issues, ranging from unrequited love to poverty and despair. The genre of music is so popular it has spawned several magazines and TV programmes, and even a few films.

Maw lam (Doctors' Dance) is an upcountry form sung in the Lao dialect by singers dressed in ornate costumes inspired by the royal courts. You'll hear *luk thung* and *maw lam* played on taxi drivers' radios and in clubs primarily located on the outskirts of town where Isaan migrant communities congregate. Spicy food and copious amounts of local rice-based whiskies are the fuel for any of these gigs.

and Kid Koala, in addition to hosting an increasingly confident posse of local DJs who go by names like Dragon, Tee Deeper and Tui.

More local-oriented venues range from mega clubs such as Dance Fever, a favourite spot for young and trendy Thais, on Thanon Ratchadapisek, to a vibrant Thai scene within the backpacker sub-culture of Thanon Khao San, with hot venues like Café Democ and Lava.

Live music

Front-line international acts are returning to Bangkok after a lull caused by the economic crash in 1997. Most gigs – recent ones include Norah Jones, Alicia Keyes and Sting – are held at Impact Arena or Bec Tero Hall.

Local music in bars varies tremendously. The huge Tawandaeng German Brewhouse on Thanon Narathiwat features local band Fong Nam on Wednesday evenings. Led by American Bruce Gaston, the band combines the music of traditional Thai *phiphat* orchestra with rock. It's not everyone's cup of tea but give it a listen if you're in the neighbourhood. Likewise, visitors may find Thai rock and country *(see text box page 64)* a novel experience and prefer to stick to standard Western staples like R & B, blues, rock and jazz *(see text box page 66)*, all of which are yours for the picking.

T-Pop (Thai pop music) is full of plastic-looking *luk kreung* (half-Thai, half-Western) stars like Tata Young, singing bubblegum tunes to doey-eyed teens. Far more entertaining are the indie bands that have been grabbing attention since the 1990s. Indie labels like Hualampong Riddim and Panda Records provide recording opportunities outside the mainstream, and their bands play regular gigs. Small clubs and party nights feature acts such as Apartment Khunpa and Futon playing a repertoire that includes metal, electronica, ska, thrash and grunge. Every November, local and international indie music takes centrestage when Bangkok's coolest radio station Fat Radio (104.5FM) stages its two-day Fat Festival at various venues.

To add to the mix, during the cooler months, outdoor beer gardens have Thai and international bands playing a diet of pop covers.

Bars and pubs

Upmarket bars with international sensibilities are found all over central Bangkok. Try sky-high champagne and caviar (both in price and altitude) at the roof-top bar Distil on Thanon Silom, or cocktails at the exquisite modern Thai restaurant Mahanaga (Sukhumvit Soi 29) or Face Bar (Sukhumvit Soi 38). The Conrad Bangkok, on Thanon Withayu, has one of the coolest hotel lobby bars imaginable in the Diplomat Bar, while the Sofitel Silom offers reasonably priced bottles of wine with 37th-floor city panoramas at V9. The hip Thai scene constantly shifts with the whims of local image mavens, but increasingly centres on the

major Sukhumvit thoroughfares of Soi Thonglor (in venues such as To Die For and Chi, at H1) and Thanon Ekamai (Skunk).

The English and Irish pub scene is mainly concentrated on Thanon Silom and Thanon Sukhumvit, with notable venues being Bull's Head on Sukhumvit Soi 33, (which has a fine English bitter on draught), the Dubliner (Sukhumvit Soi 22) and O'Reilly's (Thanon Silom). There are also a few American-style sports bars, such as Gulliver's (Thanon Khao San and Sukhumvit Soi 5) and microbreweries like Londoner Brew Pub (corner of Sukhumvit Soi 33). All these places have variations on the usual pub grub and games formula.

LEFT: interior of the uber-cool Bed Supperclub.
RIGHT: chic Distil bar is another popular watering hole.

The gay scene

Whether tolerance towards gays and lesbians is increasing or decreasing in Thailand often depends on the nuances of context, but either way the scene is thriving and very visible. Clubs and bars around Silom Soi 2 and Soi 4 cater to a variety of gay tastes, be it quiet drinking and Thai dining at Sphinx (Soi 4), boozy cruising at Balcony (Soi 4) or hard dance at DJ Station (Soi 2). Soi 2 is exclusively gay, while Soi 4 is more of a free-for-all, its street-side tables hosting people of varying sexual inclinations blatantly ogling passers-by. Gay sex shows and sleazy gay pick-up joints with go-go boys are located around Thanon Surawong,

particularly on Soi Tawan and Duangthawee Plaza. The iconic Bangkok Gay Pride Festival (www.bangkokpride.org/en) every November is a year-end climax of parades and celebration around the Silom-Patpong area.

Red-light entertainment

The foreign press often latches on to titillating headlines, painting Bangkok as a city of sleaze, so it surprises visitors to find how small the go-go scene actually is. The go-go bars that cater to *farang* (foreigners) in Patpong 1 and Patpong 2, and Nana Entertainment Plaza and Soi Cowboy along Thanon Sukhumvit, are largely neon-lit strips with a (usually) gentle hustle from girls hanging around outside. The transsexual "ladyboys" (*katoey*) can be more aggressive, particularly after hours around Soi Nana. Asian tourists who prefer more discreet adult entertainment seek out the lounge bars along Sukhumvit Soi 33 and the massage parlours of Thanon Ratchadaphisek and Thanon Petchaburi. Soi Thaniya in Silom caters to largely Japanese men.

A ban on nudity as part of the Social Order Campaign has been largely enforced; most bars feature pole-dancing girls gyrating in bikinis, although a few illegal "upstairs" shows offer full nudity and sex acts, either simulated or real. The infamous shows where girls use their genitalia for assorted juggling of bananas, darts and ping pong balls, still appear on menu cards handed out in Patpong. Prostitution, however, extends beyond the borders of these places; most clubs and bars around town will have freelance working girls (and boys) roaming the dance floors.

Kathoey cabaret

The famous transsexual or *katoey* cabaret shows, whose artistes are making a name for themselves on the international circuit from Sydney to London have become a Bangkok staple. Mambo, on Sukhumvit Soi 22, and New Calypso Cabaret at Asia Hotel, on Thanon Phayathai, are considered the best. The shows feature saucy (and sometimes risqué) lip-synching song and dance routines performed by a revue of sequinned and feather boa-ed artistes in various stages of sex change surgery.

Theatre and dance

Arts thespian Patravadi Mejudhon stages modern dance and drama inspired by traditional and

BLUE-BLOODED JAZZ PLAYER

King Bhumibol is a keen sax player and jazz composer – he's jammed with virtually all the jazz musicians who've visited Bangkok, including Stan Getz and Bennie Goodman – and Bangkok organises jazz festivals each year to commemorate his birthday. Regular gigs in the city include the Living Room (Sheraton Grande hotel) which attracts fine resident bands and visiting guests like sax player Ernie Watts. The Oriental Hotel's Bamboo Bar has an excellent Russian jazz quartet which backs foreign singers, while Saxophone, on Thanon Phayathai is the pick of the city's stand-alone venues with Latin and big band outfits as regulars.

Buddhist themes at her open-air Patravadi Theatre in Thonburi. Performances are usually in Thai, but they are music and dance oriented, and often accessible to foreigners.

There are short performances of the classical *khon* dance-drama at tourist venues and restaurants, while more serious performances are held at the National Theatre.

Joe Louis Theatre at Suan Lum Night Bazaar, which stages Bangkok's only remaining example of *hun lakhon lek*, a traditional puppet theatre based on the *khon* dance-drama, has attracted much international press, but still struggles for local support (*see Cultural Arts page 46 for more details of the above*).

as providing many of the musicians for the Bangkok Opera, plays regular concerts throughout the year, often at the Thai Cultural Centre, off Thanon Ratchadapisek, and on Sundays in Lumphini Park during the cool season.

The International Festival of Dance & Music brings international acts for a season of opera, classical music, contemporary dance and ballet every October to November, while the Thailand Cultural Centre hosts regular concerts.

Nighttime sports

Bangkok at night isn't all booze and boogie. Hip hop kids head to the Red Bull Skate Park on Thanon Sathorn for roller blading and skate-

Opera and classical music

Multi-talented Cambridge graduate Somtow Sucharitkul, who has written Hollywood horror scripts and several books in English, including the excellent *Jasmine Nights*, set up the Bangkok Opera in 2002. Among its three or four yearly productions of classics, like *The Magic Flute*, are Somtow's own works (written in English) such as *Mae Naak*, which is based on a Thai ghost story. His works are mainly staged at the Thailand Cultural Centre.

The Bangkok Symphony Orchestra, as well

boarding, and there's disco bowling – to music and flashing lights – at several bowling alleys in the city. RCA has an indoor go-kart track and some snooker clubs allow after-hours beers.

Nobody who comes to Thailand should miss the sport of *muay thai*, frenzied kickboxing accompanied by the wailing of traditional music and animated betting on the outcome. Lumphini Stadium, the mecca of world *muay thai*, where all the best fighters appear, is slated to move in the near future to a new location on Soi Nang Linchi 3. Another venue is Ratchadamnoen Stadium at Thanon Ratchadamnoen Nok. ❑

LEFT: live jazz at the Saxophone. **ABOVE:** transsexual cabaret performers; a frenetic bout of *muay thai*.

● *See also Travel Tips (pages 218–222) for more information on nightlife and addresses of nightpots.*

SPAS AND WELLNESS CENTRES

Traditional Thai massage, herbal steam baths and compresses, and time-honoured indigenous beauty and health formulas – these and various other indulgent New Age treatments at Bangkok's plush spas promise to ease holiday-induced stress

Thailand is renowned as the spa capital of Asia, and with good reason. Thai spas have an enticing allure that stems from their link to the country's unique culture and environment. To begin with, Thai spas draw on a vast and longstanding native tradition of natural healing, offering treatments like traditional Thai massage, herbal steams and baths, and herbal compresses. These treatments use indigenous herbs and formulas that have been used for centuries in native health and beauty practices.

When it comes to service, the country's masseuses and therapists are blessed with the inherent warmth that Thai people are generally known for. This makes the Thai spa experience eminently gentle and relaxing, and adds that extra dimension of luxury. On top of this, Thailand's spas, outside of Bangkok, are mostly found in exotic beach or mountain locations. In the midst of such beautiful surroundings, the spa-goer is immersed in a self-contained world of relaxation and pampering. Add to this the increasingly creative and sophisticated interior design concepts – from minimalist Zen to tropical fantasy – and you have escapist spas with a style and service unrivalled in other countries.

Traditional Thai massage

Perhaps the most unique spa treatment for visitors to Thailand is the traditional Thai massage, a holistic therapy with roots in ancient traditional medicine, and which has been practised as a form of healing for centuries. Like

LEFT: stress-relieving yoga meditation at Devarana Spa.
RIGHT: a spa therapist giving a shoulder massage.

many aspects of Thai culture, traditional Thai massage derives its origins from ancient India; it arrived in Thailand through Buddhist missionary monks who were trained as healers. Along with the spread of Buddhist faith, traditional massage techniques became popular for their ability to relieve ailments like backache, headache, tension and fever.

Thai massage technique is linked to the ancient Indian yoga philosophy which holds that our life energy is supplied along 72,000 meridian lines that run along our bodies. This is why some of the stretching actions of Thai massage resemble the stretching poses of yoga. Thai massage focuses on 10 key energy lines along our bodies and uses pressure to release the blocked energy along those lines.

Along with releasing blocked energy, there is a spiritual element to Thai massage as well. It is believed that the masseuse is healing the recipient by offering loving care through his or her hands. In ancient times, the masseuse would say a prayer to centre the mind in a meditative mood before performing a healing massage. This meditative awareness enables the masseuse to sense the energy flow and blockages in the recipient's body, thus providing optimum healing to the affected areas. When done properly, the masseuse should feel as relaxed as the recipient, because Thai massage is supposed to be a spiritual act that nourishes both the giver and the recipient.

Unlike Western massage, Thai massage does not make use of oils or lotions, and the recipient remains fully clothed during the massage. The client is supplied with loose-fitting cotton pajamas and the massage is done on a mattress laid on the floor. The masseuse uses his or her thumbs, arms, elbows, knees and feet, and may climb all over your body and even walk on your back. Don't be alarmed if you find the masseuse suddenly straddling your groin – it's all part of the technique.

The masseuse uses a combination of pressure and stretching techniques, done in a rhythmic

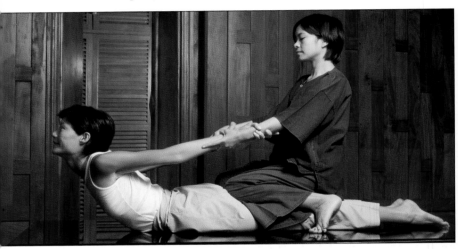

HOTEL AND DAY SPAS IN BANGKOK

For the ultimate in pampering, head for **The Oriental Spa**, located in the legendary Oriental Hotel. It is the pioneer of all Thai spas and designed in the style of a beautiful Thai teak house (48 Oriental Avenue, tel: 0-2233 9630, www.mandarinoriental.com). In the Business District, try the exquisite Thai-style **Devarana Spa** at the Dusit Thani Hotel (946 Thanon Rama 4, tel: 0-2636 3600, ext. 7006, www.devarana.com), which is imbued with the feeling of a light and airy Thai temple, or the **Shambala Spa** at the ultra-chic Metropolitan Hotel (27 Thanon Sathorn Tai, tel: 0-2625 3357, www.comohotels.co.uk), for a white-on-white experience in contemporary cool. New on the scene is the exotic **Chi Spa** at the Shangri-La Hotel (89 Soi Wat Suan Plu, tel: 0-2236 7777, www.shangri-la.com), elegantly styled to evoke the hushed calm of a temple.

Bangkok's most popular day spas – located in renovated old houses – are found in the leafy Sukhumvit area. The most elegant is **Divana Spa**, (7 Sukhumvit Soi 23, tel: 0-26616784/5, www.divanaspa.com). For a more casual, homey feel, go to **Sareerarom Spa** (117 Thonglor Soi 10, Sukhumvit 55, tel: 0-2391 9919, www.sareerarom.com) or **Rasayana Retreat** (57 Soi Sukhumvit 39, tel: 0-2662 4803-5, www.rasayanaretreat.com), which also has Thailand's only raw food restaurant offering organic meals.

and rocking motion. A Thai massage session usually lasts about two hours, during which most people fall into a relaxing slumber. However, towards the end of the massage, expect to be twisted, stretched and flipped backwards while your body is stretched into yoga-like poses by the masseuse. It is important to be relaxed and to trust that your masseuse is doing the right thing. After a Thai massage, some people may find their bodies aching in places that didn't hurt before. This is because subconscious muscle tension causes energy blockages to be released during the massage, hence the resulting discomfort. A few more massage sessions usually relieves this type of ache.

Steams, saunas and compresses

Aside from Thai massage, a number of treatments offered in Thai spas stem from the same ancient healing tradition. The use of heat therapies combined with herbal ingredients is a distinguishing trait of traditional Thai healing practices. One of the most popular is the Thai herbal steam or sauna. Their healing secret lies in the use of indigenous Thai herbs like turmeric, *prai*, lemongrass, camphor and kaffir lime. Aside from providing an overall health and skin booster, practitioners claim that Thai herbal steam can result in weight loss if done consistently over an extended period of time.

Another ancient Thai healing therapy is the use of hot herbal compresses made of medicinal herbs wrapped in a tight bundle, steamed for several hours, and then pressed against trouble areas of the body, like tense shoulders or rheumatic joints. The key to healing lies in the combination of medicinal herbs and heat.

Spa options

While Thailand is well known for its self-contained resort spas complete with accommodation and set in scenic areas, Bangkok too offers a bewildering number of spas that are popular with visitors as well as locals. The most luxurious establishments are hotel spas. These welcome the public as well as hotel guests, and usually spare no expense on design and fittings – with prices to match. Less extravagant but with a charm of their

own are the many day spas around Bangkok, usually located in renovated old houses and set among well-tended gardens. Day spa prices veer towards the mid-price range, and the treatments are just as good as hotel spas.

New on the scene is the medical spa, combining hospital health services with holistic spa therapies. Here, Western health practices such as medical check-ups and laser cosmetic surgery are offered in the same place as traditional Thai massage and Chinese acupuncture – to both fix and pamper your body at the same time. Patients can select from a variety of slimming, rejuvenation and detox fasting programmes, tailored to individual needs. ❑

MEDICAL SPAS

Billing itself as Asia's premier medical spa, **St Carlos Medical Spa** offers 17 different healing and pampering packages that include medical check-ups, luxurious hotel-style accommodation and spa meals, plus a dermatology clinic, fully-equipped fitness gym and swimming pool. (5/84 Moo 2, Thanon Tivanon, tel: 0-2975 6700, www.stcarlos.com).

Bangkok Dermatology Centre (SCB Park Plaza, tel: 0-2937 5455, www.bkkdermato.com) puts the focus on beauty, with a dermatology clinic offering the latest in laser surgery, plus spa rooms that offer pampering body massages, scrubs and reflexology treatments.

LEFT: Thai massage in progress.
RIGHT: hot herbal compress treatment at Devarana Spa.

PLACES

A detailed guide to the entire city, with principal sites
clearly cross-referenced by number to the maps

At first glance, this metropolis of nearly 10 million seems a bewildering melding of new and old and indeterminate, and of exotic and commonplace and indescribable, all tossed together into a gigantic urban maze. Years after your first contact with the city, it can still appear that way. It's hardly surprising considering that, only 60 to 70 years, ago much of what exists today was empty land. More so than with most large cities, the traveller's mental map of Bangkok needs a few anchors.

The most obvious anchor is the Chao Phraya River that Thai kings throughout the centuries have used to define their royal cities. Partly for symbolic and defensive reasons, Bangkok's founding king took a bend in the river, dug a canal between two of the river's bends and thus sliced off a parcel of land into an artificial island. In Bangkok, that royal island became known as Rattanakosin. An essential part of any city tour, its glittering highlights are many, like the Grand Palace, the temple of Wat Pho and the National Museum. As outside threats diminished, the kings established palaces in the suburbs beyond Rattanakosin. Dusit to the north is where you'll find Vimanmek Mansion and a number of parks. To the east at Pathumwan are the monster shopping malls of modern Bangkok.

South of the royal city are the enclaves where foreigners originally settled, such as Chinatown, Little India or Pahurat, and Thanon Silom, where the European riverfront community resided. Today, Silom, together with Thanon Sathorn and Thanon Sukhumvit further east, have become important business and commercial centres. At Silom's eastern end, near Lumphini Park, *soi* (side streets) lead to the raucous tumble of infamous Patpong.

Most of this urban melee is built up along one bank of the Chao Phraya River. On the other side of the river is Thonburi, where life hasn't changed much since the time it briefly functioned as the royal capital. Here, canals still thread through the colourful neighbourhoods with old wooden houses perched precariously by the water's edge.

Growth in most of Bangkok has left a confusion, most clearly demonstrated by the city's world-class traffic snarls. But, like cities anywhere, Bangkok in no way represents the country. It is a distinct entity unto itself, with treasures worth seeking out, and this alone is reason enough to visit. ❑

PRECEDING PAGES: aerial view of Bangkok's Silom and Sathorn areas; motorcycle taxis waiting for passengers. **LEFT:** bustling Thanon Yaowarat in Chinatown.

Bangkok

0 — 500 m
0 — 500 yds

Ⓢ Skytrain BTS
Ⓜ Metro MRT

RATTANAKOSIN: ROYAL BANGKOK

Rattanakosin island, bound by the Chao Phraya River and a network of canals, hosts extravagant palaces and ornate temples – a reflection of Bangkok's royal lineage – that display an eclectic mix of architectural styles

The establishment of the Thai royal district of **Phra Nakorn**, centred on the man-made island of **Rattanakosin**, marked Bangkok's rise in 1782 as the newly installed capital of Thailand. For more than a century, Rattanakosin, just a boat ride across from the earlier capital at Thonburi, acted as the pulse of the city, and this was where the seeds of a modern kingdom were planted.

Rattanakosin's foundations were based on the former capital of Ayutthaya, which was abandoned after being ransacked by the Burmese army in 1767. The new strategic enclave in Bangkok was perched at the edge of the Chao Phraya River with the majestic Grand Palace as its epicentre. As the palace took shape, the defensive moats and walls formed a protective stronghold, while canals were dug to transport people across marsh and swampland.

The city's historic anchor brims with architectural grandeur. In ancient Siam, these devotional tributes and extravagant edifices were powerful indicators that the unified nation was a force to be reckoned with. Even today, the district contains many government offices and two of Thailand's most respected universities (Thammasat and Silpakorn), in addition to being the religious nucleus of the nation.

Ceremonies, festivals and parades are frequently held in this quarter.

Rattanakosin is best explored on foot. While most visitors attempt to cram all its sights into a day, two full days allow for greater appreciation of its more secluded treasures. The area's proximity to the river means that it can be conveniently accessed by water transport, with the famous backpacker haven of Thanon Khao San (*see page 113*) just a short stroll away. A long-term project called the Krung Rattanakosin Plan to revi-

Map on page 82

LEFT: the striking Phra Si Rattana Chedi at Wat Phra Kaew.
BELOW: outside the high walls of the Grand Palace and Wat Phra Kaew.

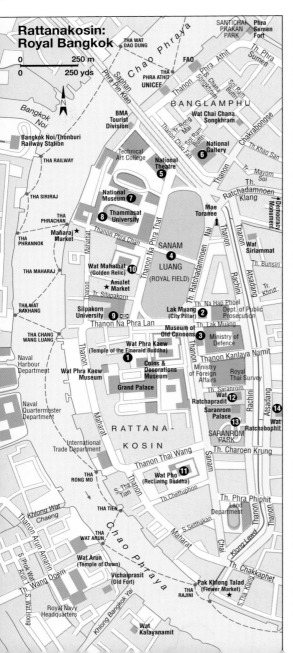

Rattanakosin: Royal Bangkok

talise the district into a historical park is already showing signs of progress, though the displacement of whole communities for the supposed greater good of the city frequently raises the hackles of its detractors.

Wat Phra Kaew and Grand Palace complex

Jostling among throngs of snap-happy tourists may not engender the most romantic vision of exotic Thailand, but the dignified splendour of two of Bangkok's principal attractions – the Wat Phra Kaew and the Grand Palace – is breathtaking in spite of the heaving crowds. The structures in this complex are an arresting spectacle of form and colour, with glistening golden *chedi*, glass mosaic-studded pillars, towering mythological gods, and fabulously ornate temple and palace structures piercing the sky.

The site originally spread over 160 hectares (65 acres) around this strategic locale by the banks of the Chao Phraya River. It was begun by King Rama I in 1782, who ordered a new residence built to house the Emerald Buddha, the country's most revered religious image, as well as a palace befitting the newly installed capital of Bangkok. The entire compound is surrounded by high crenellated walls, securing a self-sufficient city within a city.

The only entrance (and exit) to the **Wat Phra Kaew and Grand Palace ❶** complex is along Thanon Na Phra Lan to the north (daily 8.30am–3.30pm; admission charge includes entry to Vimanmek and several other sights in Dusit; tel: 0-222 2818; www.palaces.thai.net). An early morning visit is recommended, preferably when bright sunlight illuminates the buildings to their dazzling best. Make sure you are dressed appropriately *(see margin tip)* and disregard touts who linger outside the complex telling you that it is closed.

The complex is loosely divided into two, with the Wat Phra Kaew encountered first to the left (signs guide you to this sight first) and the Grand Palace and its peripheral buildings to the right. At least two hours are needed for a full appreciation, with most people lingering within Wat Phra Kaew. Most of the Grand Palace's interiors are inaccessible to public view, but the exteriors are still awesome to witness. It's worthwhile hiring the informative audio guide (B100, with passport/credit card deposit; in eight languages). If you prefer, official guides (B300) are also available near the ticket office.

Wat Phra Kaew

Wat Phra Kaew (Temple of the Emerald Buddha) serves as the royal chapel of the Grand Palace. The magnificent temple compound is modelled after palace chapels in the former capitals of Sukhothai and Ayutthaya, and contains many typical monastic structures, except living quarters for monks, a feature found in most other Thai temples.

At the main entrance to the temple compound is the statue of Shivaka Kumar Baccha, who was reputed to be the Buddha's private physician. Just behind it is the most important building in the temple compound housing the central hall (*bot*) containing the statue of the Emerald Buddha *(see page 84)*. To get to it you need to begin walking in a clockwise direction. First to capture the eye, however, on the upper terrace on the left, are the gleaming gold mosaic tiles encrusting the Sri Lankan-style circular **Phra Si Rattana Chedi Ⓐ**. Erected by King Mongkut (Rama V), it is said to enshrine a piece of the Buddha's breastbone.

In the centre is **Phra Mondop Ⓑ** (Library of Buddhist Scriptures), surrounded by statues of sacred white elephants (the white elephant, which once roamed the kingdom, is the symbol of royal power). The library was erected to hold the holy Buddhist scriptures called *Tripitaka*. The original library was destroyed by fire, ignited by fireworks during festivities to celebrate its completion. Phra Mondop is a delicate building, studded with blue and

Map on page 85

TIP

The dress code for Wat Phra Kaew and the Grand Palace is strict. Visitors must be dressed smartly – no shorts, short skirts or revealing tops, sandals or flip-flops. Suitable clothing may be borrowed from an office near the Gate of Victory, so unless you want to don stale rubber slip-ons and a gaudy sarong, dress conservatively and behave accordingly.

LEFT AND BELOW: Phra Mondop with its splendid exterior.

The multi-tiered roof of the Bot of the Emerald Buddha at Wat Phra Kaew.

BELOW: gilded *garuda* images encircle the exterior of the Bot of the Emerald Buddha.
RIGHT: worshipper outside the Bot of the Emerald Buddha.

green glass mosaic, and topped by a multi-tiered roof fashioned like the crown of a Thai king.

Adjacent to it is the **Prasat Phra Thep Bidom** ● (Royal Pantheon), This contains life-sized statues of the Chakri kings and is open to the public only on Chakri Day, 6 April. Around the building stand marvellous gilded statues of mythological creatures, including the half-female, half-lion *aponsi*. The original pantheon was built in 1855, but was destroyed by fire and rebuilt in 1903. Flanking the entrance of the Prasat Phra Thep Bidom are two towering gilded *chedi*.

Behind Phra Mondop is a large, sandstone model of the famous Khmer temple of Angkor Wat in Cambodia. The model was built during King Rama IV's reign when Cambodia was a vassal Thai state. Just behind, along the northern edge of the compund, is the **Viharn Yot** (Prayer Hall), flanked by the **Ho Phra Nak** (Royal Mausoleum) on the left and **Ho Phra Montien Tham** (Auxiliary Library) on the right.

The walls of the cloister enclosing the temple courtyard are painted with a picture book of 178 murals telling the *Ramakien* epic, the Thai version of the Indian *Ramayana*. Originally painted during the reign of King Rama III (1824–50), they have been meticulously restored.

Around the cloisters, six pairs of towering stone *yaksa* (demons), again characters from the *Ramakien*, stand guard armed with clubs, protecting the Emerald Buddha. At the complex's eastern edge are eight *prang* structures, which represent Buddhism's Eightfold Path.

The Emerald Buddha

Finally you come to the Wat Phra Kaew's most sacred structure, the **Bot of the Emerald Buddha** ●. Outside this main hall, at the open-air shrine, the air is always alive with the supplicants' murmured prayers and heavy with the scent of floral offerings and joss sticks. Remove your shoes before entering the hall. It is particularly busy on weekends and holidays when worshippers fill the main sanctuary, prostrating themselves on the marble floor before the temple's 11-metre (36-ft) tall altar.

At the top of the elaborate golden altar, in a glass case and protected by a nine-tiered umbrella, sits the country's most celebrated image, the diminutive 75-cm (30-in) tall **Emerald Buddha**, which, surprisingly, is not made of emerald but carved from a solid block of green jade. Many non-Buddhists are invariably disappointed by the size of the Emerald Buddha statue, but its power and importance should be instantly apparent from the demeanour of the pilgrims inside the hall. Photography is forbidden and it's hard to get a clear view of the statue from ground level.

Three times a year, at the beginning of each new season, the Thai king presides over the changing of the Emerald Buddha's robes: a golden, diamond-studded tunic is used for the hot season; a gilded robe flecked with blue for the rainy season; and a robe of enamel-coated solid gold for the cool season.

Of unknown origin – legend claims that the Emerald Buddha image was carved in India, but stylistically its design is 13th or 14th century Thai – the statue was found in Chiang Rai in 1434, in a temple also known as Wat Phra Kaew. The image, kept hidden in a *chedi* there for some reason, was revealed when the *chedi* was struck by lighting during a storm. Subsequently, the Lao army took the figure and brought it back to Vientiane, Laos, in the mid-16th century where it stayed put until 1779 when the Emerald Buddha was seized by the Thais. When Bangkok was established as the new capital, King Rama I brought the statue with him in 1784. The statue is claimed to bestow good fortune on the kingdom that possesses it.

The Grand Palace

Adjoining Wat Phra Kaew is the **Grand Palace**. Embodying Thailand's characteristic blend of

The Emerald Buddha is the most revered image of the Buddha in Thailand. Bathed in an eerie green light, high on its pedestal, it looks serenely down on the congregation.

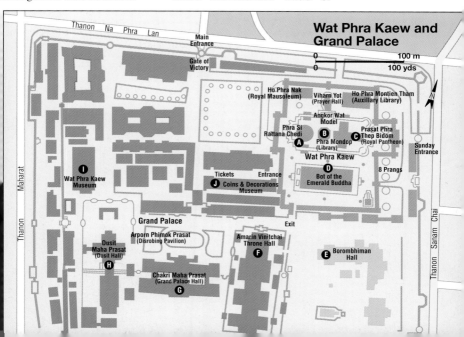

Wat Phra Kaew and Grand Palace

Thanon Na Phra Lan

Main Entrance

Gate of Victory

0   100 m
0   100 yds

Ho Phra Nak (Royal Mausoleum)

Viharn Yot (Prayer Hall)

Ho Phra Montien Tham (Auxiliary Library)

Angkor Wat Model

Phra Si Rattana Chedi

B

Prasat Phra Thep Bidom (Royal Pantheon)

A   Phra Mondop (Library)   **C**

Sunday Entrance

Wat Phra Kaew

I   Wat Phra Kaew Museum

Tickets   Entrance

J   Coins & Decorations Museum

Bot of the Emerald Buddha

8 Prangs

Grand Palace

Maharat

Thanon

Arporn Phimok Prasat (Disrobing Pavilion)

Exit

Amarin Vinitchai Throne Hall

F

E   Borombhiman Hall

H   Dusit Maha Prasat (Dusit Hall)

G   Chakri Maha Prasat (Grand Palace Hall)

Thanon Sanam Chai

A Mythical Zoo

A stroll round any Thai temple compound is like exploring a bestial forest of the imagination. Fantastical gilded creatures born from folklore and literature stand as guardians of the sacred, each with its own characteristic features and powers. Many of these creatures were born in the Himaphan Forest, the mythical Himalayan forest that surrounds the heavenly Mount Meru in Hindu and Buddhist scripture. Though Himaphan is invisible to human eyes, Thai artisans have spent centuries refining their imaginative depictions of its denizens. Here's a quick safari ride through some of the more common beasts you may encounter.

Garuda: Considered the most powerful creature of the Himaphan Forest, this half-eagle, half-man demigod is the mount of the Hindu god Vishnu. *Garuda* is the sworn enemy of the magical water serpent *naga*. *Garuda* is often depicted with *naga* caught in his talons. Since Ayutthayan times the *garuda* has been a symbol for the Royal Seal, and today, brightly coloured representations are emblazoned across official documents as well as building facades of royally approved banks and corporations.

Naga: Brother and nemesis of *garuda*, the *naga* is a semi-divine creature with multiple human heads and serpent tails. The snake has special symbolism to most of the world's faiths and cultures, and in Buddhism a great *naga* is said to have provided shelter to the meditating Buddha. A resident of the watery underworld, the *naga* is associated with water's life-giving force, as well as acting as a bridge between the earthly and divine realms. *Naga* are typically represented along steps leading into temples.

Erawan: The magical elephant *erawan* was the elephant steed for Indra, the Hindu king of the gods. The gigantic pachyderm has 33 heads, each with seven tusks so long that thousands of angels live inside them. Obviously, with such a gargantuan beast, a more modest three-headed version is usually represented. For proof of *erawan's* importance to Thais, head to Erawan Shrine *(see page 132)* at one of Bangkok's busiest intersections, where wooden elephants are presented as offerings.

Kinnaree and **Aponsi:** This exotic looking belle has the head and body of a woman with the tail and legs of a swan. Known for her talent in song and dance, beautifully crafted *kinnaree* sculptures can be seen at the Wat Phra Kaew. Perhaps a distant relative, *aponsi* is similarly portrayed as half-female, half-lion. The Golden Kinnaree is the Thai film industry equivalent of the Oscar.

Hongsa: This bird-like creature has similarities to the swan and goose, and is a prevalent motif in traditional arts and crafts. In Hindu mythology, the *hongsa* is the mount of Brahma, the god of creation. Take a drive along Utthayan Avenue in Bangkok's southern suburb of Puttha Monthon; some 1,000 golden *hongsa* birds decorate the tops of lampposts along this stretch of road.

Yaksha: Although these giant half-demon, half-god creatures appear forbidding as they guard the entrances to the temple structures at Wat Phra Kaew and Wat Arun, they are actually protectors of earthbound wealth. Led by Kuvera, they are worshipped as symbols of fertility and are also believed to protect newborn infants. ❑

LEFT: *yaksha* protector at Wat Phra Kaew.

emporal and spiritual elements, the Grand Palace has been added to or modified by every Thai king, so that today the complex is a mélange of architectural styles, from traditional Thai, Khmer and Chinese to British, French and Italian Renaissance. In the early 20th century, the royal abode shifted to the more private Chitralada Palace in Dusit district *(see page 117)*, with the Grand Palace now reserved for special ceremonies and state visits.

Palace buildings

Exit from Wat Phra Kaew. On your left and tucked behind a closed gate guarded by sentry is the French-inspired **Borombhiman Hall ❺**. It was built in 1903 as a residence for King Rama VI but is now reserved as a state guesthouse for dignitaries.

To the right lies the **Amarin Vinitchai Throne Hall ❻**, part of the three-building Phra Maha Monien complex. Originally a royal residence, it contained the bedchamber of Rama I, with the main audience hall beyond. Today, the audience hall is used for coronations and

special ceremonies. By tradition, each new king also spends the first night after his coronation here.

Next to it in a large courtyard stands the triple-spired royal residence – and the grandest building in the complex – the **Chakri Maha Prasat ❼** (Grand Palace Hall). This two-storey hall set on an elevated base was constructed during King Chulalongkorn's reign (1868–1910) to commemorate the 100th anniversary of the Chakri dynasty in 1882. An impressive mixture of Thai and Western architecture, the building was designed by British architects. The Thai spires, however, were added at the last moment, following protests that it was improper for a hallowed Thai site to be dominated by a European-style building.

The top floor contains golden urns with ashes of the Chakri kings; the first floor still functions as an audience chamber for royal banquets and state visits, while the ground floor is now a **Weapons Museum**.

The central hall contains the magnificent **Chakri Throne Room**, where the king receives foreign

Map on page 85

Sentry guard on duty outside the Chakri Maha Prasat.

BELOW: the large grounds fronting the Chakri Maha Prasat.

พระบรมมหาราชวัง
วัดพระศรีรัตนศาสดาราม
เปิดเข้าชม
เวลา 08.30น.ถึงเวลา15.30น.
DON T TRUST STRANGERS
THE GRAND PALACE
THE EMERALD BUDDHA TEMPLE
OPEN EVERYDAY
FROM 08.30 A.M. THROUGH 03.30 P.M.
THE GRAND PALACE WAT PHO

Disregard persistent touts lingering outside the Wat Phra Kaew and Grand Palace complex telling you that it is closed for a special ceremony. They usually try and steer you to shops or cajole you into taking a guided tour with them.

BELOW: Chinese-style statue outside the Dusit Maha Prasat.

ambassadors on a niello throne under a nine-tiered white umbrella, originally made for King Chulalongkorn. Outside, the courtyard is dotted with ornamental ebony trees pruned in Chinese *bonsai* style. Beside the hall, a closed-off door leads to the **Inner Palace**, where the king's many wives once lived. The king himself was the only male above the age of 12 allowed to enter the area, which was guarded by armed women.

The next building of interest is the **Dusit Maha Prasat** ❶ (Dusit Hall), built by King Chakri (Rama I) in 1789 to replace an earlier wooden structure. A splendid example of classical Thai architecture, its four-tiered roof supports an elegant nine-tiered spire. The balcony on the north wing contains a throne once used by the king for outdoor receptions. Deceased kings and queens lie in state here before their bodies are cremated on Sanam Luang.

To its left stands the exquisite **Arporn Phimok Prasat** (Disrobing Pavilion). It was built to the height of the king's palanquin, so that he could alight from his elephant and don his ceremonial hat and gown before proceeding to the audience hall.

Opposite, don't miss the superb collection of small Buddha images made of silver, ivory, crystal and other materials at the **Wat Phra Kaew Museum** ❶. On the way out, next to the ticket office is the **Coins and Decorations Museum** ❶. It has a collection of coins dating from the 11th century and also royal regalia, decorations and medals made of gold and precious stones.

Lak Muang

Every Thai city is supposed to have a foundation stone, around which the city's guardian spirits gravitate, protecting and bringing supposed good fortune to worshippers and the municipality. Bangkok was officially born into the world in 1782, when King Rama I erected the **Lak Muang** ❷ or City Pillar, to mark the official centre of the capital (daily 5am–7pm; free).

Located just across Thanon Sanam Chai from the eastern wall of the Grand Palace is the Lak Muang, a gilded wooden pillar sheltered by a Khmer-style *prang*. Resembling the Hindu Shiva *lingam*, which represents potency, it is accompanied by the taller Lak Muang of Thonburi, which was moved here when the district (and former capital) became part of Bangkok. The pillar is considered the city's spiritual core, and is watched over by a pavilion containing several golden spirit-idols. Devotees thankful their prayers have been answered usually hire resident classical *lakhon* dancers to perform here.

Museum of Old Cannons

Clearly visible across the street from the Lak Muang is a battalion of antique armoury that menacingly protects the imposing Ministry of Defence. Of passing interest to those with a military bent is the **Museum of Old Cannons** ❸ (daily 24 hours;

90-plus other *chedi*. The temple cloisters contain 394 bronze Buddha images, retrieved from ancient ruins in Sukhothai and Ayutthaya. One of the most important additions was the Reclining Buddha by King Rama III in 1832, who also converted the temple into the country's earliest place of public learning. The monarch instructed that the walls be inscribed with lessons on astrology, history, morality and archaeology. It's no wonder that locals fondly call the temple the kingdom's first university.

Wat Pho's gigantic **Reclining Buddha**, 46 metres (150 ft) long and 15 metres (50 ft) high, and made from brick, plaster and gilded in gold, depicts the resting Buddha passing into nirvana. The flat soles of the Buddha's feet are inlaid with mother-of-pearl designs, illustrating the 108 auspicious signs for recognising Buddha. Also numbering 108 are the metallic bowls that span the wall; a coin dropped in each supposedly brings goodwill to the devotee. With the building's pillars preventing full view, the head and feet are the best vantage points.

The temple's main hall is considered to be one of Bangkok's most beautiful. Girding its base are superbly carved sandstone panels depicting scenes from the *Ramakien*. The striking doors are also devoted to *Ramakien* scenes, brilliantly rendered in some of the finest mother-of-pearl work found in Asia. The ashes of Rama I are interred in the pedestal base of the hall's principal Buddha image. Standing beside the inner doorways, pairs of large stone *farang* (foreigner) guards are striking for their Western characteristics.

Wat Pho massage school

Wat Pho became, and still is, the place to learn about traditional medicine, particularly massage and meditation. The medicine pavilion displays stone tablets indicating beneficial body points for massage. Skirting the temple grounds are several small rock gardens which contain statues of hermits striking poses; these were used as diagnostic aids. Many of the old shophouses that fringe the temple walls today still peddle a range of traditional herbal remedies.

Map on page 82

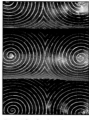

Detail of whorls on the toes of Wat Pho's Reclining Buddha statue.

LEFT: Wat Pho's main *chedi* are dedicated to Bangkok's monarchs.
BELOW: the giant Reclining Buddha.

TIP

When having a Thai massage it's important to relax completely and believe that you're in safe hands. The massage will involve some contortionist-like poses and the natural inclination is to resist when you are sometimes bent into awkward positions. Don't fight it; just relax and go with the flow. You'll avoid injuries this way.

BELOW: joggers at Saranrom Park.
RIGHT: Buddha statues on the grounds of Wat Ratchabophit.

Traditional Thai massage *(see page 69)* is based on Indian yoga philosophy, and originated from millennia-old Indian therapies which aim to release blocked energy. In Thai massage, strong thumbs dig deep into tense muscles and the body's energy points. The masseurs also bring their full body weight to bear as they stretch the recipients' bodies into yoga-like poses. The **Wat Pho Thai Traditional Massage School** offers cheap hour-long massages, and also offers courses for those wanting to learn the art (daily 10am–6pm; tel: 0-2221 2974). Most masseurs around the country claim to have received tuition here, and the hands-on training has proved a staple career option for many of Thailand's blind population.

Wat Ratchapradit

While not as grand as the other temples in this regal district, **Wat Ratchapradit ⑫**, located to the northwest of Wat Pho at Thanon Saranrom, does offer visitors a more intimate appreciation of royally connected divine edifices (daily 5am–10pm, chapel 9–9.30am and 5–7pm). Begun in 1864 on a reclaimed coffee plantation purchased by King Mongkut (Rama IV), this quaint grey marble-clad temple is yet another example of his, and later King Chulalongkorn's (Rama V), continuing preoccupation with infusing Thai architecture with pervasive Western traits.

The elaborate interior murals were added during King Chulalongkorn's reign. These depict annual Thai ceremonies such as Loy Krathong, as well as a rendition of King Mongkut, a keen and accurate astronomer, observing an eclipse. Some of Mongkut's ashes were later enshrined beneath the main Buddha image by Chulalongkorn. There are two Khmer-style *prang* to the side of the main hall, and beyond you can spot the Chinese pagoda in Saranrom Park next door.

Saranrom Park

Just behind Wat Ratchapradit, the manicured landscape of **Saranrom Park ⑬** is the perfect place to wind down after a full day of palace and

temple tours (daily 5am–8pm; free). The park was originally a garden attached to Saranrom Palace, which was supposed to have been the retirement retreat for King Mongkut. However, he passed away before the palace was completed. Livened with bridges, ponds, a European-style cherub-spouting fountain and a Chinese pagoda, this green space has been opened to the public since the 1960s. At the park's centre is a memorial erected by King Chulalongkorn for his wife Queen Sunanda, who tragically drowned in a boating accident in 1880. At the park's main gates, drink vendors sell freshly-squeezed juice to the legion of joggers – so grab a seat on a park bench and cool off with a drink.

Wat Ratchabophit

Athough it is located on the opposite bank of Khlong Lord canal and Rattanakosin, **Wat Ratchabophit ⓮** (daily 5am–8pm, chapel 9–9.30am and 5.30–6pm; free) is easily accessed from Saranrom Park. This infrequently visited sanctuary at Thanon Fuang Nakhon is recognisable for its characteristic amalgamation of local temple architecture and period European style, an unusual design fusion that places the main circular *chedi* and its circular cloister in the centre. Started in 1869 by King Chulalongkorn (Rama V), the complex took well over two decades to complete.

Built into the northern side of the yellow tile-clad cloister, the *bot* (ordination hall) is covered in brightly patterned Chinese ceramic tiles, known as *bencharong*. The windows and entrance doors to the hall are exquisite works of art, with tiny pieces of mother-of-pearl inlaid in lacquer, in an intricate rendition of the insignias of the five royal ranks. The doors open into one of the most surprising temple interiors in Thailand, with a Gothic-inspired chapel of solid columns that looks more like a medieval cathedral than a Thai temple. The courtyard doors are carved in relief with jaunty-looking soldiers wearing European-type uniforms. Wat Ratchabophit was built before King Chulalongkorn made his first trip to Europe, so its design is all the more remarkable. ❏

Map on page 82

The walls of Wat Ratchabophit are decorated with brightly patterned Chinese ceramic tiles called "bencharong".

Restaurants

Thai

Coconut Palm
394/3-5 Th Maharaj. Mobile tel: 01-827 2394. Open: daily 10am–7pm. $
Family-style restaurant serving far better meals than its Western-style fast food interior suggests. The small range of soups and curries (red, green, *tom yam* and the coconut soup, or *tom kha gai*) disappear by lunchtime. For dinner, try excellent dishes like rice noodles with spicy and sour sauce.

Poh Restaurant
Tha Tien Pier. No phone. Open: daily 6pm–10pm. $
The lovely setting at this pierside restaurant compensates for its ordinary menu. Sit upstairs for the best view across the river to Wat Arun. Serves squid, mussels and shrimp with rice or noodles, a few curries and numerous fish dishes. Stays open well after the kitchen closes.

Rub Ar-roon
310 Th Maharaj. Tel: 0-2622 2312. Open: daily 8am–6.30pm. $
Chinese shophouse with a small range of coffees, toasted sandwiches and not-too-spicy local food (although you can ask for it to be spicy). This was a pharmacy 80 years ago, and the herbal display cabinets are still in place, adding to the nice wine bar/bistro atmosphere (although the only alcohol is beer). Some outside seating available.

Sor Tor Lor
Royal Navy Club, Tha Chang. Mobile tel: 01-257 5530. Open: daily 11am–8pm. $
Part of the Royal Thai Navy Club, but open to the public, this riverside operation is perched on a large wooden deck. Good for fish and seafood standards like spicy steamed snapper with Thai lime, curried crab and fried prawns with garlic. Also tasty *pad thai* noodles. Tables also available inside.

HIGHLIGHTS OF THE NATIONAL MUSEUM

Bangkok's National Museum, one of the largest in Southeast Asia, is a good place to start learning more about the history and culture of Thailand

The National Museum's three main galleries are spread over a handful of old and new buildings. Thai history from the Sukhothai period (13th–14th centuries) to the Rattanakosin period (1782–the present) is covered in the Sivamokhaphiman Hall, while behind the hall, the Prehistoric Gallery has 5,000 year-old exhibits from the Ban Chiang archaeological site in the northeast. The south wing exhibits Buddha images and artefacts from the Srivijaya and Lopburi periods, while the north wing displays exhibits from the Lanna, Sukhothai, Ayutthaya and Rattanakosin periods. The rooms in the Wang Na, or Front Palace *(see side bar opposite)*, display fine art masterpieces, mostly from the Rattanakosin period, with treasures in the form of gold, carvings, enamelware, musical instruments, ceramics, clothes, weapons and palanquins.

In front of the old palace is the Buddhaisawan Chapel, once the private chapel of the Prince Successor and a good example of Rattanakosin architecture. Today, it houses the second holiest image in Thailand, Phra Buddha Sihing, a Sukhothai-style Buddha image. Beautifaul murals cover the wall of this chapel.

LEFT: ceramic figures of various animist spirits were used both for decoration and religious purposes in the home.

ABOVE: this Buddha head, found in Khon Kaen, northeast Thailand, shows a combination of Dvaravati and Lopburi art styles.

THE FIRST THAI MUSEUM

King Chulalongkorn, or Rama V (pictured above) established the country's first public museum in 1874 in the Grand Palace. The collections were based on those of his father, King Mongkut (Rama IV). In 1926 the museum was moved to what was the Wang Na (Front Palace), the abode of the second-in-line to the throne called the "second king" or the Prince Successor. This vast palace, dating from 1782, once extended across Khlong Lot up to the Grand Palace and included a large park. When his heir-apparent attempted a violent over-throw, Chulalongkorn abolished the office in 1887 and tore down most of the buildings. The Wang Na is one of the remnants of the original palace and today it houses a variety of artefacts in Rooms 4–15. Look out especially for Room 6, which contains a beautifully carved *howdah*, or elephant seat, made of ivory.

Chulalongkorn's statue can be found in the Issaretrachanusorn Hall, which also exhibits the beds of Phra Pin Klao, the thrones of King Chula-longkorn and King Vajiravudh, and intricate Chinese and European-style furniture.

: the Sala Samranmukhamat pavilion was originally located in Dusit and was moved to the National Museum during the reign of King pok, or Rama VII (1925–35). Such open-sided pavilions, commonly temples and palaces, are used for meetings or as resting places.

antastically elaborate and gilded teak chariots are used uneral ceremonies for carrying the urn of the deceased he crematorium. The Wechayanratcharot chariot above (left) was built during the reign of King Rama royal cremation ceremony of Princess Sri Sudarak.

LEFT: this Khmer-style female statue in the Dvaravati Room is one of the few found in Thailand. Heads were frequently ripped off statues and bas reliefs torn from walls at ancient sites as it was easier to smuggle out smaller pieces.

THONBURI

This small area of winding canals had a brief moment
of glory as the country's capital in the 19th century;
the royal connection left behind a legacy of exquisite
temples in a placid landscape and a lifestyle
defined by the canals and the river

Bangkok's original heart and veins is the mighty Chao Phraya River and the canals that splay off it. This extensive network of waterways provides the opportunity for several waterborne tours, which show how entwined the city and its riverine life was and indeed still is. It's a very different world to the sights inland and provides a more tangible view of Bangkok's humble origins.

Thonburi

Established by King Taksin after the fall of Ayutthaya in 1767, **Thonburi** served as Thailand's third capital for 15 years prior to Bangkok's establishment in 1782. Taksin spent most of his reign conquering factions of rebels after his throne, leaving time only late in his reign to embellish his city. Thonburi, as many residents understand, means "Town of Riches". It was not until 1971 that Thonburi was combined as a part of Bangkok Metropolis. It can be reached by numerous bridges, the oldest of which is **Memorial Bridge** (or Phra Buddha Yodfa Bridge).

While Thonburi is short on major tourist attractions and only has a few high-end hotels, it has a more easy-going atmosphere than frenetic Bangkok across the Chao Phraya River. Bereft of the gleaming tower

blocks of downtown Bangkok, life in this residential half of the capital primarily revolves around the network of canals and the river (see photo feature on pages 104–5).

The canals worth exploring include **Khlong Bangkok Noi**, which winds into **Khlong Bangkok Yai** downstream, as well as connecting to **Khlong Om** upstream. Once a source of fresh daily produce, the **floating markets** at **Wat Sai** and **Taling Chan** have become little more than tourist souvenir stops

Map
on page
100

LEFT: silhouette of
Wat Arun at dusk.
BELOW: a longtail boat.

TIP

One of the best times to visit Wat Arun is late afternoon, when there are fewer visitors. When you are done, take the ferry across the river to Tha Tien pier where you will enjoy great sunset views of Wat Arun from the popular but rundown bar-shack called Boh on the wooden pier.

BELOW: detail of a porcelain-encrusted *prang* of Wat Arun.

these days. The further down the canals you venture, the narrower and calmer the waterway becomes. With rickety teak houses, vendors selling produce from boats, fishermen dangling rods out of windows and kids frolicking in the water, the sights along Thonburi's canals are reminiscent of a more peaceful bygone era.

Canal and river cruising

The major canals are serviced by public **longtail boats** (*see text box page 101*). But as services can be erratic at certain times of the day – most commuters travel into the city in the mornings and return in the afternoons – it might be better to hire your own private longtail exploration of the canals.

Getting from pier to pier along the Chao Phraya River is best served by the **Chao Phraya Express** boats, which operate from the southern outskirts up to Nonthaburi in the north. For shuttling from one side of the

river to the other, make use of the cheap **cross-river ferries**; these can be boarded at the many jetties that also service the Chao Phraya Express boats (*see page 208 for details on river and canal transport*).

Wat Arun

When King Taksin first moored at the Thonburi bank of the Chao Phraya River at sunrise after sailing down from the sacked capital of Ayutthaya, he supposedly found an old temple shrine and felt compelled to build a fitting holding place for the sacred Emerald Buddha. Eventually known as **Wat Arun ❶** or the Temple of Dawn (daily 8.30am–5.30pm; admission charge), the temple was originally attached to Taksin's new palace (Wang Derm).

After Taksin's demise, the new King Chakri (Rama I) moved the capital (and the Emerald Buddha) to Bangkok, but the temple kept the interest of the first five kings. Over

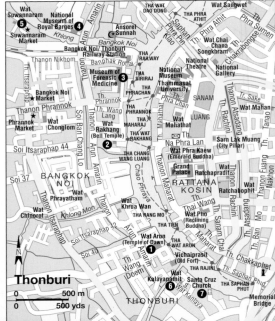

the years, the temple grew in size and ornamentation. In the early 19th century King Rama II enlarged the structure and raised the central *prang* (Khmer-style tower) to 104 metres (345 ft), making it the country's tallest religious structure.

Recycling piles of broken ceramic that was leftover ballast from Chinese merchant ships, Rama III introduced the colourful fragments of porcelain that cover most of the temple's exterior. When builders ran out of porcelain for this large edifice, the king asked his subjects to contribute broken crockery to complete the decoration. Artisans fashioned the pieces into flowers or used them to embellish the costumes of the gods and mythical figures that ring each tier.

The great *prang* represents the Hindu-Buddhist Mount Meru, home of the gods with its 33 heavens. The peak of the *prang* is topped by a thunderbolt, the weapon of the Hindu god Indra. There are four smaller *prang* standing at each corner of the temple with niches containing statues of Nayu, the god of wind, on horseback. Between the minor *prang*

are four beautiful *mondop*, smaller towers placed at the key points. The niches at the foot of each stairway contain images of the Buddha in the four key events of his life: birth, meditation (while sheltered by a seven-headed *naga* serpent), preaching to his first five disciples, and at death. The entire complex is guarded by mythical giants called *yaksa*, similar to those that protect Wat Phra Kaew.

Wat Rakhang

Further upriver, directly across from the Grand Palace complex, is **Wat Rakhang ②**, which has a lovely collection of bells (daily 6am–6pm; free). King Taksin liked the chime of the original temple bell and had it moved to Wat Phra Kaew, donating five bells as replacement.

Hidden at the rear of Wat Rakhang is the red-painted *ho trai* (wooden library), a three-part stilted building that King Rama I lived in as a monk before becoming king and when Thonburi was the capital. The late 18th-century building is considered an architectural gem and is decorated with murals from the *Ramakien*.

Map on page 100

Numerous small bells hang from Wat Rakhang's temple towers and gently chime in the afternoon breeze, adding to the ambience of this riverside temple.

BELOW: roof detail at Wat Rakhang.

Touring by Longtail Boat

Some of the sights in this chapter are best done by private longtail boat. Longtail boat operators (found at major piers like Tha Thien and Tha Chang) are notorious for overcharging tourists, so bargain hard and set a price before embarking; B400–500 an hour (per boat) is a rough guide. Discuss beforehand where you want to visit and how much time you want to spend at each place. Bear in mind that once underway, it may be difficult to swtich itineraries as boat drivers speak little or no English. Ask for a slow ride so that photos can be taken and the ambience enjoyed. And be sure to sit near the front of the boat as the rear engines are extremely noisy.

The Museum of Forensic Medicine

To the north are several museums located within the **Siriaj Hospital** complex on Thanon Phrannok. The most well known is the **Museum of Forensic Medicine** ❸ (Mon–Fri 8.30am–4.30pm; free; tel: 0-2419 7000). Green arrows point the way from the hospital grounds to the museum, located on the 2nd floor of the Forensic Department. The stomach-churning exhibits are definitely not for the queasy. Mummified corpses of Thailand's most notorious criminals, deformed foetuses in formaldehyde and a gallery of disturbing post-mortem photographs are among the exhibits here.

Museum of Royal Barges

On the north bank of the Khlong Bangkok Noi canal, which was a major waterway during King Taksin's reign, is the **National Museum of Royal Barges** ❹ (daily 9am– 5pm; admission charge, photography fee extra; tel: 0-2424 0004). A crammed canal bank community nearby provides a stark contrast to the regal opulence of the wooden barges. The dry-dock warehouse displays eight vessels from a fleet of over 50 that are rarely put to sail except on auspicious occasions, such as the 1999 celebrations marking King Bhumibol's 72nd birthday. On that day, a flotilla of 52 barges, manned by 2,082 costumed oarsmen from the Royal Thai Navy, carried the King along the Chao Phraya River to Wat Arun, where the monarch offered new robes to monks in a ceremony known as *kathin*. Because such ceremonies are so rarely held, it's a spectacle not to be missed – the next one is due in 2006.

The Royal Barges date back to 14th-century Ayutthaya, with the present fleet constructed in the early 20th century. In the old days, the royal family, like everyone else, would travel by boat. The king would sit in the largest of the barges, the magnificent *Suphannahongse*, which was made from a single trunk of teak stretching over 46 metres (151 ft). The model on display was built in 1911 and based on the design of its 18th-century predecessor.

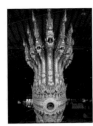

Seven-headed "naga", or serpent, adorning the prow of the "Anantanaganaj" barge at the Museum of Royal Barges.

BELOW:
Suphannahongse and *Narai Song Suban* (foreground) barges.
RIGHT:
Santa Cruz Church.

Map on page 100

Other barges at the museum include the *Anantanaganaj*, second-in-rank and built in 1914; its prow features a *naga*, the seven-headed king of the serpents. The *Narai Song Suban*, its prow adorned by the god Vishnu riding a *garuda*, was built in 1996 to commemorate the King Bhwmibol's Golden Jubilee.

Wat Suwannaram

From the museum pier, it's a five-minute boat journey up Khlong Bangkok Noi canal to the historic temple of **Wat Suwannaram ❺** (daily 6am–5pm; free). Perched on the opposite bank to the museum, have a look at the grand murals contained within the temple's main building. If the building is locked, look for a monk, who will willingly open the doors and windows to reveal the magnificent, if slightly deteriorated paintings, which tell the story of the Buddha's previous 10 lives. The intricate artwork, which adorns every corner of the temple's interior, was commissioned by King Rama III and is considered to be among the finest examples of 19th-century painting.

Wat Kalayanamit

South of Wat Arun, at the mouth of Khlong Bangkok Yai canal, are two sights worth visiting. The first is **Wat Kalayanamit ❻**, a 19th-century temple with Chinese-style embellishments (daily 8am–5pm; free). Built at the behest of Rama III, the tall main *viharn* (sermon hall) contains an impressive seated Buddha image. This, together with a large bronze bell in the grounds, are the largest of their kind in the country.

Santa Cruz Church

From the temple ask the monks to point you in the right direction to **Santa Cruz Church ❼**, the spire of which is visible from a couple of streets away (Mon–Sat 5–8pm, Sun 9am–8pm; free). The pastel-coloured church, topped by an octagonal dome, has been rebuilt twice since it was first constructed in the 18th century. The present edifice dates from 1913. The neighbourhood surrounding the church was once part of a flourishing Portuguese district that migrated here after Ayutthaya was abandoned. ❑

Buddha image at Wat Kalayanamit.

Restaurants

Thai

Krua Rakang Thong
306 Soi Wat Rakhang, Th Arun-Amarin, Sirirat. Tel: 0-2848 9597. Open: daily 11am–11pm. $
This old-style riverfront restaurant with views of Wat Arun and the spires of the Grand Palace is a good sunset spot for king prawns in sweet and sour tamarind sauce, spicy northeastern salads, and exploded catfish, diced and fried till crumbly, then added to coconut soup.

Patravadi Restaurant
Patravadi Theatre 69/1 Soi Wat Rakhang, Th Arun-Amarin, Sirirat. Tel: 0-2412 7287-8. Open: Mon–Fri 11am–9pm, Sat–Sun 11am–10pm. $
www.patravaditheatre.com
Garden café, located within Bangkok's premier fringe theatre near Wat Rakhang, with views of performances. Serves curries and a long list of veggie dishes. Enjoy coffee, tea or juice with blueberry pie or brownies.

Sirirat Market
Th Phrannok. Open: daily 7am–8pm. $

Rough and ready food stalls in this general goods market offer local fare: spicy sausages, grilled mussels, satay, deep-fried chicken, stir-fries, noodles, and one-plate rice dishes.

Supatra River House
266 Soi Wat Rakhang, Th Arun-Amarin, Sirirat. Tel: 0-2411 0305. Open: daily L and D. $$
www.supatrariverhouse.com
Former family home of owners Patravadi Mechudhon (of Patravadi Theatre fame) and her sister. Excellent Thai cuisine is served on the riverbank terrace or in one of two Thai-style houses. On Fri and Sat, traditional music and dance accompanies your dinner. Take the express boat to Tha Maharaj pier and transfer to the opposite bank on Supatra's free shuttle boat.

PRICE CATEGORIES

Price per person for a three-course meal without drinks:
$ = under US$10
$$ = US$10–$25
$$$ = US$25–$50
$$$$ = over US$50

LIFE ON THE CHAO PHRAYA RIVER

Bangkok's notorious traffic problem drives most visitors into taking river transport during their stay; few return to the roads willingly

Tourists enjoy travelling on the Chao Phraya River more than the average Bangkok resident. This is no surprise as the city grew up around the banks of the Chao Phraya and many of its oldest and most spectacular buildings are best seen from the vantage point of a river craft. River travel also has some very obvious benefits in a city choking with traffic and pollution. Speeding in a *reua dan* (express boat) from one *tha* (pier) to another with the wind cooling your face it's hard to imagine, as you pass under a bridge jam-packed with cars, why anyone would travel any other way in Bangkok. The answer is the same all over the world: people love cars, public transport is thought to be inadequate, and in Bangkok no one walks anywhere if they can help it. There is a variety of water transport, from express boats *(pictured below)* – which travel up and down the length of the river, to cross-river ferries (for getting from side of the river to the other) and longtail boat taxis (which mainly ply along the *khlong* or canals). See page 208 of Travel Tips for more details.

ABOVE: the truly authentic Thai floating market is more or less a thing past. Head for the floating market at Damnoen Saduak *(see page 171* in mind that what you are going to see is staged just for tourists. Bus tourists from Bangkok arrive after 10am so in order to beat the crowd there well before that and hire a private longtail boat to tour the marke

ABOVE: if you can't afford to stay at the Oriental Hotel, do the next b thing: have a drink at its Riverside Terrace and watch the riverine life

HOW THE *KHLONGS* DEVELOPED

Bangkok's origins date back to the 16th century when a canal was dug across a loop of the Chao Phraya River to cut the distance between the sea and the then Thai capital at Ayutthaya, 85 km (55 miles) north. Over the years, monsoon floods scoured the banks of the canal until it widened to become the main course of the river. On its banks rose two towns, Thonburi on the west and Bangkok on the east. The abandoned river loop became Khlong Bangkok Noi and Khlong Bangkok Yai, the principal canals that run through Thonburi. Bangkok's founding king, Rama I, established Rattanakosin as the nucleus of the new capital in 1782 by digging three concentric canals, turnig it into an easily defensible island. Houses were built on bamboo rafts and people primarily travelled by boat. In the mid 20th century, Bangkok abandoned boats for cars. Canals were filled in to make roads, and houses were built on land. The result? Congested streets in the hot season that become flooded in the monsoon season. Some say it was a bad trade, though with the reopening of Khlong Saen Saep, the canals are undergoing a welcome rebirth.

LEFT: other than ferrying passengers, the Chao Phraya River is also used to transport all manner of goods, from rice and fresh produce to cement and building materials. Here, a longtail boat is used to transport large water urns from its production centre in the village to the city.

life on the Chao Phraya Rver is mainly lived outdoors; mestic and social activities take place on wooden decks he house, creating close-knit communities. The river been the lifeblood of these riverside communities, and , moving to land-based housing is not an option.

THE OLD CITY AND DUSIT

Bangkok's Old City is embellished with yet more gilded temple stuctures and historic monuments that recall its chequered history. To the north is the area of wide boulevards and open space known as Dusit, the enclave of the Thai monarchy and government

Dominated by the wide boulevard of Thanon Ratchadamnoen, this section of the "Old City" contains all the peripheral buildings and temples that lie just outside Rattanakosin island. The area once marked the outskirts of the city, with the canals of Khlong Banglamphu and Khlong Ong Ang ferrying in supplies from the surrounding countryside. At the turn of the 20th century hardly any roads cut into the landscape, with the neighbourhood occupied by traditional craftspeople and performing artisans. Devotional structures were the main protrusions on the skyline.

Time has drastically altered the area's visual appeal, yet there is still a strong sense of the past, making this is one of the city's most pleasant areas to explore. Aside from tourist attractions, most foreigners head to the district of Banglamphu for cheap accommodation and entertainment in the well-known backpackers haven of Thanon Khao San.

Thanon Bamrung Muang

Thanon Bamrung Muang was once an old elephant trail and was one of the city's first paved tracks. A one-stop shop for all your Buddhist accessories, the stores may be drab in design, but the scores of gold and amber cloth-shrouded Buddha images, candles, alms bowls and other religious paraphernalia make for excellent photography.

Thanon Giant Swing

Thanon Bamrung Muang intersects a large square with the City Hall at its northern end and Wat Suthat and the Giant Swing opposite. In former days, the **Giant Swing** ❶ (Sao Ching Cha) was the venue for an annual Brahman ceremony dedicated to the god Shiva. As crowds gathered, four sturdy men would pump

Map on page 108

LEFT:
seated Buddha
images lining the
cloisters at Wat Suthat.
BELOW:
the Giant Swing.

themselves back and forth to set the giant swing in motion, trying to grab bags of coins suspended on a 15-metre (49-ft) tall pole with their teeth. Not surprisingly, many plummeted to the ground, either injuring or killing themsleves, and the festival was halted in the 1930s during the reign of Rama VII. With the swing itself now removed, the tall red-painted timber frame has become little more than a curious street marker.

Wat Suthat

Detail of wall murals at Wat Suthat.

Standing tall behind the Giant Swing, **Wat Suthat 2** is considered one of the country's six principal temples (daily 8.30am–9pm; admission charge). Begun by Rama I in 1807, it took three reigns to complete. The temple is noted for its enormous *bot*, or ordination hall, said to be the tallest in Bangkok, and for its equally large *viharn* (sermon hall), both of them surrounded by cloisters of gilded Buddha images.

The 8-metre (26-ft) tall Phra Sri Sakyamuni Buddha is one of the largest surviving bronze images from Sukhothai, and was transported by boat all the way from the northern kingdom. The base of the image contains the ashes of King Ananda Mahidol (Rama VIII), older brother of the present king. The wall murals date from the reign of King Rama III; most intriguing are the depictions of sea monsters and foreign ships on the columns.

Accounts vary, but it is said that Rama II himself carved the ornate teakwood doors of the *bot*. Incised to a depth of 5 cm (2 in), they follow the Ayutthaya tradition of floral motifs, with tangled jungle vegetation hiding small animals. The temple courtyard is a virtual museum of statuary, with stone figures of Chinese generals and scholars. They came as ballast in rice ships returning from deliveries to China and were donated to temples.

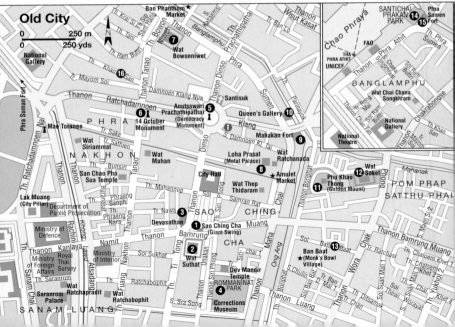

Devasathan

West of the Giant Swing along Thanon Dinso is a row of three adjoining Brahman shrines called **Devasathan** ❸ (daily 9am–5pm, chapel Thur and Sun only 10am–4pm; free). Built in 1784 at the same time as the Giant Swing and recently renovated, the three chapels house images of Shiva, Ganesha and Vishnu. Although the Thais are largely Buddhists, certain Brahman beliefs have been integrated into their faith system (*see margin*).

Rommaninat Park

Southwest of Wat Suthat, a short walk along Thanon Siri Phong brings you to **Rommaninat Park** ❹ (daily 5am–9pm; free). With the original watchtowers still standing, this lively city park is a fun example of how punishment can be turned into recreation. The old prison was built in 1893 and after over a hundred years of service, was transformed into a public park to celebrate Queen Sirikit's birthday. Livened up with ponds, fountains and a large bronze sculpture of a conch shell, this green

spot is busy in the mornings and evenings with joggers, while aerobics and weight-lifting takes place in an open area. Around the perimeter is the small **Corrections Museum**, housed in a former prison building and displaying various tools of castigation (Mon–Fri 8.30am–4.30pm; free).

Democracy Monument

Behind City Hall, north along Thanon Dinso, is a roundabout anchored by the **Democracy Monument** ❺. Designed by Italian sculptor Corrado Feroci (also known as Silpa Bhirasri), the 1939 monument is a celebration of Thailand's 1932 transition from absolute to constitutional monarchy. Marked by four elongated wings, the central metal tray contains a copy of the constitution. Almost every detail and measurement of the monument has symbolic relevance. A rallying point for civil discontent in May 1992, the monument became the scene of a bloodbath after the army violently suppressed peaceful demonstrations against the military dictatorship. More than 100 protesters were killed during the incident.

Map on page 108

Since the 14th century, long-haired and white-robed Brahman priests have been a fixture in Thai royal life. They are in charge of royal statecraft and rite-of-passage ceremonies. They have also introduced Hindu gods, such as Shiva, Brahma, Indra and others, who appear in Thai art and architecture.

LEFT: the Democracy Monument.
BELOW: Devasathan shrine has strong Hindu influences.

The 14 October Monument is a shrine to the people who died in the 1973 demonstrations against Thailand's military dictatorship.

BELOW: the pointed metal spires of the Loha Prasat.

14 October Monument

Just a short walk west from the Democracy Monument, along Thanon Ratchadamnoen Klang towards the corner of Thanon Tanao, brings you to another chiselled edifice to the democratic struggle in Thailand, the **14 October Monument** ❻. While not as grandiose as the Democracy Monument, this sombre granite memorial remembers fallen victims of the 1973 mass demonstrations against authoritarian rule. The central spire has the names of 73 of the victims inscribed in Thai, surrounded by a small amphitheatre. Beneath is an exhibition room, meeting rooms and a mini-theatre. Given the government's past denial of this traumatic event, it's somewhat remarkable that this pertinent 21st century tribute – it was erected in 2002 – stands at all.

Wat Bowonniwet

Due north of the 14 October Monument along Thanon Tanao is **Wat Bowonniwet** ❼, a modest looking monastery with strong royal bonds (daily 8am–5pm; free). Built in 1826 during the reign of Rama III, King Mongkut (Rama IV) served as abbot of the temple for a small portion of his 27 years as a monk. More recently the present King Bhumibol (Rama IX) donned saffron robes here after his coronation in 1946.

Home to Thailand's second Buddhist university, the temple is known for its extraordinary murals painted by innovative monk-artist Khrua In Khong. Krua had never travelled outside Thailand, but had looked at Western art reproductions and understood the concept of perspective. Unlike the flat, two-dimensional paintings of classical Thai art, these recede into the distance and are characterised by muted, moody colours. Also interesting are the subjects: antebellum southern American mansions, horse racing tracks and people dressed in the fashions of 19th-century America.

Thanon Ratchadamnoen

Stretching all the way from the Grand Palace to the Dusit Park area, the wide **Thanon Ratchadamnoen** (Royal Passage) splits into three sections and is modelled after Paris' famous boulevards. Built at the turn of the 20th century, the tree-lined avenue has some of the city's widest and least cluttered pavements.

Part of a recent spruce up, the somewhat austere-looking 1930s buildings that line both sides of Thanon Ratchadamnoen Klang have been given a lick of paint and numerous public benches added along the pavements to offer rest for the weary. Plans are underfoot to embellish the avenue further, replacing local businesses with tourist-driven boutique shopping (along the lines of Paris' Champs-Elysées) and diverting the traffic flow away from view. On royal birthdays, the area is turned into a sea of decorative lights, flags and royal portraits. Don't be surprised if all traffic and pedestrians

are abruptly halted by legions of police – it means a royal cavalcade is on its way.

Loha Prasat and Wat Ratchanatda

Just at the point where Thanon Ratchadamnoen Klang crosses the Pan Fah canal bridge, veering left into Ratchadamnoen Nok, are several noticeable structures on both sides of the busy intersection. More evocative of Burmese temple structures, the **Loha Prasat ❽** (Metal Palace) shares the same grounds as **Wat Ratchanatda** (sometimes spelt as Rajanadda) and is the main attraction here (both daily 9am–5pm; free).

Originally meant to be the temple's *chedi*, Loha Prasat's unusual architecture is said to draw from an Indian design dating back some 2,500 years ago. Built by Rama III in 1846, two tiers square the central tower, peaked by 37 iron spires which symbolise the virtues needed to attain enlightenment. On each floor of the monastery is a network of corridors leading to cramped meditation cells. Outside the

entrance is a manicured forecourt with the **Mahachesdabodin Royal Pavilion**. The ornate wooden pavilion is actually just over a decade old, one of the first additions in a grand scheme to redevelop the area. Its rich gleaming embellishments have made it an appropriate setting for special ceremonies. Just behind the temple is a thriving amulet market *(see below)*.

Mahakan Fort

Across Thanon Maha Chai from Wat Ratchanatda is one of only two surviving remnants of the 14 original fortified watchtowers that once protected the old city wall. With development having consumed the wall and other towers, the white octagonal turret of **Mahakan Fort ❾** is the only structure to survive, along with Banglamphu's larger Phra Sumen Fort *(see page 113)*. With the canal approach to the city deemed less threatening than the river, this small tower is certainly not the most formidable of structures. Closed to the public, the cannons here were only recently disarmed.

Map on page 108

Mahakan Fort, one of only two remaining watchtowers that guarded the old city walls of Bangkok.

BELOW: an amulet seller outside Wat Ratchanatda.

Armed with Amulets

The thriving amulet market behind Wat Ratchanatda is proof of Thais' superstitious belief in talismans. Most commonly worn as pendants on heavy neckchains and resembling modern-day bling bling, these amulets are thought to ward off evil, and bring power and fortune to the wearer. The most common amulets are religious in nature. Blessed by monks, images of Buddha or holy men are pressed into terracotta, bronze or gold. Other less religious amulets have specific intent – attracting men or women, or heightening sexual ability. The amulets at Wat Ratchanadda are more expensive than those in the market around Wat Mahathat *(see page 92)*.

During World War II, the Golden Mount served as a watch-tower, with guards armed with signal flags to warn of enemy invaders.

BELOW: the climb to the top of the Golden Mount is rewarding for its views of the Rattanakosin area.

Queen's Gallery

Just opposite Mahakan Fort on the corner of Thanon Phra Sumen is the modern cream-coloured **Queen's Gallery** (daily except Wed 10am–7pm; admission charge; tel: 0-2281 5360; www.queengallery.org/en). One of the capital's more recent viewing spaces to open, the five-floor gallery has exhibitions of modern and contemporary paintings, predominantly locally produced works.

Golden Mount

Standing tall south of Mahakan Fort, the elevated spire of the **Golden Mount** (Phu Khao Thong) was for many years Bangkok's highest point (daily 7.30am–5.30pm; admission charge). Started by Rama III as a huge *chedi*, the city's soft earth made it impossible to build and the site soon became an artificial hill overgrown with trees and shrubbery. King Mongkut added a more modest *chedi* to the abandoned hill, and later King Chulalongkorn completed work on the 78-metre (256-ft) high plot.

The summit is reached by a stairway that curves around the side of the hill, and is shaded by trees and dotted with small shrines along the way. A part of Wat Saket (*see below*), the gilded *chedi* is said to contain a Buddha relic from India. The climb is fairly exhausting, but the summit rewards with panoramic scenes of historic Rattanakosin surrounded by Bangkok's urban sprawl.

Wat Saket

At the bottom of the Golden Mount stands one of the capital's oldest temples, **Wat Saket** (daily 8am–5pm; free). Upon returning from Laos in 1782 with the Emerald Buddha, General Chakri stopped here and took a ceremonial bath before making his way back to Thonburi to be crowned King Rama I. The temple's name was later changed to Saket, which means "the washing of hair".

The temple is also associated with a more grisly history as it was used as the old city's main crematorium. Disease epidemics broke out regularly during the 19th century, killing an estimated 60,000 people. The bodies of the dead were taken out of the city to the temple through the Pratu Pii (Ghost Gate) for cremation; if the families were too poor to pay for the ceremony, they were left for the vultures. Be sure to visit the main hall, which is adorned with fine murals and usually ignored by tourists.

Monks' Bowl Village

Skirting the western edge of the Golden Mount is **Thanon Boriphat**, a street lined with timber merchants and wood carvers, chiselling away at doors, lintels and even birdcages. Further along the some road are the narrow alleyways that run off **Soi Ban Baat**. This area, known as **Monk's Bowl Village**, is home to the only surviving community of traditional alms bowl makers, who have been hammering out these metal receptacles here since the capital's beginnings in the late 18th century.

Early birds may be privy to saffron robed monks walking barefoot along the streets at dawn collecting food offerings from merit-seeking alms givers. The bowl is known as a *baat* and was traditionally handcrafted from eight pieces of metal, representing the eight spokes in the wheel of Dharma. Cashing in on the tourist market, signs in English guide you to this small community of skilled artisans, where you hear the distant tap-tap of hammers. Finished in enamel paint, the bowls sell for about B500.

Santichai Prakan Park and Phra Sumen Fort

Called the village (*baan*) of the *lamphu* tree, the **Banglamphu** district was originally settled by farmers who fled the old capital of Ayutthaya after it was abandoned. The riverbank once held several princely mansions for nobles, a few of which survive on Thanon Phra Athit as offices of large companies and international agencies like UNICEF.

The riverfront from Saphan Phra Pin Klao bridge along the length of Thanon Phra Athit to **Santichai**

Prakan Park ⑭ is one of the city's few easily accessible river paths. It offers sweeping views up towards the relatively new Rama VIII Bridge. This lovely bankside park (daily 5am–10pm), always busy with activity of some sort, fringes the white-washed octagonal **Phra Sumen Fort ⑮**, and is said to have the only surviving *lamphu* trees left in the neighbourhood. The fort, built in 1873 and restored in 1999, is one of two remaining defences of the old city wall (*see also page 111*). It is not open to the public.

Nearby **Thanon Phra Athit** is a lively street of "art bars", frequented by budding artists from nearby Silpakorn University. The colourful and cosy venues, which hold regular exhibitions and cultural events, are a marked contrast to the backpacker-crammed watering holes just a stone's throw away on Thanon Khao San.

Thanon Khao San

Since the early 1980s, **Thanon Khao San ⑯** (or Khao San Road as it's popularly referred to) has been a self-contained ghetto for the backpacking

Map on page 108

Alms bowls, or "baat" are used by monks to collect food from faithful Buddhists every morning.

LEFT: skilled artisans hammering out alms bowls for monks at Soi Ban Baat.
BELOW: Khao San, a magnet for budget travellers.

Backpacker land Khao San Road has become so popular that it's even spawned its own website, called www.khaosanroad.com. Its packed chock-a-block with tips on cheap guesthouses, food and nightlife, as well as offbeat advice on how to wash your dreadlocks without unravelling them!

BELOW:
streetside hair-braiding service at Thanon Khao San.

globetrotter. Once a rather seedy gathering of cheap guesthouses, rice shops and pokey bars, as portrayed in Alex Garland's novel *The Beach*, Banglamphu's nerve centre has undergone a significant upgrade in recent years. The arrival of boutique hotels like Buddy Lodge, along with new bars and international chains like Starbucks have taken some of its edge away, but this neon-lit street still throngs. All the needs of a shoestring traveller are found here – Internet cafés jostle for space alongside shops offering hair-braiding, tattooing, body-piercing, used books, clothing, ethnic jewellery, and bootleg CDs and DVDs.

Sadly, many of the so-called "world" travellers who stay here see relatively little of what larger Bangkok has to offer, content to drink at the open-front bars and recount road tales to one another. Fortunately, the surge in Khao San's popularity among Bangkok's youth means that locals now head here for evening fun, bringing local flavour to the international mix. Even well-heeled tourists should explore the Khao San experience once.

North to Dusit Park

Crossing Khlong Banglamphu, Thanon Ratchadamnoen Klang turns into Ratchadamnoen Nok, with the pleasant, tree-lined boulevard leading down to a broad square in front of the old National Assembly building. Known as **Royal Plaza**, the square is watched over by a bronze **Statue of King Chulalongkorn** (Rama V) on horseback. Chulalongkorn was responsible for the construction of much of this part of Bangkok, which was once a rustic royal retreat from the city and the Grand Place.

Chulalongkorn was the first Thai monarch to venture to Europe and his travels obviously left a lasting impression on the architecture and layout of this district, which looks as much European as it is Thai. A

Map on page 114

great reformer and modern thinker, Chulalongkorn abolished slavery, put the country on the road to modernisation, and kept the colonialists from knocking at Thailand's door. Revered as a god, on the anniversary of his death each year on 23 October, the square is thronged with people honouring him by laying wreaths at the base of the statue. With the present king resident in nearby Chitralada Palace and the day-to-day governance taking place in Parliament House, this area is still the heartbeat of the nation.

Ananta Samakhom

As you head down the broad boulevard of Thanon Ratchadamnoen Nok, in the distance you will see the monumental edifice of the **Ananta Samakhom Throne Hall** ⓰, an Italian-Renaissance style hall of grey marble crowned by a huge dome (daily 8.30am–4.30pm; admission charge or free with Grand Palace entrance ticket). It is the tallest building within the manicured gardens of **Dusit Park**, a royal oasis livened up by canals, bridges and fountains.

Built in 1907 by King Chulalongkorn as a grandiose hall for receiving visiting dignitaries and other state ceremonies, it was used for the first official meeting of the new parliament after Thailand became a constitutional monarchy in 1932. A Parliament House has since been built behind the throne hall. Used for state occasions, the highlight of the rich interior is the dome ceiling frescoes depicting the Chakri monarchs from Rama I to Rama VI.

Vimanmek Mansion

Behind Ananta Samakhom Throne Hall is the **Vimanmek Mansion** ⓱, billed as the world's largest golden teak building (daily 9.30am–4pm; admission charge, or free with Grand Palace entrance ticket; tel: 0-2628 6300; www.thai.palaces.net;

compulsory guided tours every 30 minutes; visitors dressed in shorts must wear sarongs that are provided at the door; shoes and bags have to be stowed in lockers).

Originally built in 1868 as a summer house for King Chulalongkorn on the east coast island of Ko Si Chang *(see page 186)*, the king ordered the three-storey mansion dismantled and reassembled on the Dusit grounds in 1901. Made entirely from golden teak and without a single nail used in the construction, the gingerbread fretwork and octagonal tower of this 72-room lodge looks more Victorian than period Thai. The king and his large family lived here for only five years, during which time no males were allowed entry. The mansion was occupied on and off during the next two decades before being abandoned as storage space. It was restored for the Bangkok bicentennial 50 years later and given a new lease of life.

Vimanmek (meaning Palace in the Clouds) offers an interesting glimpse into how the royal family of the day lived. Only 30 of the rooms are open

Ananta Samakhom Throne Hall, which dates back to 1907, is more European than Thai in character.

BELOW: Vimanmek, the world's largest golden teak building.

TIP

Be sure to keep your admission ticket to the Wat Phra Kaew and Grand Palace *(see page 82)*. This allows you access to many of Dusit's sights for free, like the Ananta Samakhom Throne Hall, Vimanmek Mansion, Abhisek Dusit Throne Hall, and the Royal Elephant Museum.

BELOW: the Abhisek Dusit Throne Hall.

to the public and the tour is rather brief given the fact that there are so many treasures to see. A highlight is the king's bedroom, which has a European-style four-poster bed, and the bathroom, which houses what was probably Thailand's first bathtub and flushing toilet. The plumbing, however, was a little primitive – the waste had to be carried out via a hidden spiral staircase beneath. Among the porcelain and hunting trophies are rare finds like the first typewriter to have Thai characters.

In the pavilion on the south side of the mansion are free performances of Thai dance and martial arts every day at 10.30am and 2pm.

Abhisek Dusit Throne Hall

To the right of Vimanmek is the **Abhisek Dusit Throne Hall ⓳** (daily 9.30am–4pm; admission charge, or free with Grand Palace entrance ticket). Constructed in 1903 for King Chulalongkorn as an accompanying throne hall to Vimanmek, the ornate building is another sumptuous melding of Victorian and Moorish styles, but still retaining its

distinctly Thai sheen. The main hall is now used as a showroom-cum-museum for the SUPPORT foundation, a charitable organisation headed by Queen Sirikit which helps preserve traditional arts and crafts. On view are examples of jewellery, woodcarving, nielloware, silk and wicker products. Next to the museum is a shop where the handiwork of village artisans is on sale.

Royal Elephant Museum

Just east of the Abhisek Dusit Throne Hall is the **Royal Elephant Museum ⓴** or Chang Ton (daily 9.30am–4pm; admission charge, or free with Grand Palace entrance ticket). Formerly a stable for three very rare "white" elephants, it was converted into a museum; on display is a large model of one of the present king's prized living pachyderms, tusks, photos of a Brahman ceremony conferring royal status upon white elephants *(see text box below)* and other paraphernalia associated with this royal creature. Regarded as a national symbol and emblazoned on the Thai flag,

White Elephants

To the uninitiated, white elephants look nearly the same as everyday grey ones. It is only by a complicated process of examining skin colour, hair, eyes and genitalia that an elephant's albino traits can be determined. Historically, the white elephant has denoted regal power in Southeast Asia. The number of white elephants a king owned, which had to be fed rare foods and housed in special quarters, signified his power. If the king suspected a minor prince was becoming too powerful, he would give him a white elephant. The prince would go bankrupt trying to feed and house it; hence, the term "white elephant" denotes a gift that is too costly to maintain.

Map
on page
114

according to local tradition every white elephant found in Thailand rightfully belongs to the king.

Dusit Zoo

To the east is the **Dusit Zoo** ㉑ (daily 8am–6pm; admission charge; tel: 0-2281 2000). The grounds were originally part of the Royal Dusit Garden Palace, where King Chulalongkorn had his private botanical garden. The 19-hectare (47-acre) site became a public zoo in 1938. The zoo has around 300 different species of mammals, almost a 1,000 bird species, and around 300 different kinds of reptiles, but conditions at some of the animal enclosures are less than adequate. More worthy of observation are the packs of local families, who converge on the zoo at weekends, picnicking and adding colour to the mix.

Chitralada Palace

East of the Dusit Zoo, a thick tree-shaded fenced moat and sentry guards protect the grounds of the **Chitralada Palace** ㉒, the permanent home of the present monarchy. Once a rural retreat known as Sompoy Field, where King Vajiravudh (Rama VI) would seek creative solitude away from court life at the Grand Palace, it was built in 1913. Not open to the public, keen observers might spot some agricultural equipment along the fence perimeter, where King Bhumibol himself conducts experiments in agricultural sustainability for the benefit of his people.

Opposite the palace on Thanon Sri Ayutthaya is the **Royal Turf Club** horseracing track. Races are held here every other week.

Wat Benjamabophit

To the south of the Chulalongkorn statue is **Wat Benjamabophit** ㉓ (Marble Temple) on Thanon Rama V, the last major temple built in central Bangkok and the best example of modern Thai religious architecture (daily 8am–5.30pm; admission charge). Started by King Chulalongkorn at the turn of the century, the *wat* was designed by the king's half-brother Prince Naris together with Italian architect Hercules Manfredi. Completed in 1911, these two collaborators fused elements of East and West to dramatic effect. The most obvious of these must be the walls of Carrara marble from Italy, the cruciform shape and the unique European-crafted stained-glass windows depicting Thai mythological scenes. The *bot*'s principal Buddha image is a replica of the famous Phra Buddha Chinarat of Phitsanulok, with the base containing the ashes of King Chulalongkorn.

Behind the *bot* is a gallery holding 53 original and copied significant Buddha images from all over Buddhist Asia, providing a useful educational display. The temple is most interesting in the early morning, when merit-makers gather before its gates to donate food and offerings to the line of bowl-wielding monks – unlike elsewhere where monks walk the streets searching for alms. ❑

Ayutthayan-style Buddha image in the "abhaya mudra" (reassurance) posture at a gallery in Wat Benjamabophit.

BELOW: worshippers at a night service at Wat Benjamabophit.

RESTAURANTS

Chinese
Yee Lao Tang Jua Lee
45-47 Th Kalayana Maitri.
Tel: 0-2221 8447. Open:
daily L and D. $$
Air-conditioned restau-
rant with only Thai script
outside (look for the fish
drawing), but with an Eng-
lish menu within. Chinese
specialities, from various
dim sum and stir-fried
scallops with XO sauce to
double-boiled bird's nest
with ginko nuts feature
prominently. Busy in the
week with mainly office
workers nearby while
Chinese families con-
verge at weekends.

Indian
The Indian Spice
30 Soi Rambutri. No phone.
Open: daily 11am–11pm. $
A seven-table Indian café
down the Thanon Phra
Arthit end of Soi Ram-
butri. Start with crispy
samosas, then choose
from a range of *naan*,
paratha and other
breads to dip into lamb
korma, chicken *jalfreezi*,
and vegetable and lentil
curries. Five-course meat
or vegetarian *thali* avail-
able for the very hungry.

International
**Baan Phra Arthit
Coffee & More**
102/1 Th Phra Arthit.
Tel: 0-2280 7878-9. Open:
Mon–Fri 11am–11pm,
Sat–Sun 11am–midnight. $
Mochas and cappucci-
nos in a refined old

house that was once the
Goethe Institut. Along
with the cheesecakes,
meringues and Black
Forest gateaux, there's a
choice of salads and
snacks like Chiang Mai
sausage and quiche,
with lasagna and chicken
curry among the mains.
Comfortable sofa seat-
ing to lounge on while
reading magazines.

Primavera
56 Th Phra Sumen.
Tel: 0-2281 4718. Open:
daily 9am–11pm. $–$$
European coffee shop
interior of mainly dark
woods. Top billing on a
short menu goes to
pizza, along with liver
pâté and fried calamari
as starters. The Austrian
owner dresses his sal-
ads with pumpkin seed
oil, which he swears is
what Arnie Schwarzeneg-
ger was reared on. Rea-
sonable choice of ice
creams and coffees.

Israeli
Chabad House
108/1 Soi Rambutri.
Tel: 0-2282 6388. Open:
Sun–Thur noon–9pm, Fri
noon–4.30pm. $
Run as a charitable
business by the
synagogue in the same
building, this Israeli-run
café offers nicer (and
cleaner) surroundings
than most other Middle
Eastern-style eateries in
the neighbourhood. And
all the food is kosher of

course. Good falafel,
salads, hummus and the
usual *tahina*-based dips
to accompany a wide
choice of mains.

Italian
La Bella Italian Cuisine
45-47 Soi Rong Mai, Th
Chao Fah. Tel: 0-2282 6858.
Open: daily 1pm–1am. $–$$
Good for a change from
the Khao San scene, this
Italian place is on a quiet
soi, and set in a walled
garden with a fountain
and wicker chairs. Try
the pasta with four
cheeses, pizza *diavola* or
grilled lamb, and finish
with *zabaglione*. Not
haute cuisine, but
decent food for the price.

Thai
Chote Chitr
Th Praengphutorn.
Tel: 0-2221 4082. Open:
Mon–Sat 10am–9pm. $
This restaurant has been
in this row of shop-
houses on the edge of a
quiet community square
close to Wat Ratchapra-
dit since the early 20th
century. It retains its
chalkboard menus of
tom yum goong, spicy
salads and its famed
mee krob (sweet crispy
noodles). Also sells *ya
dong* (herbal liquors).

Kaloang Home Kitchen
2 Th Sri Ayutthaya, Dusit.
Tel: 0-2281 9228, 0-2282
7581. Open: daily
11am–10pm. $–$$
Located behind the

National Library where
Thanon Sri Ayutthaya
peters out at the river-
bank boatyards, Kaloang
has retained its rustic
charm even though much
else around it has
careened into the 21st
century. Serves a good
choice of Thai stan-
dards, but most people
go for the grilled fish and
terrific seafood, such as
curried crab.

Kinlom Chon Saphan
11/6 Samsen Soi 3.
Tel: 0-2628 8382-3. Open:
daily 5pm–midnight. $
Live tanks of fish and
seafood in the driveway
advertise the speciality
at this riverfront restaurant directly opposite the
spectacular Rama VIII
Bridge. Diners sit on the
open-air wooden terrace
for leisurely meals of
steamed shrimp in spicy
sauce, curried crab and
charcoal-grilled fish. A
few Western dishes bal-
ance the menu.

Krua Nopparat
130-132 Th Phra Arthit.
Tel: 0-2281 7578. Open:
Mon–Sat 10.30am–9pm. $
The restaurants around
Thanon Khao San are apt
to get jaded with their
faceless backpacker cus-
tomers, so good, tradi-
tional home cooking is
quite a rarity in these
parts. This tiny shop-
house has relied on local
customers for nearly 30
years, and consequently
serves very reliable food.

Don't be put off by the plain formica tables and wooden chairs.

May Kaidee

117/1 Th Tanao. Tel: 0-2281 7137. Open: daily 8am–11pm. $
www.maykaidee.com
Serving vegetarian food since 1988, May has a growing reputation for her meat-free Thai standards. Second outlet at nearby **111/1-3 Th Tanee**. Isaan-style (from northeast Thailand) vegetarian dishes with mushrooms, tofu and soya beans, and *massaman* curry with tofu, potatoes and peanuts are popular selections. Dessert of black sticky rice with coconut, banana and mango is heavenly. May also gives cooking lessons. To find this place, take the *soi* next to Burger King, and turn left.

Methavalai Sorn Daeng

78/2 Th Ratchadamnoen Klang. Tel: 0-2221 2378. Open: daily 10am–11pm. $$
Popular old-style Thai-Chinese upmarket restaurant with linen tablecloths and tacky salmon-coloured floral chairs. Decent food includes the famous *nam phrik platu* chilli sauce with mackerel), double-boiled duck soup with preserved lemon, and spicy banana flower salad. Right by the Democracy Monument roundabout.

Mitr Go Yuan

86 Th Dinso. Tel: 0-2224 194. Open: Mon–Sat 11am–10pm, Sun 4pm–10pm. $

Traditional shophouse set-up that's busy at lunch and after 5pm with workers from the nearby City Hall, who rave about its *tom yum goong* (clear and spicy prawn soup) and spicy Thai salads. This eatery is famous with locals, and attracts occasional celebrities – like Thailand's super-model Luk Ked, whose photo is on the wall.

Nan Faa

164 Th Dinso. Tel: 0-2224 1180. Open: daily 8am–8pm. $
Thai-Chinese café that specialises in slow roasted duck and goose basted with honey. Also has *dim sum* and – if you are adventurous – traditional family dishes like stewed pig's ears and pig's feet. If you can't get a seat here, go two doors away to **Tien Song**, which serves similar food in larger (and air-conditioned) surroundings.

Pen Thai Food

229 Soi Rambutri. Tel: 0-2282 2320. Open: daily 7am–7.30pm. $
Khun Sitichai has had this spot since 1980, long before the first backpackers appeared at his tables. And his menu has changed little. His spicy catfish curry, soups and deep-fried fish are still displayed outside in metal pots and trays in street-stall fashion. And at B20–40 each, his prices haven't changed much either.

Roti-Mataba

136 Th Phra Arthit. Tel: 0-2282-2119. Open: Tues–Sun 7am–10pm. $
A whole army of women here make the Muslim-style breads – like flat unleavened *roti* and meat-stuffed *mataba* – by the hundreds in this incredibly busy shop-house. Dip the crisp *roti* into their delicious *massaman* and *korma* curries of fish, vegetable or meat. There are only a few tables inside and on the pavement, so be prepared to wait.

Siam House Baan Khunying Phuen

591 Th Phra Sumen. Tel: 0-2281 6237. Open: daily 10am–11pm. $
A fine Sino-Portuguese house originally belonging to Thailand's first consular to Singapore, an adopted son of King Rama IV. Sparsely decorated (just a few family photos), it also has outdoor seating in front of Khlong Banglampu. Very popular in the evenings with Thai folks. Usual Thai standards, plus Western-style steaks.

Sunset Bar & Garden Restaurant

Sunset St, 197 Th Khao San. Tel: 0-2282-2565. Open: daily 8–2am. $
The food on Thanon Khao San is generally average, and Sunset Garden restaurant is no exception. What it does have is a European piazza-like location in the shadow of a beautiful old

house with a Starbucks cáfe and an art gallery. A peaceful retreat from the main street hustle.

Thip Samai

313 Th Mahachai. Tel: 0-2221 6280. Open: daily 5.30pm–3.30am. $
A very basic but legendary café that does several versions (and nothing else) of *pad thai*, the fried noodle, dried shrimp, roasted peanut and bean sprout meal that is often claimed as Thailand's national dish. If it's closed, try **Pad Thai Goong Pa**, next door. Located close to the Golden Mount (Phu Thao Khong).

Tom Yum Kung

Th Khao San. Tel: 0-2629 2772. Open: daily 3pm–2am. $
www.tomyumkungkhaosan.com
This restaurant is proof that Thanon Khao San is more than just backpackers and American break-fasts; Tom Yum Kung is perennially packed with young partying Thais. The venue is a town-house set back from the main street with more seating under the stars. Popular eats are the eponymous soup, stir fries and sizzling seafood hot plates.

CHINATOWN

Bangkok's Chinese and Indian communities have made Chinatown their own by building shrines and temples as well as thriving businesses that serve both their people and the Thais. Loud, boisterous and frenzied, this is Bangkok at its visceral best

Chinatown was settled by Chinese merchants in the 1780s, after being asked to relocate here so that the Grand Palace could be built. In 1863, King Mongkut built Thanon Charoen Krung (New Road), the first paved street in Bangkok, and Chinatown soon began mushrooming outwards from the original dirt track of Sampeng (now officially Soi Wanit 1). Other adjacent plots of land were given to the Indian and Muslim communities. Later, a third artery, Thanon Yaowarat, was built between Charoen Krung and Sampeng roads, in the process becoming the main artery of Chinatown and the Thai name for the area.

Naturalised as Thai citizens, the Chinese still manage to retain a distinct character to this day, creating a multicultural mix that pervades all levels of society. The influence of the Chinese upon Bangkok's, and indeed the country's, economic development cannot be overstated. Their work ethic has taken them from pulling rickshaws and slaving as coolies to the highest ranks, with the nation now governed by Thai-Chinese telecommunications magnate, Prime Minister Thaksin Shinawatra.

With narrow roads and lanes teeming with commercial bustle this is one of the capital's most traffic-clogged districts. Exploring on foot allows you to soak up the mercantile atmosphere. Away from downtown's plush mega-malls, Chinatown is a raw experience of Bangkok past and present: old shophouses, godowns (warehouses), temples and shrines, all swelling with activity.

Sampeng Lane

The **Sampeng** area is considered the old pulse of Chinatown and has had a rowdy history. What began as a mercantile pursuit soon degenerated into a raunchy entertainment area.

Map on page 122

LEFT: Thanon Yaowarat in Chinatown is a hive of activity just before Chinese New Year.
BELOW: dried food products for sale in Chinatown.

The golden-domed Sri Guru Singh Sabha temple is where Bangkok's Sikh community congregates.

By 1900 it had a reputation as "Sin Alley", with lanes leading to opium dens, gambling houses and buildings whose entrances were marked by *khom khiew* (green lanterns). A green-light district was like a Western red-light district; while the lanterns have disappeared, the term *khom khiew* still signifies a brothel today. Eventually, however, Sampeng lost its sleaze and became a bustling lane of small shops selling goods imported from China.

The stretch of **Sampeng Lane ❶** (or Soi Wanit 1) between Thanon Ratchawong and Thanon Mangkon is covered by awnings that shield market stalls supplying all the basics for the average Thai Chinese household. Not a lot of quality here, but for fun kitsch and tacky bargain hunting it's certainly worth a rummage. Aside from cheap clothing, footwear, sticky confectionary, costume jewellery and plastic novelties, you could stumble across Chinese scroll painters.

Wat Chakrawat

From Sampeng Lane, cross Thanon Chakrawat and turn left to get to **Wat Chakrawat ❷** (daily 8am–4.30pm; free). The temple comprises an odd amalgam of buildings. Dating from the Ayutthaya period, it has a small artificial hill topped by a *mondop* and a small grotto with a statue of a fat, laughing monk. According to legend, the statue was built to honour a devout but very handsome monk who was constantly pestered by women while deep in meditation. His devotion to Buddhism led him to stuff his face to obesity and the women soon lost interest. Also in the grotto is a curious black silhouette on the wall. Adorned with gold leaf, it is supposed to be Buddha's shadow.

Thais with a litter of puppies or kittens they cannot feed usually leave them at the *wat*, to be fed the leftovers from the monks' daily meals. This particular *wat*, how-

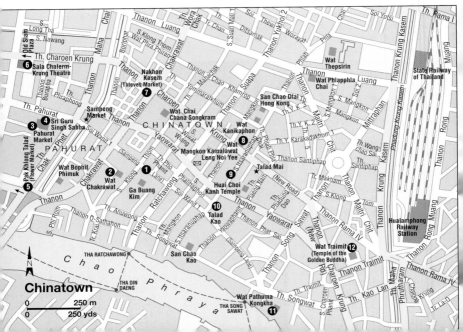

Thanon Yaowarat and Nakhon Kasem

Parallel to Sampeng Lane is Thanon Yaowarat, which in places looks much like a Hong Kong street with its forest of neon signs. It is best known for its gold dealers; daily prices are scrawled on the windows of shops painted red for good luck. Prices are quoted in baht for an ancient unit of weight measurement that is equal to 15 grams (half an ounce).

Between Thanon Yaowarat and Thanon Charoen Krung, at the corner with Thanon Chakrawat, is **Nakhon Kasem ❼** or Thieves' Market (daily 8am–8pm). A few decades ago, this was a black market for stolen goods. It later developed into an antiques dealers' area, but today, most antiques stalls have gone. You are more likely to find items of a less glamorous description and run-of-the-mill household appliances these days. Nevertheless, if you search hard, it's still possible to find a few shops selling old grandfather clocks, musical instruments and Buddha images.

Wat Mangkon Kamalawat

On Thanon Charoen Krung near Soi Itsaranuphap is the towering gateway of **Wat Mangkon Kamalawat ❽** or **Leng Noi Yee** (Dragon Flower Temple) as it's also known (daily 8.30am–3.30pm; free). The most revered temple in Chinatown, from early morning onwards it's a constant swirl of activity and incense smoke. As with the whole of this district, the temple is overrun at Chinese New Year.

Built in 1871, the temple is one of the most important centres for Mahayana Buddhism (most Thais practice Theravada Buddhism) in all of Thailand. Elements of Taoism and Confucianism are also prevalent. The dragon-crowned roof overlooks a courtyard containing several temple structures that house altars and images of gilded Buddhas, the Four Heavenly Kings and other Taoist deities.

Soi Itsaranuphap

The most interesting lane in Chinatown is **Soi Itsaranuphap ❾** (Soi 16), which runs south from Thanon Phlab Phla Chai and and passes a 19th-century Thai temple called **Wat Kanikaphon** (daily 6am–4pm; free). It is better known as Wat Mae Yai Fang, after the brothel madam who built it to atone for her sins.

Around the entrance to Soi Itsaranuphap are shops selling "hell money" and miniature houses, Mercedes cars, household furniture and other items made of paper for the Chinese *kong tek* ceremony. The items are taken to the temple and burnt to send them to deceased relatives. Other shops sell the red-and-gold-trimmed shrines the Chinese install in homes to propitiate the spirits.

Talad Kao and Talad Mai

Soi Itsaranuphap has two of the city's best-known markets. Closer to the corner with Sampeng Lane is the two-century old **Talad Kao ❿** (Old Market) while a little off Soi Itsaranuphap (closer to Thanon Charoen Krung) is the newer **Talad**

Map on page 122

Bundles of "hell money" found at shops along Soi Itsaranuphap are legal tender only in the netherworld.

BELOW: the main altar inside Wat Mangkon Kamalawat.

Map on page 122

The solid gold Buddha image at Wat Traimit was found purely by accident.

BELOW: morning scene at Talad Kao.

Mai (New Market), which has been plying its wares for a century. The old market wraps up by late morning, while the newer one keeps trading until sundown. These fresh markets have a reputation for high-quality meat, fish and vegetables, and overflow during Chinese New Year. With raw and dried fish, pungent spices, and stoves boiling away, wandering here can overwhelm the senses. These days Talad Kao seems to be losing ground to its younger rival, which has been attributed to bad *feng shui* after the stretch of lane around the old market was widened recently, allowing profit to flow away.

Wat Pathuma Kongkha

Back on Sampeng Lane, continue east; halfway down on the left is the striking seven-storey **Tang To Kang** building that once served as Chinatown's central gold exchange. In the side alleys are small Chinese shrines; farther down on the right are shops selling cinnamon and other spices.

Near the end of Sampeng Lane are shops that bear Muslim names. The merchants here trade gems.

Marking the eastern end of Sampeng is **Wat Pathuma Kongkha** , also called **Wat Sampeng**, (daily 8am–5pm; free). One of Bangkok's oldest temples and dating back to the Ayutthayan period, it was here that criminals of noble birth were executed for crimes against the state.

Wat Traimit

Just east of the point where Thanon Yaowarat meets Thanon Charoen Krung, across from the Odeon Circle China Gate, is the unremarkable looking **Wat Traimit** (daily 8am–5pm; admission charge). The real treasure lies within, the famous **Golden Buddha**. Found by accident in the 1950s at a riverside temple, the 3-metre (10-ft) tall stucco figure was being transported to its present site when the crane lifting it snapped and sent the statue smashing to the ground, breaking one corner. A glint of yellow showed through the crack, revealing an image of solid gold weighing some 5.5 tonnes. Truly a hidden treasure, the gleaming image is said to date from 13th-century Sukhothai, and was probably encased in stucco during the Ayutthayan period to conceal its true worth from Burmese invaders, and remained undetected for centuries.

Hualamphong Station

East of Wat Traimit is the city's main railway terminus, **Hualamphong Railway Station**, a fine example of Thai art deco style. King Chulalongkorn (Rama V) initiated Thailand's first rail line from here in 1891, carrying passengers on the relatively short distance to Paknam. The European structure was constructed between 1910 and 1916. A renovation in the late 1990s has made the station a far more comfortable and convenient transit point. The recently opened metro line terminates here and is a convenient point to head off to your next port of call. ❑

RESTAURANTS

Chinese

Hua Seng Hong Yaowaraj

438 Th Charoen Krung Soi 14. Tel: 0-2627 5030. Open: daily 9am–9pm. $–$$
An ex-shophouse that is now a glassed-in restaurant with marble top tables, wooden chairs and air-conconditioning. Still a raucous Chinese lunch venue though, selling all-day dim sum from an outside counter and all manner of congee, hot and sour soup, barbecued pork, fish maw and braised goose dishes inside.

Noodle N' More

513/514 Th Rong Muang. Tel: 0-2613 8972. Open: daily 11am–11pm. $
This branch of a Hong Kong noodle restaurant has a good corner location close to Hua Lamphong Station and a modern café interior. Upstairs seating by the window has great street views. Serves good range of noodle dishes including "mixed", with wonton, pork, duck and crab meat), plus all-day dim sum, rice with mixed dishes and a few novel desserts, like sesame dumpling with ginger.

Shangrila Yaowarat

06 Th Yaowarat.
el: 0-2224 5933. Open: aily 10am–10pm. $$
his busy Cantonese lace dishes out casual afé-style dim sum

lunches, then brings out the tablecloths and napkins for dinner. Menu includes drunken chicken with jellyfish, smoked pigeon, and live seafood from the tanks on the ground floor. Or choose from the displays of roasted duck, steaming dim sum and freshly baked pastries.

Indian

Punjab Sweets and Restaurant

436/5 Th Chakraphet. Tel: 0-2623 7606. Open: daily 8am–9pm. $
Bangkok's Little India (Pahurat) sits at the western edge of Chinatown. Its alleyways are crowded with tailors and tiny Indian cafés, of which this is one of the best. Its meat- and dairy-free food includes a good choice of curries and dosa (rice-flour pancakes) from South India, and Punjabi sweets wrapped in edible silver foil.

Thai

Laem Thong

894 Th Charoen Krung Soi 12. Tel: 0-2224 3591. Open: daily 8am–4pm. $
The glass-fronted displays of non-Chinese Thai dishes are not that common in this part of town, so head here if you feel like having red curry with pork or spicy fried chicken with ginger. Despite plastic chairs

and tiled walls, its air-conditioning promises comfortable dining.

Ped Tun Jao Thaa

941-947 Soi Wanit 2.
Tel: 0-2233 2541. Open: Mon–Sat 10am–5pm. $
Streetside outfit famous for duck with rice or noodles. A mere 10 tables inside and out, but its popularity is obvious from the non-stop packaging of take-away and delivery orders, and the fact it's now taken over the next-door shophouse from where it does an equally brisk business selling stir-fried noodles with pork, shrimp and squid.

Thailand Tonight

Royal Orchid Sheraton, 2 Captain Bush Lane, Th Withayu. Tel: 0-2266 0123. Open: daily 6.30–10pm. $$$
Not quite Chinatown but on its outskirts. Upmarket Thai-theatre restaurant with a river view that's a relaxing antidote to the heat and hassle of Chinatown. You sit in an open-air stage set, like a traditional village square with wooden buildings and the food is laid out buffet-style in a "market". The show has classical dancing, masked khon theatre and sword dancing.

Yok Yor

Yok Yor Marina, 885 Somdej Chao Phraya Soi 17.
Tel: 0-2863 0565/6. Open: daily 11.30am–11pm. $$
www.yokyor.co.th

Open-air and indoor seating at this restaurant bustling with locals and tourists. The Thai and seafood dishes are mostly decent, but the main attractions are the lovely riverside setting and the Thai cabaret show, which features comedy, singing and katoey (transvestite) acts. Stars occasionally do a short spot (they tour the city playing several venues in one night).

Thai Food Stalls

Soi Texas

Th Padung Dao. Open: 9am–2am. $–$$
Named after its **Texas Suki** restaurant, this atmospehric soi (narrow sidestreet) also has **Nam Sing** (famous for its Chinese specialities like bird's nest soup), and several seafood eateries. The best of these are **Rut and Lek** and **T & K** (open from 6pm daily), both at the entrance of the soi. You can't go wrong with crab and seafood, either cooked in curry, charcoal-grilled or fried with garlic and chilli.

PRICE CATEGORIES

Price per person for a three-course meal without drinks:
$ = under US$10
$$ = US$10–$25
$$$ = US$25–$50
$$$$ = over US$50

PATHUMWAN AND PRATUNAM

When shopping in multiple monster malls becomes oh so tedious, Jim Thompson's House, Suan Pakkad Palace and Lumphini Park offer alternative pleasures in the commercial heart of downtown Bangkok. But children will probably prefer the Snake Farm

The commercial heart of downtown Bangkok, **Pathumwan** is a sprawl of shopping malls, all connected by the Skytrain. It's mainly a consumerist's paradise, yet there are still plenty of sights more reminiscent of an older and more traditional Bangkok. Cleaved in the early 19th century, the man-made canal **Khlong Saen Saep** enabled the capital to spread north to **Pratunam** and beyond. To the east is Thanon Withayu (Wireless Road) where a string of embassies are found along with upmarket expatriate housing.

Just a short walk to the end of Soi Kasemsan 2 from the National Stadium Skytrain station is the protected oasis of **Jim Thompson's House Museum** ❶ (daily 9am–5pm; admission charge includes compulsory guided tour of the museum; tel: 0-2216 7368; www.jimthompson house.com). Jim Thompson (*see photo essay on pages 138–39*) was the American silk entrepreneur responsible for the revival of Thai silk. An architect by training, Thompson arrived in Thailand at the end of World War II, serving as a military officer. After the war he returned to Bangkok, where he became interested in the almost redundant craft of silk weaving and design.

Thompson mysteriously disappeared in the jungles of Malaysia's Cameron Highlands in 1967 but his well-preserved house still stands today by the banks of the Khlong Saen Saep canal. Thompson was an enthusiastic collector of Asian arts and antiquities, many of which adorn his traditional house-turned-museum. The garden surrounding the house is a luxuriant mini tropical jungle and is an attraction in itself.

The museum comprises six teak structures, which were transported from Ayutthaya and elsewhere to the silk weaving enclave of Ban Khrua,

Map on page 130

LEFT: Jim Thompson's House, viewed from the lush gardens.
BELOW: bustling shoppers at the Mahboonkrong shopping centre.

just across Khlong Saen Saep, before being reassembled at its current spot in 1959. From the windows of the house, it's easy to imagine how scenic the view would have been some 40 years ago, looking across the lush gardens, or "jungle" as Thompson called it, to the canal and its daily life.

Window displays at Siam Square mainly target the young.

Next to the old house is a wooden annex, housing a pond-side café with an elegant upstairs bar and restaurant, while opposite is the **Art Centre at Jim Thompson House**, a contemporary gallery that holds regular exhibitions of local and international art and crafts. Before leaving, be sure to stop by and pick up some silk accessories from the branch of **Jim Thompson Thai Silk Company**.

Siam Square

As downtown Bangkok loses character to a growing conglomeration of faceless air-conditioned malls, **Siam Square ❷**, along Thanon Rama I, retains its maverick air as one of the city's few remaining street-side shopping enclaves. This maze of low-rise shops and restaurants is a favourite hangout for students, who mainly congregate in the area known as Centre Point. Apart from the ubiquitous

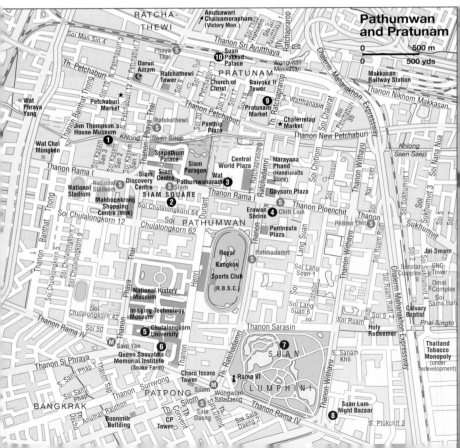

Hard Rock Café, there are few shops here catering to tourists; the lanes are mainly crammed with stores selling street wear and teenage gear along with tuition and language schools, tiny cafés and ice-cream shops.

Malls along Thanon Rama 1

Cross the footbridge over Thanon Phaya Thai from Siam Square and head into the bewildering mayhem of **Mahboonkrong** shopping centre, better known as MBK. A monster mall, MBK is always busy with Thai youngsters, especially at weekends when they crowd around the shops selling a cluttered variety of fake designer clothing, sunglasses, watches, cheap leather and fashion accessories, gold jewellery and electronics. Get your portrait painted on the ground floor in one of several art studios, while on the 7th floor is **SF Strike Bowl** (10-pin bowling) and **SF Music City**, a trendy karaoke lounge.

Across from Siam Square along Thanon Rama 1 are the connecting malls of **Siam Centre** and **Siam Discovery Centre**. Pleasantly less crowded, Siam Discovery Centre stocks international brand names and elegant home accessories, while Siam Centre is the turf for the younger set, with its CD warehouse store, local designer wear and sports and surf clothing shops.

Movie-buffs are spoilt for choice with five cinemas within a stone's throw of each other. Siam Square has three ageing movie houses, **Scala**, **Siam** and the **Lido**. Across at Siam Discovery Centre is the ritzy EGV cinema, while up on MBK's 7th floor is the youthful **SF Cinema City**.

Next to Siam Centre is the recently opened **Siam Paragon** mall. As well as housing a slew of designer brand name shops, the mall also has Southeast Asia's largest aquarium at **Siam Ocean World** (daily 9am–10pm; tel: 0-2687 2000; admission charge; www.siamoceanworld.co.th). The aquar-

ium has over 30,000 marine creatures, and visitors can ride in a glass-bottomed boat and dive with sharks.

Wat Pathumwanaram

Commercial development in this busy part of the city has suffocated the few early structures that still survive. Few people know that hidden to the rear of Siam Centre is the **Srapathum Palace**, which still operates as a royal residence and is not open to the public. The palace was given to King Bhumibol's late father, Prince Mahidol Adulyadej, in the early 20th century and became the home of Bhumibol's late mother until she passed away in 1995.

The palace's expansive grounds include **Wat Pathumwanaram** ❸ (daily 8.30am–6pm; free). Given its busy location between the new Siam Paragon mall and Central World Plaza *(see next page)*, you'd expect the temple to be overrun with guilt-ridden shoppers seeking spiritual salvation. Fortunately, this sanctuary is an oasis of calm in this busy area. The temple holds the ashes of Prince Mahidol as well as that of his wife.

Map on page 130

 TIP

The main shopping areas in downtown Bangkok are now linked by the Skywalk – a covered elevated walkway beneath the Skytrain tracks – connecting Chidlom, Siam Square and National Stadium Skytrain stations along Thanon Rama 1. This means you can walk from one mall to another under shade and without having to cross the streets.

BELOW: monk at the main altar of Wat Pathumwanaram.

*Wooden elephants –
which represent
Brahma's elephant
mount, Erawan, sold
outside the Erawan
Shrine. In March
2006, the shrine was
destroyed by a mental
patient, but it was
restored less than
three months later.*

BELOW: offerings
at Erawan Shrine.
RIGHT:
Gaysorn Plaza lobby.

Central World Plaza

Next door looms the huge granite block of **Central World Plaza**. Certainly not the city's best shopping centre, its spacious walkways are propped either end by the large Zen and Isetan department stores, ensuring a constant flow of Japanese customers. The mall is more a draw for entertainment. If you get too hot under the collar, head for the **World Ice Skating** rink on the 7th floor (Mon–Fri 10am–9pm; admission charge; tel 0-2255 9500). Or cool off at its multi-screen cinema, or any one of numerous restaurants and cafés. During the cooler season, the large forecourt at the front transforms into an open-air evening beer garden.

Erawan Shrine

At the end of Thanon Rama I is the chaotic junction where the street intersects with Thanon Ratchadamri and changes its name to Thanon Ploenchit, before metamorphosing later into Thanon Sukhumvit. At the corner of Thanon Ratchadamri and Thanon Ploenchit stands the **Erawan Shrine ❹** (daily 8am–10pm). The

aromatic haze of incense hits you before you actually see the shrine.

Attracting locals and Asian tourists in droves, the shrine is dedicated to the four-headed Hindu god of creation, Brahma. Originally erected on the site of the former Erawan Hotel, rebuilt as the present Grand Hyatt Erawan, the initial spirit house was deemed ineffective after a spate of unfortunate events (including deaths) slowed the hotel's construction. After astrological consultation, this plaster-gilded 1956 replacement halted the unlucky run, and ever since then the shrine has been revered for its strong talismanic powers.

Vendors line the enclosing fence selling floral garlands and wooden elephants (symbols of Brahma's elephant mount, Erawan). Supplicants who have their prayers answered buy these as offerings, while some even hire a resident troupe on site to perform *lakhon* dances.

Thanon Ploenchit malls

Behind Erawan Shrine, along Thanon Ploenchit, is the new **Erawan Bangkok**, a boutique mall connected

to the swish Grand Hyatt Erawan and professing to offer a complete leisure experience, with not just chi-chi shops and eateries, but also a wellness and beauty centre. Across the street, **Gaysorn Plaza** is an expensive designer mall that is relatively quiet save for the trickle of "hi-so" spenders and wannabe window shoppers. The upper level accommodates tasteful arts and home decor stores.

North along Thanon Ratchadamri, just opposite the Central World Plaza, is **Narayana Phand**, a large treasure trove of Thai arts and crafts. The three-floor emporium is your one-stop shop for all manner of Thai arts and crafts, from classical Thai musical instruments and ornate ceremonial headgear to paintings and Thai silk purses. However, the onslaught of goods rather diminishes the uniqueness of many of its pieces.

Chulalongkorn University

South of Siam Square along Thanon Phaya Thai are the verdant grounds of **Chulalongkorn University ⑤**, the country's oldest and most prestigious institution of higher learning. Combining both Thai and Western architectural styles, the university was named in honour of King Chulalongkorn (Rama V). Located on two blocks of the city's most coveted real estate, the college regularly comes to life with campus events.

The campus grounds on the same side as MBK hosts two contemporary galleries. The **Jamjuree Gallery** (Mon–Fri 10–7pm, Sat 12–6pm; free; tel: 0-2218 3709) displays both student shows as well as more experimental exhibits by rising artists, whereas the **Art Centre** (Mon–Fri 8am–7pm, Sat 9am–4pm; free; tel: 0-2218 2964), at the Centre of Academic Resources, holds exhibitions by Thailand's internationally recognised artists. The university's **Museum of Imaging Technology** by the lakeside may be of interest to photo

buffs; it documents the development of photography in Thailand (Mon–Fri 9am–3pm; admission charge; tel: 0-2218 5581).

Royal Bangkok Sports Club

East of Chulalongkorn University along Thanon Henri Dunant is the members-only **Royal Bangkok Sports Club** (tel: 0-2255 1420 for race info). Dating from the early 1900s, the horse racing club quickly became the favourite recreational spot for the city's upper class. The grounds also served as Bangkok's only airfield before Bangkok International Airport was eventually built. Attracting large crowds of feverish gamblers, non-members are only allowed through the gates on alternate Sundays for the races.

Snake Farm

Travellers to the tropics often worry about encounters with dangerous beasties and a visit to the **Queen Saovabha Memorial Institute ⑥**, popularly called the **Snake Farm**, will either allay or enforce such trepidations (Mon–Fri 8.30am–4.30pm,

Map on page 130

A young volunteer at the Snake Farm gingerly handles a python as he poses for a photograph.

BELOW: showtime at the Snake Farm.

BELOW: tranquil lake at Lumphini Park.
RIGHT: Suan Lum Night Bazaar – a haven for food and shopping.

Sat–Sun 8.30am–noon; admission charge; tel: 02-252 0161-4). Located south of Chulalongkorn University, it was founded in 1923 as the Pasteur Institute. Now operated by the Thai Red Cross, the institute's principal work lies in the research and treatment of snakebites and the extraction of antivenins. Venom-milking sessions (Mon–Fri 11am and 2.30pm, Sat–Sun 11am; slide show 30 mins before) are the best times to visit, when various snakes are pulled from the pit and generally goaded for a squealing audience.

Of Thailand's six species of venomous snake, the King Cobra is the largest and most common. A single yield of venom from the King Cobra is deadly enough to send some 50,000 mice to an early grave; fortunately the King Cobra's basic diet is other snakes. Willing spectators can drape a snake around their necks for a one-of-a-kind photo memento.

Lumphini Park

Green spots are few and far between in Bangkok, but in the heart of downtown at the intersection of Thanon Rama IV and Thanon Ratchadamri is **Lumphini Park ❼**, Bangkok's premier outdoor retreat (daily 4.30am–9pm; free). Named after Buddha's birthplace in Nepal, the park was given to the public in 1925 by King Vajiravudh (Rama VI), whose memorial statue stands in front of the main gates.

Embellished with lakes (with pedal boats for hire) and a Chinese-style clock tower, sunrise or sunset sees elderly Chinese practising *t'ai chi*, sweaty joggers, mass aerobic sessions, bodybuilders lifting weights at the open-air gym, and youngsters playing the team sport of *takraw* using a rattan ball.

Suan Lum Night Bazaar

Across from Lumphini's Thanon Withayu (Wireless Road) gates, the **Suan Lum Night Bazaar ❽** (daily 3pm–midnight) is a more sanitised and cooler alternative to Chatuchak Weekend Market *(see page 158)*. Geared for tourists, the open-air bazaar offers souvenirs, clothing, handicrafts, antiques, jewellery and home decor. There is also a large beer

garden with live music and plenty of local and international food options, traditional massage, and a German pub. Also found at Suan Lum Night Bazaar is the Thai equivalent of a Punch and Judy show at the **Joe Louis Theatre** (nightly at 7.30pm; admission charge; tel: 0-2252 9683; www.joelouis-theater.com). Sakorn Yangkeawsot, who goes by the moniker Joe Louis, is responsible for reviving the fading art of *hun lakhon lek*, a unique form of traditional Thai puppetry *(see pages 46 and 218)*.

Pratunam area

Head north cross over Khlong Saen Saep canal and Thanon Petchaburi to the narrow lanes of **Pratunam Market ❾** (daily 9am–midnight). This bustling warren of stalls is more a lure for residents than tourists, but with cheap piles of clothing, fabrics and shoes, it's of interest to any bargain hunter.

The area is shadowed by Thailand's tallest building, **Baiyoke II Tower**, whose 84th floor observation deck (daily 10am–10pm; admission charge) offers eye-popping views of the city and beyond.

If hungering for a byte, cross Thanon Petchaburi from Pratunam to Bangkok's biggest mall devoted to IT, **Panthip Plaza**. Frequented by more than just tech-heads, the competitively priced stores stretch over six floors, selling all manner of electronic devices, hard and software, entertainment discs (both genuine and counterfeit).

Suan Pakkad Palace

Most tourists make a beeline for Jim Thompson's House, missing out on an equally delightful abode, the **Suan Pakkad Palace ❿** (daily 9am–4pm; admission charge includes a guided tour; tel: 0-2245 4934; www.suan pakkad.com). Located a short walk along Thanon Sri Ayutthaya from Phaya Thai Skytrain station, the

quirkily named Suan Pakkad or "Cabbage Patch", refers to its former use as farmland before the palace was constructed in 1952. The former residence of the late Prince and Princess Chumbhot, who were prolific art collectors and gardeners, Suan Pakkad comprises five teak houses sitting amid a lush garden and lotus pond.

Converted into a museum, the wooden houses display an eclectic collection of antiques and artefacts, including Buddha images, Khmer statues, paintings, porcelain, musical instruments and ancient pottery from Ban Chiang. At the rear of the garden stands a mid 17th-century **Lacquer Pavilion**, which Prince Chumbhot discovered in a temple near Ayutthaya and carefully restored as a birthday present for his wife. Depicting scenes from the life of the Buddha, the *Ramakien* and the vernacular life of the period, the pavilion's black and gold leaf panels are considered masterpieces.

On the same grounds is the **Khon Museum**, a small but interesting expose on the classic Thai dramatic art form of *khon*. ❑

Map on page 130

The facade of the Lacquer Pavilion at Suan Pakkad Palace.

BELOW: interior of Suan Pakkad's Lacquer Pavilion.

RESTAURANTS

Brazilian

Fogo Vivo

Gnd Fl, Unit G02-G03 President Tower Arcade, 973 Th Ploenchit. Tel: 0-2656 0384. Open: daily L and D. $$
www.fogovivo.com

A Brazilian all-you-can-eat churrascaria restaurant in which waiters roam the room with skewers of grilled meats and seafood. Options include Argentinean grass-fed beef, pork, chicken, Australian lamb, and prawns. A decent salad bar, Brazilian cheese bread and gaucho rice offer reprieve from the protein overload.

French

Auberge DAB

Fl 1, Mercury Bldg, 540 Th Ploenchit. Tel: 0-2658 6222/3. Open: daily L and D. $$$

Very formal silver service ambience of red leather and clubby wood panelling attracts the upper echelons of Thai society for the speciality Plateau de L'Auberge, a seafood tier of oysters, lobster, crab, prawns, langoustine and sea snails. A good main course choice is rack of lamb, and creme brulee for dessert.

Cáfe Le Notre

Gnd Fl Natural Ville Executive Residences, 61 Soi Lang Suan. Tel: 0-2250 7050/1. Open: daily 6am–10.30pm. $–$$

Inheriting the Parisian panache of its main operation, this stylish café has a mini menu of starters, salads and mains to supplement its wonderful cakes and pastries. Great quality (despite being in a serviced apartment block) at the price.

Indonesian

Bali Restaurant

15/3 Soi Ruam Rudi. Tel: 0-2250 0711. Open: Mon–Sat 11am–11pm. $

One of the few Indonesian restaurants in Bangkok, Bali corners the market in satay with peanut sauce, chicken rendang (with coconut milk and spices) and ikan pepes (marinated fish in banana leaf). Vegetarian options include tapioca leaf curry or gule daun singkong. Restrained interior of batiks, paintings, puppets and masks.

International

Madison

Four Seasons Hotel, 155 Th Ratchadamri. Tel: 0-2251 6127. Open: daily L and D. $$$

Fine dining on the likes of roasted foie gras, shimenji mushrooms, sea bream and Belon oysters from Europe as well as US prime-grade aged beef and Tasmanian lamb – reared on coastal meadows. If you can't decide on dessert, go for the warm guanaja tart, pomelo soup and fresh marinated mango – all on the same plate. Tony Chi-designed interior features an open-style kitchen. Sunday there is a fabulous brunch blow-out.

Italian

Biscotti

Four Seasons Hotel, 155 Th Ratchadamri. Tel: 0-2255 5443. Open: daily L and D. $$$

A power dining mecca of terracotta, marble and wood in another stylish Tony Chi-designed outlet. The large and busy open kitchen sets the tone for its excellent Italian cuisine, while the open space is ideal for being seen. Packed with business people for lunch and a who's who list of Thai society for dinner.

Calderazzo

59 Soi Lang Suan. Tel: 0-2252 8108/9. Open: daily L and D. $$–$$$

Clever lighting and lots of wood, stone, metal and glass create a warm and exceptionally stylish atmosphere for good homey southern Italian food such as grilled vegetables in hazelnut pesto, hand-rolled rag pasta with goat cheese sauce, lamb loin in red wine, and heavenly profiteroles filled with ice cream and drenched in warm chocolate sauce.

Gianni's

51/5 Soi Tonson. Tel: 0-2252 1619. Open: daily L and D. $$–$$$

Larger than life Gianni Favro was perhaps Bangkok's first non-Thai celebrity chef. His original Italian restaurant in Soi Tonson serves all the classics – vitello tonata, osso bucco, tiramisu – and has proven so enduringly popular that Gianni now has other branches around the city.

Holy Pizza

442 Siam Sq Soi 7. Tel: 0-2654 6373. Open: 11am–10pm. $

Well, not quite Italian but a Thai take on Italian pizza. Proclaiming itself as "the quickest way to heaven", this Thai-owned parlour serves pizzas like Holy Hot Chic (very hot chicken with onion and basil leaves) and Spicy Esarn (Northeastern sausage, shredded ginger, chilli and garlic) along with more regular pastas and pseudo-Italian fare.

Japanese

Shin Daikoku

Fl 2, Intercontinental Hotel, Th Ploenchit. Tel: 0-2656 0096/7. Open: daily L and D. $$–$$$

Dine on high-quality sushi and sashimi, matsuzaka beef or superb ishikarinabe salmon and enoki mushrooms in miso soup. Modern bamboo cabinets divide the teppanyaki room from the restaurant proper.

Spanish

Rioja

1025 Th Ploenchit.
Tel: 0-2251 5761-2. Open:
Mon–Fri L and D, Sat–Sun
11am–11pm. $$
Bangkok's only authentic Spanish restaurant offers fine Iberico ham from the famous black pig, shrimp carpaccio on sour cream with salmon roe, Rioja-style oxtail stew, and an exceptional seafood *paella*, which is large enough to feed two. Spanish-style desserts are mainly custard-based. Of the two dining rooms, the cellar-like *bodega*, with its stone floor, dark woods and timber beams, is more appealing.

Thai

Coca

16/3-8 Th Henri Dunant, cnr Siam Square Soi 7.
Tel: 0-2251 6337. Open:
daily 11am–11pm. $
www.coca.com
One of a chain of restaurants offering communal dining with a pot of hot broth in the centre of the table for cooking morsels of fish, meat and vegetables, fondue-style. Dunk the food into a small bowl of sweet and spicy chilli sauce before popping it into your mouth. Delicious.

Curries & More

3/3 Soi Ruam Rudee.
Tel: 0-2253 5405-7. Open:
daily 11am–11.30pm. $$

A branch of the famous **Baan Khanitha** (at 49 Soi Ruam Rudee 2 and 31/1 Sukhumvit Soi 23) serving tasty Thai food with the spices toned down to suit international palates. Charming townhouse setting with sculptures, paintings and ceramics. The *kaeng leuang* (yellow curry) is excellent. It also has some international dishes (pasta, pies, crepes and excellent apple crumble).

I Din Klin Krok

232/1 Siam Sq Soi 2.
Tel: 0-2252 0331. Open:
11am–9pm. $
Popular student hangout selling design-your-own *somtam* (green papaya salad). Choose from a base of shredded green papaya, carrot, coconut or mango and add extras like pickled crab or preserved egg. Also has Isaan (northeastern Thai) staples, including a good fried spicy morning glory with lemon.

Inter

432/1-2 Siam Sq Soi 9.
Tel: 0-22551 4689. Open:
daily 10am–10pm. $
Popular lunch and snack-time hangout for students and teachers from nearby Chulalongkorn University. Spicy steamed shrimp with lemon featured on the menu with more usual fare such as crispy fried catfish salad and grilled mussels hot plate. Simple decor, with two large windows to watch the world go by.

Khanom Chine Bangkok

Gnd Fl, Mah Boon Krong, 444 Th Phyathai.
Tel: 0-2620 9403. Open:
daily 10.30am–10pm. $
This place specialises in the delicious street food noodle dish called *khanom chine* amid brushed concrete walls, clever spotlighting and a wall of windows. Don't miss the traditional northern-style curry (or choose from several other versions) and the good *tom yum kai jeaw* (*tom yum* with omelette).

Lan Som Tam Nua

392/2 Siam Sq Soi 5.
Tel: 0-2251 4880. Open:
daily 11.15am–9pm. $
Modern, funky, bustling Isaan (northeastern Thailand) restaurant so popular there are cushions outside for people waiting to be seated. The action whirls around an open kitchen where staff make a great fiery mixed salad (*somtam mua*) with noodles and northeastern sausage, and other excellent Isaan dishes. Thai-only menu, so some finger pointing or gesticulating is neccessary.

Le Lys

75/2 Langsuan Soi 3.
Tel: 0-2652 2401. Open:
daily noon–10.30pm. $
Charming wooden house with large windows and a homey interior of silk fabrics, Thai and Chinese pottery. The Thai-French owners favour tamarind-flavoured soups (*tom som* with stuffed squid) and delicious baby clams in curry sauce. Terrace

and garden seating alongside games of pétanque.

Sara-Jane's

Gnd fl Sindhorn Bldg 130-132 Th Withayu. Tel: 0-2650 9992-3. Open: daily noon–10pm. $
American Sara-Jane, a long-time Bangkok resident, pulls off a very authentic Isaan menu of the ferociously spicy salads and grilled beef staples of northeast Thailand. Locals who like raucous dining pack this office block outlet. Has a few less successful Italian dishes.

Thai Food Stalls

Mah Boon Krong Food Centre

Top Fl, Mah Boon Krong, 444 Th Phyathai. Tel: 0-2217 9491. Open: daily 10am–9pm. $
Huge Thai food court in a centrally located shopping mall. Large variety of tasty local dishes available (noodles, rice, salads, desserts, duck, chicken, vegetarian). Buy vouchers as you go in, choose from as many stalls as you like and sit down anywhere. Redeem unused vouchers for cash on your way out. If streetside food puts you off, this is a good alternative.

PRICE CATEGORIES

Price per person for a three-course meal without drinks:
$ = under US$10
$$ = US$10–$25
$$$ = US$25–$50
$$$$ = over US$50

JIM THOMPSON'S THAI HOUSE

In a city increasingly dominated by Western architecture, this offers a glimpse of Thailand's rich cultural heritage

Jim Thompson began his collection shortly after World War II, when the value of Thai antiques was still unknown. His assemblage includes precious Buddha images, porcelain, traditional paintings, and finely carved furniture and panels collected from old homes and temples throughout Thailand. The traditional Thai house where his collection is contained is painted with the red-brown hue characteristic of Thailand. The house features a dramatic outward-sweeping roof covered with rare tiles designed and fired in Ayutthaya. Curving gracefully in a *ngo* (peak), the wide roof allows the airy rooms to remain open all year long, sheltered from the downpours of the rainy season. The entire structure, enveloped by lush tropical greenery, stands elevated a full storey above the ground as protection against flooding.

ABOVE: the only air-conditioned room in the original house and the lush gardens, the study is where Jim Thompson spe hours at work. Occupying centrestage in the study is a ing limestone Thai Buddha image from the 8th centur or early Dvaravati period.

TOP: decorated with 19th-century paintings of the *Jataka* tales, and luxury silk sheets and pillows, the bedroom reflects Thompson's impeccable taste.

LEFT: part of the museum's extensive collec exquisite sandstone Buddha images, some c date back to the early 7th century.

ABOVE: resembling more an exotic jungle than well-manicured grounds, the garden reflects its former owner's preference for untamed nature. The gardens are a fabulous contrast to the bustling city just outside the Thompson sanctuary.

THE KING OF THAI SILK

One Easter day in 1967 Jim Thompson went for a walk in the jungles of the Cameron Highlands in Malaysia and never came back. After years of speculation the mystery of his disappearance is still unsolved. Born in Delaware, USA, in 1906, Thompson worked as an architect before joining the army in 1939. He fought in Europe and Asia during World War II, and when the war ended, he served in Bangkok in the Office of Strategic Service (the forerunner of the CIA). Thompson later returned to Bangkok, where inspired by swatches of silk he had collected during his trips in Thailand, decided to track down traditional silk weavers. He found one lone community of Muslim weavers at the canal-side Ban Khrua (he eventually built his own house just opposite the canal). Utilising new techniques and dyes that raised the silk's quality to unrivalled standards, he set up the Thai Silk Company, later exporting his creations around the world. Thompson is one of the most celebrated *farang* (Westerner) in Thailand and his silks remain a treasured part of Thailand's culture.

ABOVE: the dining table, which is set with 17th-century blue-and-white Chinese porcelain, consists of two antique *mahjong* tables joined to form a single unit. Adorning the cupboards along the walls of the dining room are other valuable pieces of blue-and-white porcelain and fine paintings.

ABOVE: this exquisite gilded lacquer book chest is from Ayutthaya and dates back to the 17th century.

BANGRAK AND SILOM

The so-called *farang*, or foreigner, area of the 19th century, with historic places of worship, mercantile buildings and venerable hotels, is a bustling commercial area by day. At night, a very different sort of trade flourishes in the fleshpots of Patpong

Gravitating eastwards from some of the Chao Phraya River's premier riverfront real estate, Thanon Silom is the principal route that intersects the business district, ending at Thanon Rama IV with Lumphini Park beyond. Parallel to Silom are Sathorn, Surawong and Si Phraya roads, all of which make up the district of **Bangrak** – "the village of love". Despite the proliferation of girlie bars along Silom's notorious den of Patpong, it's the rattle of commerce rather than sweet seduction that resonates strongest.

During the mid 19th-century, major canal construction meant the city had to expand outwards from the royal district on Rattanakosin Island. Running parallel to the river, Thanon Charoen Krung (New Road), which cuts across China-own, was one of the city's earliest paved thoroughfares, which in turn sprouted fledgling communities, like the rich Bankolem quarter. Today, the old waterside neighbourhood has been usurped by upmarket riverbank development in the form of luxury hotels and the River City shopping centre. However, exploring the quiet side streets still reveal elements of its former historic splendour.

But it's not all starchy office blocks and unbridled sleaze that make up Bangrak. Between the River

City shopping centre and Shangri-La hotel is what is regarded as the old *farang* (foreigner) district. Easily navigable, the lanes in this pocket still hold a few buildings from its days as a 19th-century port settlement. It was once home to numerous foreign banks, commercial and diplomatic offices and colonial-style mansions, along with the capital's first hotels and inns. Today, the narrow winding alleys in this area still reveal the intimacy and community spirit of this traditional neighbourhood.

Map on page 143

LEFT AND BELOW: Thanon Silom by night and day.

The Sala Rim Naam restaurant at the Oriental Hotel puts on a nightly show of traditional Thai dance-drama accompanied by a Thai set dinner.

BELOW:
the elegant Authors' Lounge at the Oriental.
RIGHT:
Assumption Cathedral.

Holy Rosary Church

Located behind the River City shopping centre and just off an alley housing a bustling market is the **Holy Rosary Church ❶** or Wat Kalawa (daily 6am–9pm; free). Portuguese Catholics erected the original edifice in 1787 after they moved from the sacked capital of Ayutthaya. After a fire burnt down the wooden church, it was rebuilt again around 1890. The neo-Gothic sanctuary features some of Thailand's best examples of stained glass.

Continue south of the River City shopping centre, and just next door to the **Royal Orchid Sheraton** hotel is the city's oldest embassy, the 1820s **Portuguese Embassy**. It is best viewed from the riverside.

Oriental Hotel

Continue south to the legendary **Oriental ❷** hotel. Founded in the 1870s, the Oriental's reputation is well known; it has consistently been rated as one of the world's best. A riverside retreat for the influential and wealthy, the Oriental's grandeur has endured through the years. However, the exteriors of two newer and modern buildings, the Garden Wing (1958) and River Wing (1976) added to the original Author's Wing somewhat detract from its classic feel. To best imbibe its old world atmosphere, have afternoon tea in the elegant **Authors' Lounge** and muse over the literary greats that have passed through its doors, such Somerset Maugham, Noel Coward and Graham Greene. The **Riverside Terrace** is another charming spot to settle down with a drink. Some regard the Oriental as stuffy but there is no denying its charm.

Assumption Cathedral

Turn right outside the Oriental Hotel towards the river; a side road on the left leads to a small tree-lined square dominated by the **Assumption Cathedral ❸** (daily 6am–9pm; free). Built in 1910, the red-brick cathedral is surrounded by a Catholic mission. Its ornate interior is topped with a domed ceiling hovering over a large sacristy with gilded pillars. Looming behind it in stark contrast is the unmistakeable State Tower *(see page 144)* building.

Oriental Hotel area

Continue to the Tha Oriental ferry point; just to its left is the white-washed and Venetian-inspired **East Asiatic Company ➍**. Erected in 1901, it was once the most visible riverside structure in this area; today, it awaits redevelopment. To the left of the Oriental hotel are two early 20th-century buildings, the romantic **China House** restaurant (run by the Oriental hotel) and next door, the former **Commercial Company of Siam** (currently closed and undergoing major renovations). A side road to the left leads to the charming **OP Place**. Dating from 1905, this old-world building was one of the city's first department stores.

Continue past Haroon Mosque to the recently restored **French Embassy**, hidden behind high walls and an imposing gate. Then head towards the riverside where the crumbling but wonderfully atmospheric 19th-century **Old Customs House** stands. Currently used as a fire station, plans are afoot for its development into a boutique hotel or an arts centre.

Thanon Silom

Taking its name from irrigation windmills that used to occupy the area, Thanon Silom and its former canal transported life inland. Today, Silom's charm has all but dissipated amidst aggressive commercial progress, with shopping and nightlife the principal attractions. The Skytrain (BTS) and metro (MRTA) lines intersect at the top of Thanon Silom (with Thanon Rama IV), with the Skytrain continuing westwards, close to the Chao Phraya River at the Saphan Taksin Skytrain station.

Thanon Silom along with Thanon Sathorn are considered the city's main business arteries, but come dusk, the shift from day to night

Map on page 143

The imposing gates of the French Embassy. Take a peek from the outside as entry is forbidden.

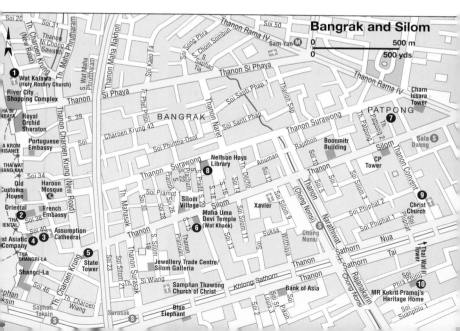

The towering entrance facade of the Maha Uma Devi Temple.

trade becomes apparent when the office workers depart and a bevy of attractive females and males (and those of indeterminate sex) begin to converge in the area.

Recently built and standing tall at the river-end junction of Thanon Silom and Thanon Charoen Krung, the faux-classical and ostentatious **State Tower ❺** is worth mentioning for its fashionable rooftop drink and dine venue called **The Dome**. With some of Bangkok's best panoramas, The Dome's **Sirocco** *(see page 148)* on the 63rd floor claims to be the world's highest outdoor eatery.

Heading up Thanon Silom, on the right at No. 919/1, is the soaring **Jewellery Trade Centre**, proof of how significant the precious stone market is in Thailand and in the region, while its connecting **Silom Galleria** houses art galleries and antiques shops over several levels.

Further up Thanon Silom, on the left, is the tourist-oriented **Silom Village**, brimming with shoppers and diners, with traditional music and dance performed in a couple of its establishments.

Maha Uma Devi Temple

About a quarter of the way up Thanon Silom on the right, on the corner of Soi Pan, is the vibrantly coloured Hindu **Maha Uma Devi Temple ❻** (daily 6am–8pm; free). Named after Shiva's consort, Uma Devi, the temple was established in the 1860s by the city's Tamil community, whose strong presence is still prevalent in the area. It is known to Thais as Wat Khaek, meaning "guests' temple" (*khaek* is also a less welcoming term used by locals for anyone from the Asian subcontinent).

On holy days, the temple throngs with a lively spectrum of worshippers, including many Indian, Thai and Chinese, who find devotional comfort in the images of Vishnu Uma Devi's son Ganesh, as well as the Buddha. The structure is prominent for its 6-metre (20-ft) high facade, which is adorned with an ornate diorama of religious statuary.

Patpong

Come nightfall, the upper end of Thanon Silom transforms into a pleasure haven to entertain customers of all persuasions. Stall vendors set up a **night market** along Thanon Silom from Soi 2–Soi 8, commandeering the narrowing pavements in either direction, including the fleshpot of **Patpong ❼** (Soi 1 and Soi 2). The market plies mainly tourist tat, including counterfeit watches, fake name-brand bags and clothes, CDs and DVDs, as well as some menacing-looking combat knives. Every few steps dodgy-looking men try to push VCDs and DVDs of porn flicks on unsuspecting pedestrians.

With its slew of trashy go-go bars and anything-goes strip clubs, Patpong's sleazy image is still deserved, although government clampdowns on nightlife over the years have almost reduced this slice of vice to little more than amusing eye candy. Developed on the site of

a former banana plantation by the late millionaire Khun Patpongpanit, the playground first found favour among affluent locals and foreign airline crews – before American GIs descended here in droves on R&R from Vietnam in the late 1960s and 70s. Despite incessant touts claiming a freakish assortment of sex shows, today's tamer experience is a blitz of neon, relentless techno beats and gyrating bikini-clad dancers on bar tops.

Adjacent **Patpong 2** is an alley of box-shaped beer bars that also accommodates the 24-hour supermarket Foodland. Watching leering drunks and working women cruising the shopping aisles for late night liaisons is a spectacle in itself.

A few lanes east from Patpong, pumping **Silom Soi 4** attracts throngs of beautiful and young (both straight and gay) revellers to its compact dance clubs and bars. Nearby **Silom Soi 2** is similar in appeal, though designated for gay partiers. And further on still, the hostess bars along **Soi Thaniya** cater for an exclusively Japanese clientele.

Neilson Hays Library

Many of Thanon Silom's even numbered lanes cut through to parallel **Thanon Surawong**, which has seen little of the district's commercial development. Of interest to bookworms, however, is the **Neilson Hays Library** ❽ at 195 Thanon Surawong, an early 20th-century cultural haven for the city's foreign residents (Tues–Sun 9.30–4pm; tel: 0-2233 1731; www.neilsonhayslibrary.com). Stacked with over 20,000 tomes, this nostalgic throwback, which takes its name from Jennie Neilson Hays (a founder of the Bangkok Ladies Library Association), manages to keep a foot in the present moment by exhibiting works by modern artists in the small domed **Rotunda Gallery**.

Soi Convent area

Opposite Silom Soi 4 is a street known as **Soi Convent**, a busy tree-shaded lane that starts with a barrage of street side food stalls and continues with several restaurants catering for various tastes – from Irish pub grub to fancy fusion. Just at the corner with Thanon Sathorn is the

Map on page 143

TIP

The market vendors around Patpong are more unscrupulous than elsewhere in the city, quoting ridiculously inflated prices that are some 50–75 percent higher than what they are actually prepared to accept. Bargain hard!

LEFT:
Patpong in the flesh.
BELOW: vendors at Patpong market.

Map
on page
143

TIP

If you would like to be a dab hand at Thai cookery, sign up for cookery lessons at the Blue Elephant restaurant. Priced at B2,996 per person, four dishes are taught during the half-day hands-on sessions (tel: 0-2673 9353; www.blueelephant.com /bangkok).

BELOW:
MR Kukrit Pramoj's Heritage Home.
RIGHT:
view of Thanon Sathorn, with the Metropolitan hotel in the foreground.

Anglican **Christ Church ❾** (daily 8am–5pm; free). Originally established as the English Chapel in the mid 19th-century, the present Gothic-style building was built in 1905.

Thanon Sathorn

Thanon Sathorn grew on either side of the central canal toiled by Chinese labourers towards the end of the 19th century, which in turn encouraged the growth of an affluent neighbourhood of colonial-style mansions for the city's local and foreign elite. Modern Sathorn evokes little of this historic charm, though the odd period piece still exists – like the stylish **Blue Elephant** Thai restaurant *(see page 149)*, which once housed the Thai-Chinese Chamber of Commerce.

Today, Thanon Sathorn is home to a number of obstrusive office towers, as well as several embassies. Several noteworthy buildings stand out, including the slim **Thai Wah II Tower** with its gaping arch, standing tall between two of the capital's hippest boutique hotels, the **Sukhothai** and **Metropolitan**.

Looking more like a creation of a child's fantasy than a bank headquarters, the **Bank of Asia**, at the corner of Thanon Sathorn and Soi Pikun, was designed by the country's foremost modern architect Dr Sumet Jumsai, and is affectionately dubbed the "robot building".

Kukrit Pramoj's Home

Halfway down Thanon Sathorn, tucked away on Soi Phra Phinij, is **MR Kukrit Pramoj's Heritage Home ❿** (Sat and Sun 10am–5pm; admission charge; tel: 0-2286 8185). Born of royal descent (signified by the title Mom Ratchawong – MR), the late Kukrit Pramoj had a brief stint as prime minister during the disruptive 1970s, but is better remembered as a prolific author and cultural preservationist. This splendid wooden home, now a museum, comprises five stilt buildings that are reminiscent of the traditional architecture of the Central Plains. The ornate garden adds to a sense of serenity, and the home is livened by antique pottery, memorabilia and photos of the famous statesman. ❑

RESTAURANTS

Chinese

China House

Oriental Hotel, 48 Oriental Ave. Tel: 0-2236 0400. Open: daily L and D. $$$
Elegant, pristine white Sino-Portuguese colonial townhouse set apart from the hotel – and small enough to believe you're dining at home. Super *dim sum* lunch and dinner specials like "Monk Jumped Over the Wall", supposedly named after Chinese monks, who – seduced by the beautiful aroma – jumped over a temple wall to try this dish.

Mei Jiang

Peninsula Hotel, 333 Th Charoen Nakhorn. Tel: 0-2861 2888. Open: daily L and D. $$$
Superb Cantonese restaurant on the river. An elegant interior of glass chandeliers, silk upholstered teak furniture and beautiful wall hangings sets the scene for delicious hot and sour soup, duck smoked with tea, and grouper with soy sauce. Good wine list and a selection of teas.

French

Bistingo

1/1 Saladaeng Soi 1. Tel: 0-234 2225. Open: Mon–Fri L and D, Sat D. $$–$$$
Light French-Mediterranean food served in a delightful old house with a few terrace tables

overlooking the floodlit, palm-strewn garden. The menu offers excellent traditional dishes such as fish soup as well as more contemporary preparations like red snapper with crab quenelle seasoned with lime and olive oil. North African influences define the taste in some dishes.

Le Bouchon

37/17 Patpong Soi 2. Tel: 0-2234 9109. Open: Mon–Sat L and D, Sun D. $$–$$$
This atmospheric seven-table bistro gains a certain frisson from its location in Patpong – very French and slightly naughty, like a Marseille dockyard diner. Very popular with local French expats for its simple home cooking and friendly banter at the small bar where diners wait for seats while sipping aperitifs.

La Boulange

2-2/1 Th Convent. Tel: 0-2631 0355. Open: daily 7am–8pm.
Enticing French bakery and patisserie with takeaway outlets in supermarkets around the city. This branch serves freshly baked croissants and brewed coffee to the breakfast crowd, all-day snacks such as *croque monsieur*, pâtés, omelettes and salads, and daily specials like duck confit and quiches.

D'Sens

Dusit Thani Hotel, 946 Th Rama IV. Tel: 0-2236 9999. Open: Mon–Sat L and D. $$$$
This branch of the three Michelin-starred Le Jardin des Sens, in Montpellier, France, is full of delicate and delicious surprises. Chefs Jacques and Laurent Pourcel work wonders in their kitchen with dishes like cep (porcini) mushrooms and duck liver ravioli in a frothy truffle sabayon. Desserts are equally outstanding. The retro decor includes Paul Smith's striped carpets and a curtain of glass beads. An oversized aquarium and amazing city views will grab your attention.

Le Normandie

Oriental Hotel, 48 Oriental Ave. Tel: 0-2236 0400. Open: Mon–Sat L and D, Sun D. $$$$
Formal French dining with jacket and tie required for the men. Concoctions like goose liver dome with Perigord truffles, and sole fillets with Oscietra caviar cream sauce verge on brilliance. In the stately, marmalade-coloured interior, crystal chandeliers hang from a quilted silk ceiling while the floor to ceiling windows overlook the Chao Phraya River. Save this experience for a special night out.

Indian

Indian Hut

311-2-5 Th Surawong. Tel: 0-2237 8812. Open: daily 11am–11pm. $$
Rich north Indian food served on two floors. The *murg malai tikka* (chicken in fresh cream and cheese) and the spicy *murg lazeez* (chicken in a tomato and onion sauce) are both mouthwatering selections. Diners can easily spot the restaurant by its sign, which mimics the Pizza Hut logo.

Tamil Nadu

Silom Soi 11. Tel: 0-2235 6336. Open: daily 11.30am–9pm. $
This simple south Indian café serves the workers in this area close to Bangkok's most ornate Indian temple. The house speciality is *masala dosa*, a pancake made of rice flour and *urad dal*, stuffed with potato and onion curry and served with coconut chutney. You can also order meat and vegetable curries to eat with the plain *dosa*.

PRICE CATEGORIES

Price per person for a three-course meal without drinks:
$ = under US$10
$$ = US$10–$25
$$$ = US$25–$50
$$$$ = over US$50

International/Fusion

Cy'an
Metropolitan Hotel, 27 Th Sathorn Tai. Tel: 0-2625 3333. Open: daily B, L and D. $$$–$$$$
Serves inspired Mediterranean-Asian seafood amid the cutting-edge minimalism of this hip new hotel. Spanish and Moroccan flourishes bring sweet and spicy flavours to seared tiger prawns, and tortellini with pine nuts, raisins and parmesan. Or try Wagyu beef with anchovy and caper butter and tender slow-grilled vegetables. An amazing 22 wines are available by the glass.

Eat Me
Fl 1, 1/6 Piphat Soi 2, off Th Convent. Tel: 0-2238 0931. Open: daily D. $$$
Very popular restaurant with art exhibitions often featuring edgy young artists promoted by the nearby H Gallery. The food is modern Australian, featuring dishes such as charred scallops with mango, herb salad, pickled onion and citrus dressing. Low lighting and a fragmented layout lend intimacy. On cool nights ask for a table on the terrace. Excellent wine list of mainly Australian varietals.

Jester's
Peninsula Hotel, 333 Th Charoen Nakhorn, Khlong San. Tel: 0-2861 2888. Open: daily D. $$$
Exciting East-West fusion of ingredients like crispy duck pancakes with mustard vinaigrette, and grilled pork loin on chilli crab with fermented black bean broth. Creative desserts end the meal. Beautiful river view through a wall of glass, and ultra modern detailing in the decor goes perfectly with the cutting-edge *Buddha Bar* soundtracks.

Sirocco
Fl 63 State Tower Bangkok, 1055 Th Silom. Tel: 0-2624-9555. Open: daily D. $$$
www.thedomebkk.com
Spectacular 200-metre (656-ft) high rooftop restaurant with magnificent views over the river. Greco-Roman architecture and a jazz band add to the sense of occasion. The Italian and Mediterranean food is inconsistent, but who cares? This is a must-visit, if only for the views. In the same complex, there's good seafood in the classy **Distil Bar**, and an expensive Italian eatery called **Mezzaluna**.

V9
Fl 37 Sofitel Silom Bangkok, 188 Th Silom. Tel: 0-2238 1991. Open: daily D. $$
The no mark-up policy at this wine bar cum restaurant means you can get decent stuff from B500 a bottle, which is very cheap for Bangkok. Add 37th-floor views and you can have a very affordable romantic dinner. The food is served in "tasting trees" with six dishes in each, such as roast duck salad with Vietnamese dressing, or lobster with three pepper sauces.

Italian

La Scala
Sukhothai Hotel, 13/3 Th Sathorn Tai. Tel: 0-2287 0222. Open: daily L and D. $$$
Asian modernist interior of teak, bronze, terra cotta and glass brickwork with a central open kitchen where diners sit around to watch culinary theatre. If you don't fancy dishes like roasted fillet of turbot with fennel, black olives and dill, order the thin-crust pizzas fresh from the wood-fired oven.

Scoozi
174/3-4 Th Surawong. Tel 0-2267-0344. Open: L and D. $$–$$$
Set on two floors of a beautiful 120-year-old house with private rooms and a bar area. Features southern Italian cuisine and an accent on imported seafood: snow crabs, lobster, oysters and mussels. Its stand-alone pizza bar in front of the house serves delicious thin-crust pizzas with innovative toppings.

Zanotti
Gnd fl, Saladaeng Colonnade, 21/2 Soi Saladaeng. Tel: 0-2636 0002. Open: daily L and D. $$$
www.zanotti-ristorante.com
Chef-owner Gianmaria Zanotti has created a restaurant that people visit for the buzz as much as for the food. The homey Italian fare from the Piedmont and Tuscany regions includes over 20 pasta dishes and quality seafood and steaks charcoal-grilled over orange wood from Chiangmai. Good selection of wines by the glass. Vivid Rincicotti paintings on the walls liven up the ambience.

Japanese

Aoi
132/10-11 Silom Soi 6. Tel: 0-2235 2321/2. Open: daily L and D. $$
Black stone walkways invoke a cool calm in this unfussy restaurant serving well prepared Japanese food. Downstairs is a sushi bar, with two floors of private and semi-private rooms available for a surcharge. As usual, set meals are much cheaper than the à la carte options.

Korean

Nam Kang
5/3-4 Silom Soi 3. Tel: 0-2233 1480. Open: daily 11am–10pm. $$
A favourite with Korean expatriates, Nam Kang serves many *yangban* dishes usually associated with upper class dining. The speciality is the herbal cure-all *samgyetang* (whole chicken stuffed with rice and ginseng and served in soup). Also try *gucholpan* (small pancakes of shredded vegetables and meat with soy sauce and sesame oil).

Thai

Anna's Café
114 Soi Saladaeng, Th Silom. Tel: 0-2632 0619/20. Open: daily 11am–10pm. $

Incredibly popular for both lunch and dinner, this large, open restaurant combines good modern Thai and international food at ridiculously cheap prices for these chic surroundings. Its small menu has a tasty version of the northern Thai classic *khao soy*, (a Chinese-influenced soupy curry over soft noodles and topped with crispy noodles) and creative spaghetti options that blend cream sauces with Asian spices. Try the decadent toffee banoffee for dessert. Best to make reservations.

The Blue Elephant
233 Th Sathorn Tai.
Tel: 0-2673 9353. Open: daily L and D. $$–$$$
www.blueelephant.com/bangkok
One of a few very upmarket Thai restaurants located outside hotels, this is part of a Belgian-owned international chain. The menu mixes Thai standards with a few fusion dishes like foie gras in tamarind sauce. The food is excellent, but the flavours are slightly toned down to suit Western palates. Housed in a beautiful century-old restored building that was the former Thai-Chinese Chamber of Commerce.

Café de Laos
16 Silom Soi 19. Tel: 0-2635 2338/9. Open: daily L and D. $–$$
Most northeastern Isaan food is served at rough and ready street stalls or

shophouses. This place is unusual as it occupies a handsome 100-year-old wooden house. Serves all the famous Isaan dishes like green papaya salad (*somtam*) and *laab* (spicy minced meat salad with ground roasted rice). Photos of old Laos on the walls add a nice touch.

Harmonique
22 Charoen Krung Soi 34. Tel: 0-2237 8175. Open: Mon–Sat 10am–10pm. $–$$
Charming restaurant occupying several old Chinese shophouses with leafy courtyards and filled with antiques. Because there's usually a large contingent of Western diners, the spices used in the Thai cooking are too subdued for many locals. Still, the food is generally good, and it's a relaxing place to hang out.

Jim Thompson's Saladaeng Café
120/1 Saladaeng Soi 1. Tel: 0-2266 9167. Open: daily 11am–10pm. $
www.jimthompson.com
Drink mulberry tea straight from the farms of the famous Thai silk merchants in this predictably elegant little restaurant. The small menu has Thai salads and curries, plus pastas, sandwiches and burgers. Garden seating is arranged around a small lotus pond. There's another branch beside the Jim Thompson House in Thanon Rama I.

Kalpapruek
27 Th Pramuan. Tel: 0-2236 4335. Open: Mon–Sat 8am–6pm, Sun 8am–3pm. $
The original restaurant of a rapidly expanding chain, this is one of the city's few surviving Royal Thai kitchens. It features some of the Western influences first brought to Thai cooking through palace connections. On the street is a small popular café-restaurant, and inside, a covered garden area and bakery.

Krua Aroy Aroy
Th Pan, Silom. Tel: 0-2635 2365. Open: daily 10am–6pm. $
Opposite Silom's Maha Uma Devi Temple, with a sign reading "Delicious, Delicious, Delicious", this simple and unpretentious wooden-stool café features regional Thai dishes seldom found on the same menu. Curries include *nam ngeow* (pork broth with chicken's blood) and *nam ya ka ti* (minced fish in coconut milk). Noodle specials come deep-fried (*mee krob*) or cold (*khanom jeen*).

Mali
43 Pitak Court, Th Sathorn Tai, Soi 1. Tel: 0-2286 7311-7 (ext 171). Open: daily 8.30am–11pm. $
Diners crowd this tiny, simple Thai-Western restaurant for the consistently good country-style Thai cooking. The hot-plate dishes, *laab* salads and red curry with vegetable and coconut are all excellent.

New York cheesecake and apple pie feature as desserts, with Sarah Vaughan and Ella on the sound system. Very friendly, and popular with diplomatic staff from nearby embassies.

Noodi
Th Silom. Tel: 0-2632 7989. Open: daily 11–4am. $
One of a new generation of cafés that sell cheap Asian streetfood in funky fast-food surrounds: in this case, a wallpaper montage of black and white photos and glass jar displays of the noodle varieties that feature on the pan-Asian menu. Great for munchies after the bars shut. One of several outlets in the city.

Silom Village
286 Th Silom. Tel: 0-2234 4448. Open: daily 11am–11.45pm. $$
www.silomvillage.co.th
The food is better than you might expect at this touristy theatre restaurant set in wooden houses and a courtyard. The cultural show of music, dancing and martial arts accounts for the inflated prices. Nearby stalls sell souvenirs and local produce. Indoor and outdoor shows nightly from 8pm.

SUKHUMVIT

This area best defines cosmopolitan Bangkok. Pockets of Arabs and Indians dominate the business and this is where the city's growing expat community nests in luxury condos and houses. Leafy parks, shopping and nightlife spots give Sukhumvit added buzz

Thanon Sukhumvit, a bustling, traffic-clogged artery, pushes the urban sprawl eastwards, continuing all the way to the Cambodian border. Once a dirt track surrounded by marshland, Thanon Sukhumvit was built in the 1930s and became Thailand's first proper road, transporting vehicles beyond the capital. Today it's the efficient Skytrain that provides the fastest means of transport between the plethora of upmarket shops, restaurants and entertainment venues that line Thanon Sukhumvit.

Although thin on key tourist attractions, Thanon Sukhumvit is where most of the city's growing expatriate community nests. Plush condo towers line the lanes that splay either side of the main street, home to ever increasing numbers of European, American and Asian expatriates. As the local economy bounces back from the 1997 Asian meltdown, extravagant boutique-style apartment buildings are taking root at a staggering rate.

Sukhumvit is also one of the capital's most cosmopolitan areas; communities of Africans and Arabs congregate in the hookah cafés around Soi 3, and there is a sizeable contingent of Indian-Thai residents who have prospered from many of the businesses in the vicinity.

Sukhumvit's side roads

Starting at the trail of bars collectively nicknamed as "Soi Zero" that huddle under the expressway, Sukhumvit's early blocks burst with a profusion of tailors, pool halls, beer bars and hotels. Proffering typical tourist souvenirs, fake goods and general tat, the night market crowds the pavements from Soi 5–11, replaced later at night by a slew of makeshift food and drink stalls. Thronging with after-hours imbibers, the plastic stools and tables are a response to the government's

Map on page 152

LEFT:
outdoor sculpture at Benjakitti Park.
BELOW:
Nana Entertainment Plaza is a hub for go-go bars.

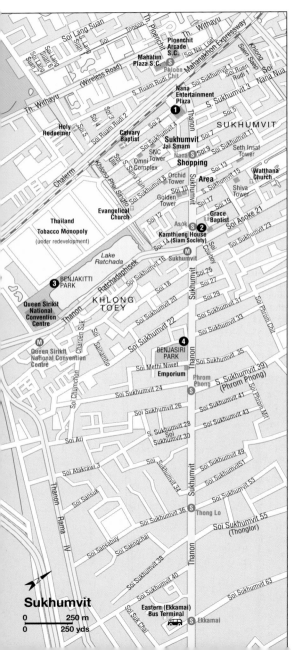

Sukhumvit

0   250 m
0   250 yds

recent curbs on the opening hours of licensed entertainment venues.

The area has a lascivious veneer, anchored by the three-storey clutch of raucous go-go bars at the **Nana Entertainment Plaza ❶** on Soi 4. Working girls soliciting customers can be found along street corners from Soi 5 to Soi 19. Further along the road across the Soi 21 (Soi Asoke) intersection is Sukhumvit's other notorious neon strip devoted to pole dancing, **Soi Cowboy**.

However Sukhumvit's overall appearance is far from sleazy, with many of the city's best nightspots dotted within the winding side streets. Leading the charge is **Soi 11**, where both **Q Bar** and the hip **Bed Supperclub** sit nearby one another.

Kamthieng House

One of Sukhumvit's oldest buildings is the headquarters of the **Siam Society** at Sukhumvit Soi 21 (Soi Asoke), founded in 1904 to promote the study and preservation of Thai culture (Tues–Sat 9am–5pm; tel: 0-2661 6470-77; www.siam-society org). There's an excellent library full of rare books on Thai history, old manuscripts and maps. For visitors with more than just passing curiosity, look out for the society's regular lectures on regional history and culture. Non-members may attend by paying a nominal fee.

On the same grounds is the **Kamthieng House ❷**, a small pocket of northern Lanna culture transported to Bangkok (same opening hours as Siam Society but admission charge applies). The 150-year-old wooden home once stood on the banks of Chiang Mai's Mae Ping River before being carefully reassembled here and opened as an ethnological museum. Presenting audio-visual displays on northern folk culture and daily life, the home is reputedly still inhabited by the ghosts of three former residents.

Sukhumvit's parks

South of the Sukhumvit Soi 21 (Soi Asoke) intersection is the **Queen Sirikit National Convention Centre**, which hosts mainly large-scale business, cultural and entertainment events. The centre looks out at the city's newest green space, **Benjakitti Park ❸** (daily 5am–8pm; free), an activity-orientated park overlooking the artificial **Lake Ratchada**. Opened at the end of 2004 as the first stage in the redevelopment of the adjacent Tobacco Monopoly grounds, this "Water Zone" will be followed in the future by a large "Forest Zone". Embellished with large fountains and cascading water displays, it is busiest in the early morning and evening when joggers and cyclists circle the lake on two designated paths.

Further east along Sukhumvit near Soi 24 is the area's other green lung, **Benjasiri Park ❹** (daily 5am–8pm; free). Opened in celebration of the present queen's 60th birthday, the small metropolitan garden is livened by a large pond, fountains and noteworthy sculptures by some of the country's most respected artists. For the physically inclined there are basketball courts, a skate park and a swimming pool with Thai pavilions to relax under.

Emporium area

On the corner of Soi 24, where the Phrom Phong Skytrain station is found, is Sukhumvit's premier shopping magnet, **Emporium**. This is a great place to watch Bangkok's affluent parade in their finest togs and splash out at its many desiger stores. There is also a department store of the same name, numerous eateries including an international food hall and local-style food court, and a cineplex. The side lanes around Emporium are cluttered with upmarket furniture and decor shops, bakeries, coffee bars, galleries and restaurants.

Further east, just off Thong Lo Skytrain station is **Soi 55** (Soi Thonglor), lined with garish wedding studios, as well as boutique shopping arcades like the uber-stylish **H1** and **Playground**. It also signals a recent trend to build well-heeled shopping enclaves in more residential neighbourhoods. ❑

Map on page 152

TIP

Sukhumvit's odd and even streets (soi) are out of synch. For instance Soi 24 beside Emporium mall is opposite Soi 39 on the other side of the street.

LEFT: the plush interior of Emporium shopping mall.
BELOW: Kamthieng House, formerly a home, now an ethnological museum.

RESTAURANTS

American

Bourbon Street

29/4-6 Washington Square, Sukhumvit Soi 22. Tel: 0-2259 0328-9. Open: daily 6am–midnight. $$
www.bourbonstbkk.com
Bar and restaurant with decent Cajun-Creole food from around New Orleans. Main courses of either jambalaya, barbecued pork ribs, blackened chicken and crayfish pie made with crayfish fresh from the owner's farm in Kanchanaburi, are all recommended, followed by traditional pecan pie for dessert. Hearty American breakfasts are also available with pancakes and home-made sausages.

New York Steakhouse

JW Marriott Hotel, 4 Sukhumvit Soi 2. Tel: 0-2656 7700. Open: daily D. $$$$
Top-notch restaurant with a relaxed atmosphere despite the formal trappings of club-like dark woods and high-backed leather chairs. Start with the yummy Manhattan clam chowder before sinking your teeth into the grain-fed Angus beef, sliced at the table from a silver trolley. The beef here is imported chilled, not frozen – which accounts for the high prices. Long martini list and refined wines to accompany your meal. Reservations are essential.

Ethiopian

Abyssinya Café

16/11 Sukhumvit Soi 3. Tel: 0-2655 3436. Open: daily noon–midnight. $
Ethiopian café food served on huge rounds of the country's unique, spongy *teff* bread, which has a sour flavour ideal for spicy dishes like *yedoro kei watt* (red chicken stew). Use the bread to help pick up the food with your hands. A few vegetarian dishes round out the menu.

French

Le Banyan

59 Sukhumvit Soi 8. Tel: 0-2253 5556. Open: Mon–Sat 6–10pm. $$$
Great little French restaurant with a formal but appealingly eccentric air. Maitre d' Bruno Bischoff is the perfect foil to diminutive Michel Binaux, who prepares many dishes tableside often looking very amused. Try the speciality of pressed duck or pan-fried foie gras with apple and fresh morel mushrooms.

Philippe Restaurant

20/15-17 Sukhumvit Soi 39. Tel: 0-2259 4577-8. Open: Mon–Sat L and D. $$
Small restaurant with very good classic French fare. The grand staircase sweeping down from the mezzanine and Gauloise-invoking nicotine-tinged colour scheme make a comfortable setting for delicious roast lamb loin with duck liver sauce or trout with lemon butter and almond. Good selection of reasonably priced wines.

German

Bei Otto

1 Sukhumvit Soi 20. Tel: 0-2262 0892. Open: daily 11am–midnight. $$
Three-in-one venue of bar, restaurant and bakery run by long time resident Otto Duffner. Must-tries are the home-made Turinger and Nuremburger sausages, home-baked breads and apple strudel. The cooked meat platter, which will satisfy two hearty appetites, is ideal ballast for German beer.

Greek

Athena

594 Soi Ekamai. Tel: 0-2392 7644. Open: daily 10am–11pm. $$
www.acropolitan.com
Enjoy the Mouskouri and Theodorakis soundtracks in Bangkok's only authentic Greek taverna. Good home-style dishes include *souflaki*, eggplant moussaka and the famous Greek salad called *horiatiki*, with tomatoes, olives and feta cheese. Alternatively, down a few shots of ouzo for a Friday or Saturday night out of mezze snacks and plate smashing.

Indian

Akbar

1/4 Sukhumvit Soi 3. Tel: 0-2253 3479. Open: daily 10.30am–1am. $
One of the oldest Indian restaurants in Bangkok, it serves North Indian fare, such as *tandoori* chicken, *vindaloo* and *korma* curries, on two floors decorated like a curio shop with Arabic lanterns, Indian rugs, fairy lights and wooden parrots. The chairs have quilts and bows; the waitresses wear floral dresses. Everything's charmingly over the top at this eatery.

Hazara

29 Sukhumvit Soi 38. Tel: 0-2713 6048-9. Open: daily D. $$
www.facebars.com
Tasty north Indian fare, such as peppery *khadai kheenga* (shrimps stir-fried with bell peppers), in a glorious setting embellished with Asian antiques and artefacts. It is housed in a traditional Thai cluster complex and comprises the trendy Face Bar, a Thai restaurant called Lan Na Thai, a patisserie, a function space and a spa.

Rang Mahal

Rembrandt Hotel, 19 Sukhumvit Soi 18. Tel: 0-2261 7100. Open: Mon–Sat L and D. $$
Feast on city views in silk upholstered rooms with Indian wood carved panelling, lots of mirrors and

ive music while dining on mouthwatering Mogul specialities. Great curries, huge *tandoori* prawns and a choice of meat and vegetable *thali* and set meals for the indecisive. Posh, and very popular with the local Sikh community.

International

Bed Supperclub
26 Sukhumvit Soi 11. Tel: 0-2651 3537. Open: Sun–Thur 7.30pm–midnight, Fri–Sat 7.30pm–1am. $$$
www.bedsupperclub.com
Extraordinary tubular construction with an all-white interior where diners lie on beds and cushions to eat the brilliant fusion cuisine whipped up by chef Dan Ivarie. Choose from multi-choice three-course set menus. Also mixed media shows including dance, theatre and video. Next-door is **Bed Bar**, one of the city's top clubs and popular with Bangkok's trendy.

Crepes & Co
8 Sukhumvit Soi 12. Tel: 0-2251 2895. Open: Mon–Sat 9am–midnight, Sun 8am–midnight. $$
Reliable creperie that specialises in unusual fillings along with the expected crepe suzette. Also has *tajine* stews and other Moroccan dishes, and Greek favourites like *kotopolou* (a tomato and chicken casserole) and eggplant *melizana*. The tasteful wooden interior with Berber-style tented

ceiling and world music on the sound system gives the place a cosmopolitan atmosphere.

Greyhound
Fl 2 Emporium, Th Sukhumvit. Tel: 0-2664 8663. Open: daily 11am–9.15pm. $$
www.greyhound.co.th
Trendy modern Thai café serving European-influenced dishes such as the signature Thai anchovy spaghetti with chilli. Meals are chalked up on giant blackboards and there are glass-fronted displays of mouth-watering cakes. The all-white interior has *de rigueur* exposed ceiling pipes and outside there's seating with balcony views of the Emporium mall shoppers.

Kuppa
39 Sukhumvit Soi 16. Tel: 0-2663 0450. Open: Tues–Sun 10.30am–10.30pm. $$
Bangkok's sophisticated thirtysomethings browse magazines and enjoy their *tête-à-tête* over espressos in a huge room of comfortable sofas, blond wood and brushed metal, with a giant coffee roaster in the corner. Decent international and Thai food. Art gallery upstairs.

Offshore Fish and Chips
7/8 Sukhumvit Soi 23. Tel: 0-2661 7830. Open: daily 11am–2am. $
Bangkok's only UK/Australian style fish and chippie. For better flavour pay the few baht extra for the cod, rather than the standard fish, and don't

forget the mushy peas. Also has steak and kidney pie, mince and onion pie, and all the battered edibles you'd expect in Sydney or London.

The Old Dutch
9/4 Sukhumvit Soi 23. Tel: 0-2258 9234. Open: daily 8.30–2am. $
Appealing Dutch diner with an old European coffeehouse ambience, and strewn with books and magazines for patrons to read. The extensive menu lists cheese fondue, fish and chips, stews, sandwiches and salads, plus standard Thai dishes. Cheap wine and beer. Surprisingly non-seedy, despite its closeness to the raunchy red light district of Soi Cowboy.

To Die For
H1 Place, 998 Sukhumvit Soi 55 (Soi Thonglor). Tel: 0-2381 4714. Open: daily 11–2am. $$
French-Italian bar-restaurant set in a trendy boutique mall. Celebrity owners, like film director Nida Sudasna, help draw customers for homey meals of beef pockets stuffed with anchovy and capers, or asparagus and Parma ham deep-fried in filo pastry. Or come here just to drink designer cocktails in the funky warehouse interior.

Italian

Café Buongiorno
22 Sukhumvit Soi 33. Tel: 0-2662 3471. Open: Tues–Sun 10am–11pm. $$
Sipping cappuccino in

this elegant, secluded house in a walled garden it's hard to believe you're a stone's throw from the hostess bars of Soi 33. The menu culls dishes from the owner's family archives, including great cakes and breads. They're also keen promoters of Italian culture and host occasional plays in the garden.

Giusto
Sukhumvit Soi 23. Tel: 0-2258 4321. Open: daily L and D. $$$
Split into bar area, private rooms and an octagonal, glass-walled main dining space, this Italian restaurant has stylish fittings with burgundy and black and white decor, giving the feel of a luxury designer shop. Specialities include skewered fish, seafood and meats presented on "gallows" on the table and foie gras terrine. Interesting wine list.

La Piola
31/4 Sukhumvit Soi 11. Tel: 0-2250 7270. Open: Mon–Sat L and D. $$–$$$
Popular trattoria with no menu, but a daily changing "light" and "full" set meal according to what's available in the market. The owners are food

importers whose tasting sessions for buyers were so well appreciated they opened this restaurant. The full meal has cold cuts, soup, two pastas, one fish and one meat dish, dessert, coffee and home-made limoncello.

Pizzeria Limoncello
17 Sukhumvit Soi 11.
Tel: 0-2651 0707. Open: Tue–Sun L and D. $–$$
The Bangkok pizza boom, which started in 2003, had several established restaurants opening dedicated pizza parlours. This one has the signature buzz of owner Gianmaria Zanotti of Zanotti's *(see page 148)* and big tasty pizzas from the wood-fired oven. Its summery lemon and blue interior is full most nights, so book ahead.

Rossini's
Sheraton Grande Sukhumvit, 250 Th Sukhumvit.
Tel: 0-2649 8888. Open: L and D. $$–$$$
A faux mediaeval castle interior with cobbled floor, brick-arched doorway and domed ceiling gives a relaxed formality to this excellent restaurant. Start with timbale of blue crab and lobster tartar with scented avocado and move on to lobster and watercress-stuffed tortellini flambéed with vodka. Good wine choice by the glass.

Japanese

Shin Daikoku
Sukhumvit 32/8 Soi Wattana, Sukhumvit Soi 19.
Tel: 0-2254 9980-3. Open:

daily L and D. $$
A peaceful ambience amid bamboo partitions and private rooms around a Japanese garden-style fishpond. Among the standard *nigiri sushi* and *sashimi* options are a traditional nine-course *kaiseki* set meal, sea urchin from Hokkaido and noodle dishes such as *chasoba* (tea-flavoured chilled buckwheat noodles with scallion and wasabi).

Korean

Jang Won
202/9-19 Sukhumvit Plaza, cnr Sukhumvit Soi 12.
Tel: 0-2251 2636. Open: daily 9am–midnight. $$
One of many Korean café-restaurants in this plaza and the neighbouring *soi*. Diners sit in blond wood family-sized booths to enjoy Seoul food such as *ugeoji haejangguk* (spicy beef and vegetable soup), *dolsot bibimbap* (rice and beef cooked in hot stone pots) and sizzling plates of *bulgogi* beef.

Middle Eastern

Nasir Al-Masri
4/6 Sukhumvit Soi 3/1.
Tel: 0-2253 5582. Open: daily 10am–4am. $
This area is often called Soi Arab because of its numerous Middle Eastern operations selling kebabs and Lebanese style dips. "Nasir the Egyptian" also has specialities from home, such as *fuul* (mashed beans in oil) and

molokhaya (a spinach-like vegetable mixed with garlic). Outside, men smoke shiny metal shisha pipes, reminiscent of downtown Cairo.

Swiss

Chesa
5 Sukhumvit Soi 20.
Tel: 0-2261 6650. Open: daily 11am–11pm. $$
Modern take on a traditional Swiss restaurant-bar complete with a *stammtisch* (a large communal table). Disregard the wall-mounted papier-mâché cows' heads and feast on very tasty Steinpilz risotto (with boletus mushrooms), cheese fondue or raclette with baby potatoes and pickles.

Thai

Baan Khanitha
36/1 Sukhumvit Soi 23.
Tel: 0-2258 4181. Open: daily L and D. $$
This first outlet of the well known Baan Khanitha (second restaurant at **49 Soi Ruam Rudee 2**), is located in a charming old house with a lush garden. Busy with mainly Japanese and Western customers dining on tasty foreigner-friendly flavours ranging from Chiang Mai sausage and spicy salads to various curries, such as red duck with grapes.

Basil
Sheraton Grande Sukhumvit, 250 Th Sukhumvit.
Tel: 0-2649 8888. Open: L and D. $$–$$$
One of few hotel Thai

restaurants that doesn't over-compromise home-grown flavours for the delicate stomachs of tourists. The teak interior has a modern, clean-lined elegance, bereft of clutter. For something unusual, pick the stir-fried wild boar with chilli paste or papaya salad with bananas from the extensive menu of mainly traditional staples. Three kinds of rice dishes available if plain white does not entice.

Cabbages & Condoms
10 Sukhumvit Soi 12.
Tel: 0-2229 4610. Open: daily 11am–10pm. $–$$
Renowned for its promotion of family planning (its owner is former senator Mechai "Mr Condom" Viravaidhya, who has done much for AIDS awareness in Thailand). The two-storey restaurant, with mainly outdoor seating, has a pleasant ambience with glowing lamps in the courtyard and decent Thai standards. Free condoms as you leave.

Kalpapruek on First
Fl 1, Emporium, cnr Sukhumvit Soi 24.
Tel: 0-2664 8410-1. Open: daily 11am–10pm. $
This clone of the all-white industrial design trend that engulfed Bangkok in the late 1990s is notable for its fusion-style meals based on the owners' royal recipes, such as spicy pork casserole, concocted some 60 years ago. Dishes are

prepared at the original restaurant off Thanon Silom *(see page 149)*.

Lemon Grass
5/1 Sukhumvit Soi 24.
Tel: 0-2258 8637. Open: daily L and D. $$
A favourite with both Thais and expats, this was one of Bangkok's earliest Thai restaurants with "international sensibilities" (read spices toned down for foreigners). It's a little faded now, but still has the attraction of a house and garden. The food, despite being less fiery than purists would demand, is excellent. Try the satay or minced chicken with ginger and cabbage leaves.

Mahanaga
2 Sukhumvit Soi 29.
Tel: 0-2662 3060. Open: daily L and D. $$$
www.mahanaga.com
With its beautiful and spacious interior of Thai statuary, North African accents and Indian glass mosaics, this is one of the finest examples yet of modern international-ism in Bangkok dining. The less inspired fusion dishes such as lamb chop in *massaman* curry don't ruin the overall splendour of the interior.

Rosabieng
3 Sukhumvit Soi 11.
Tel: 0-2253 5868. Open: daily 11am–11pm. $
A handsome white town-house with al fresco eating in the spotlit garden, where a band plays Thai and international pop and jazz

standards nightly. The waiters rush the crowded tables with standard Thai curries and plates of crispy fried morning glory, and shrimp and mango salad. A giant TV screen shows soccer.

Ruen Mallika
189 Sukhumvit Soi 22.
Tel: 0-2663 3211-2. Open: daily 11am–11pm. $$
www.ruenmallika.com
Rama I period wooden house with garden tables and traditional floor-cush-ion seating inside. Opt for *kaeng tai pla* (pun-gent southern-style fish stomach curry), which tastes better than it sounds, *mee krob* (sweet and herby crispy noo-dles) or battered and deep-fried fresh flowers. At the end of Soi 22, turn right at the 7-Eleven into Soi Sedhi (the restaurant is on the right).

Seafood Market & Restaurant
89 Sukhumvit Soi 24. Tel: 0-2661 1252-9. Open: daily 11.30am–11.30pm. $$$
Bright barn-like dining hall with counter displays of fresh tiger shrimp, mud crab, giant sea perch and other seafood. The sign out-side says: "If It Swims We Have It". Buy your seafood, then take it to the table and ask for it to be steamed, grilled or stir-fried as you like. Touristy and expensive, but fun dining.

Vientiane Kitchen
8 Sukhumvit Soi 36.
Tel: 0-2258 6171. Open: daily 11.30–12.30am. $

Lao-Isaan food in a Thai *sala* complex around a garden where musicians play traditional music under trees laden with fairy lights. Have a shot of Thai rice whisky along with plates of *laab moo* (spicy minced pork salad), *gai yang* (grilled chicken) and *kai mot daeng* (red ant eggs). Both romantic and fun in equal measures.

Thai Food Stalls

Sukhumvit Soi 38
Open: daily 4pm–2am. $
At the entrance of this *soi* is a cluster of rough and tumble food stalls selling flavoursome local dishes. Start with the slow-cooked rice gruel *congee* and finish with *nam kaeng sai* (assorted desserts with ice), trying spring rolls, *yam poo* (spicy crab salad) and *moo krob* (crispy pork) in between sips of fresh fruit juice.

Vegetarian

Govinda
6/5/6 Sukhumvit Soi 22. Tel: 0-2663 4970. Open: daily except Tues L and D. $$
All-vegetarian high-standard Italian food, with a variety of pastas, thin-crust pizzas, cheesy risottos and bakes. Even desserts such as tiramisu and cheesecake are egg free. Also serves bread and ice cream made on the premises and imported beers. Small, cosy interior with a wooden staircase lead-ing to the mezzanine.

Tamarind Café
Sukhumvit Soi 20.
Tel: 0-2663 7421. Open: Mon–Fri 11am–11pm, Sat–Sun 9am–11pm. $
www.tamarind-cafe.com
A haven for art-loving vegetarians, this stylish all-white Bangkok branch of a Hanoi café holds photography exhibitions and has a flair for Euro-pean-Asian flavours. Tapas-style starters include tabouleh, falafel coated in sesame seeds and Thai crispy mush-rooms with a mild chilli dip. Follow up with vegetable gratin and coconut cream pie. Some rooftop seating.

Vietnamese

Le Dalat Indochine
14 Sukhumvit Soi 23.
Tel: 0-2661 7967/8. Open: daily L and D. $$
Located in an exquisitely decorated house with trees and plants every-where. The owners are related to exiled Saigon socialites and a former French colonial governor of Laos. Family photos and mementos of the old days line the walls. Tasty and elegantly-presented Vietnamese food, more subtle than Thai, and deliciously piquant.

PRICE CATEGORIES

Price per person for a three-course meal without drinks:
$ = under US$10
$$ = US$10–$25
$$$ = US$25–$50
$$$$ = over US$50

BANGKOK'S SUBURBS

Accessible getaways from the big city's relentless pace are sleepy Nonthaburi by the river, delightfully green Rama IX Royal Park, child-friendly Dream World and sprawling Chatuchak Weekend Market – where incurable shopaholics find their inner child

Map on page 160

Just a few decades back, the city's outer reaches constituted villages and farmland with little of the trappings of urban society. With lax urban planning, today's suburban sprawl veers off in all directions and can be bewildering to the uninitiated. Thai people's ability to speak English drop considerably the further out you venture, but you can also expect a more relaxing pace of life in these residential recesses. Many of the sights in this chapter can be visited as stop-offs on longer

BELOW: silk shawls on sale at the Chatuchak Weekend Market.

journeys out of town or as half- to full-day trips from downtown Bangkok; make sure taxi drivers are clear about where they're heading.

Chatuchak Weekend Market

The final stop on the Skytrain's northern line at Mo Chit station drops you at the sprawling **Chatuchak Weekend Market ❶** (Sat–Sun 7am–6pm). Reputed to be the world's biggest flea market, Chatuchak is a must-see for any visitor; even the least enthusiastic shopper cannot fail to be overawed by the sheer scale and variety of goods available. With an estimated 400,000 visitors weaving through the market's maze-like interior every weekend, Chatuchak is a heady assault upon the senses, so an early start (arrive by 9am) is essential to beat the soaring heat and ensuing claustrophobia. Navigating your way around Chatuchak is an adventure in itself. Although loosely partitioned into sections, the fun is in stumbling across hidden pockets of culture or kitsch as you meander the web of narrow alleyways. You will find everything from crafts, home decor and clothing to flowers and even pets

Numerous cafés, snack and juice bars are dotted throughout the market with many staying busy long after the stalls pack up for the day. After sunset, the edge of the market or

Thanon Kamphaengphet comes alive with a string of bars and coffee shops.

If the market overwhelms then retreat to the nearby **Chatuchak Park** (daily 4.30am–9pm; free). Built on land once owned by the State Railway, the park has a small **Hall Of Railway Heritage** museum (Sat–Sun 5am–3pm; free), with displays of old steam locomotives as well as other forms of transport, like London taxis.

Nonthaburi

The provincial riverside town of **Nonthaburi** , some 10 km (6 miles) north of Bangkok, feels a world away from hectic Bangkok. To get there, take an express boat (around 45 mins) to the end of the line at Tha Nonthaburi pier. The journey passes under bridges and weaves past tiny tugboats, gilded temples and communities of stilted houses.

At Nonthaburi, spend some time exploring the streets and markets, or charter a longtail boat to explore the island of Ko Kret (*see below*) or the scenic canal of Khlong Om. A canal trip along Khlong Om takes you past durian plantations and water-bound communities. Five minutes upriver from Nonthaburi pier brings you to the temple of **Wat Chalerm Phra Kiet**, a beautifully restored 19th-century monastery seemingly set in the middle of nowhere.

Ko Kret

Further upstream from Nonthaburi is the car-free island of **Ko Kret** ❸, best reached by chartered longtail boat from Nonthaburi to Tha Pa Fai pier on Ko Kret, the island makes for a laid-back half-day tour, allowing tourists to soak up a relaxed pace of life more typical of the rest of Thailand. The island has no roads, and can be walked round in less than two hours. While there are no specific attractions, the island is famous for its earthenware pottery studios. The villagers are primarily from the

ethnic Mon group, who migrated to Central Thailand from China and were a strong regional influence from the 6th to the 11th centuries.

Air Force Museum

Dedicated plane spotters will appreciate the nostalgic **Royal Thai Air Force Museum** ❹, tucked away in several hangars at the Royal Thai Air Force Base behind Bangkok Airport (171 Thanon Phahonyothin; daily 8am–4pm; free; tel: 0-2534 1853).

The rare planes on display include the only Model I Corsaire in existence, one of only two Japanese Tachikawas left, and Thailand's first domestically-built aircraft, the 1920s Model II Bomber Boripatr. There are also helicopters and jet-fighters on display. The museum is geared more towards organised groups than the occasional wandering tourist, with little English-language signage to guide you around.

Dream World

Those who have visited Disney World or other major US and European theme parks aren't going to be

There is not much to see in Ko Kret, but worthy of a picture is the distinctive tilting spire of Chedi Songmon. Legend has it that when the chedi eventually collapses, the Mon people will be able to return to their original homeland.

BELOW: a Mon potter at Ko Kret.

En route to Dream World, stop off at one of the flotilla of restaurant barges that moor up along Khlong Rangsit canal beside Thanon Rangsit Nakorn Nayok. They all specialise in a delicious noodle dish found only in this area.

BELOW: bumper car ride at Dream World.

rendered speechless by Bangkok's **Dream World** ❺ (Km 7, Thanon Rangsit Nakornnayok; Mon–Fri 10am–5pm, Sat–Sun 10am–7pm; admission charge; tel: 0-2533 1152; www.dreamworld.th.com/english).

Nevertheless, the park, located east of Bangkok Airport, is worthwhile if you have a bunch of teenagers with you. The park comprises Dream World Plaza, Dream Garden, Fantasy Land and Adventure Land. A sightseeing train circles Dream Garden, while a cable car and monorail offer nice views of the park and surrounding rural areas.

Thrillseekers should head for Adventure Land, the most stomach-churning section of the park. Along with the two fairly tame rollercoasters, there is a Viking swinging ship, Super Splash log flume and Grand Canyon water ride. In Snow Town, locals get to experience frosty weather, with sled rides down a slope made of artificial snow.

Safari World

Some 45 km (28 miles) northeast of Bangkok near Minburi is **Safari World** ❻, a popular destination for Bangkok families (99 Thanon Ramindra; daily 9am–5pm; admission charge; tel: 0-2914 4100-19; www.safariworld.com). Its reputation, however, took a severe beating in 2003 when it was discovered to be harbouring some 50 orangutan smuggled in from Indonesia. For a long time, the questionable orangutan boxing shows were one of the park's most popular attractions. The wildlife park is open as usual, though the apes have been seized by the authorities and the owner faces criminal persecution.

Other animals on view at the 81 ha (200-acre) park include giraffes, zebras, ostriches, rhinos and camels. Its adjoining **Marine Park** features acrobatics performed by sea lions and dolphins, as well as airborne antics by parrots and cockatoos.

Prasart Museum

Little visited, partly because of its rather remote location in Huamak, is the **Prasart Museum** ❼ (9 Soi A Krungthep Kreetha, Thanon Krungthep Kreetha; visits only by appointment Thur–Sun 10am–3pm; admission charge; tel: 0-2379 3601). Housed within a garden, the antique Thai arts and crafts on display belong to its private collector, Prasart Vongsakul. The artefacts are contained in several magnificent buildings, all of which are replicas inspired by the region's architectural classics. These elegant structures include a European-style mansion, a Khmer shrine, teak houses from Thailand's North and Central regions, as well as a Thai and Chinese temple.

Wat Thammamongkhon

At the eastern reaches of Thanon Sukhumvit at Soi 101 is the **Wat Thammamongkhon** ❽, unique for its 95-metre (312-ft) high *chedi*, which at 14 storeys is the tallest in Bangkok and offers commanding views of the low-rise eastern suburbs (daily 6am–6pm; free). Built in 1963, the *chedi* is modern in design, containing study rooms for novice monks and a lift to the top circular shrine room. At its base is the Will Power Institute, which runs classes in Buddhist meditation. The three-level glass pavilion beside the temple houses a 14-tonne Buddha image and a 10-tonne sculpture of the Chinese goddess Guanyin, both carved from a solid slab of jade.

Rama IX Royal Park

One of the city's largest green spaces, the 81-ha (200-acre) **Rama IX Royal Park** ❾ offers a delightful escape from the city (daily 5.30am–6.30pm; admission charge). Unfortunately, the park's suburban locale in Sukhumvit 103 means taking a 20-minute taxi ride from the last Skytrain station at On Nut. In a city desperately thin on public greenery, the park's opening in 1987 as a 60th birthday tribute to the king was a welcome addition.

With a dome-covered botanical garden, canals and bridges, water lily pond, as well as Chinese and Japanese ornamental gardens, the park is a delight to explore. ❑

Map on page 160

LEFT: the main hall at Wat Thammamongkhon.
BELOW: an afternoon escapade at the Rama IX Royal Park.

Around Bangkok

40 miles
40 km

CAMBODIA

Gulf of Thailand

Bight of Bangkok

BURMA (MYANMAR)

Taninthari (Tenasserim)

Bilauktaung Range

Tanintharyi (Tenasserim)

Bangkok

Ayutthaya

Lopburi

Chonburi

Ratchaburi

Kanchanaburi

Pattaya

Khao Yai National Park

Kaeng Krachan National Park

Khao Sam Roi Yot N. P.

Hua Hin

Cha-am

Phetchaburi

Hat Chao Samran

Suan Son Beach

River Kwai Bridge

Wat Museum

Rose Garden Country Resort

Damnoen Saduak Floating Market

Crocodile Farm

Ancient City

Si Racha

Ko Si Chang

Ko Samet

Rayong

Chanthaburi

Trat

Ko Chang Marine N.P.

Ko Mak Ko Kut

BANGKOK'S SURROUNDINGS

When the city seems too overwhelming, easy escapes within a 3- to 4-hour driving distance of Bangkok can provide welcome relief. Choose from ancient city ruins, sandy beaches dotted with sleepy villages, and picturesque national parks and waterfalls

Bangkok residents say that the next best thing to living in Bangkok is being able to leave it – a bit like hitting your head with a hammer: it's great when you stop. Of course the city has much to offer, but when you tire of its charms, there is an array of attractions within a few hours' drive of Bangkok. Some are strictly day trips but several, especially beach destinations, can be extended into leisurely week-long stays. Getting around in Thailand is relatively easy and very cheap. There is a good network of domestic flights to many provincial centres, and a regular if rather slow rail network. Buses are another alternative but the drivers can sometimes steer like madmen *(see pages 208–9 for details on getting there)*.

The flat, fertile Central Plains is the nearest and most accessible area from Bangkok, holding the remnants of former kingdoms as well as several expansive national parks. West of Bangkok are attractions like Rose Garden with its tourist-geared cultural shows, and its close neighbour Samphran Elephant Ground. Further west still is Kanchanaburi, the legendary site of the bridge built across the Kwai River during World War II. The area around Kanchanaburi is an outdoor adventure playground with river rafting, trekking and waterfall scaling. South of the capital are a string of beaches where Thais first began taking their summer holidays a century ago. Hua Hin is where Thai royalty and Bangkok's wealthy maintain their plush holiday homes. Kaeng Krachan National Park nearby is the country's largest forest reserve yet sees surprisingly few visitors.

The Eastern Seaboard provides ample opportunity for beach escapades. Everyone has heard of scandalous Pattaya, but further afield is the island of Ko Samet, blessed with picture-postcard white sand beaches, and Ko Chang, where resort development is taking place at breakneck speed.

Turning north, the ancient city of Ayutthaya is a grand repository for faded ruins, dating to the 14th century when it functioned as Thailand's capital. Some say the best part about Ayutthaya is getting there – on a teakwood barge winding up the sinuous Chao Phraya River. To the northeast, the main attraction is Khao Yai National Park, a favourite spot for Thais seeking picturesque mountains and waterfalls, and a break from the heat of Bangkok. ❏

PRECEDING PAGES: the three Khmer-style *prang* of Prang Sam Yot at Lopburi.

WEST OF BANGKOK

Home to the world's tallest Buddhist monument, the historic River Kwai Bridge and spectacular waterfalls in rainforest-clad national parks, this region offers attractions for both history and culture enthusiasts as well as nature lovers

Map on page 164

Further afield in Bangkok's neighbouring provinces are a number of attractions that can be visited on day trips or as pleasant overnight breaks. The western provinces are only a short distance from the capital and share a border with nearby Burma (Myanmar). Most people heading in this direction make a brief stop in Nakhon Pathom province to gawk at the huge *chedi* that dominates the town, before heading to Kanchanaburi province, famous for its so-called "Bridge over the River Kwai" and its tragic wartime associations. However, equally fascinating are the seldom-visited coastal provinces of Samut Sakhon and the lush lowlands of Samut Songkhram.

Rose Garden

Some 32 km (20 miles) west from Bangkok on Route 4 towards Nakhon Pathom is the **Rose Garden Country Resort ❶** (daily 8am–6pm; admission charge; tel: 0-3432 2588; www.rose-garden.com). It has well-landscaped gardens with roses and orchids in addition to a resort-style hotel, a cultural centre, restaurants, tennis courts, an artificial lake with paddleboats, a spa and an excellent golf course.

The premier attraction here is the Thai Village Cultural Show held daily in the garden. In a large arena, costumed actors perform folk dances to live traditional music and re-enact a traditional wedding ceremony and a Thai boxing match. Outside, after this, elephants put on their own show, moving huge teak logs as they would in the forests of the north. The elephants then carry tourists around the compound for a small fee. Otherwise, spend time browsing at the Cultural Village, with gift shops and demonstrations by weavers creating thread from silkworm cocoons.

LEFT: Erawan Falls at Erawan National Park, Kanchanaburi.
BELOW: bamboo dance demonstration at Rose Garden.

The Jumbo Queen contest which takes place at Samphran Elephant Ground annually on 1 May seeks a "well-padded lady who "best exhibits the characteristics of the majestic pachyderm to persuade people to support the cause of elephant conservation in Thailand." Strange but true. More details at www.jumboqueen.com

BELOW:
resident elephant at Samphran Elephant Ground & Zoo.

Samphran Elephant Ground

Just a stone's throw from the Rose Garden is the **Samphran Elephant Ground & Zoo**, another family-oriented attraction that provides a chance to trek on an elephant, feed the crocs and learn about the pachyderm's importance in Thai culture (daily 8am–5.30pm; admission charge; tel: 0-2284 1873; www.elephantshow.com). Other fauna on view include gibbons, macaques, pythons and a diverse flock of local birds.

At the Crocodile Show, men wrestle with these scaly creatures, while the Elephant Show explains Thailand's historical relationship with its national symbol. The war re-enactments are exciting displays, but the elephants' majesty somewhat diminishes when they're made to do silly things, like dance, race and play football in oversized shirts. After the show, you can feed the elephants or go on a 30-minute elephant trek. Each May 1st, a travesty of a beauty contest takes place here as oversized women weighing over 80 kg (176 lbs) compete for the ignominious title of **Jumbo Queen**.

Phra Pathom Chedi

Just 56 km (35 miles) west of Bangkok, beyond the Rose Garden on Route 4, is the town of **Nakhon Pathom ②**, known for the colossal **Phra Pathom Chedi**. Measuring 130 metres (420 ft) in height, this golden landmark is claimed as the tallest Buddhist monument in the world, and possibly the oldest Buddhist site in the country, dating back to 3 BC.

The original small Sri Lankan-style *chedi* was erected to commemorate the arrival of Indian Buddhist missionaries who supposedly brought Buddhism to Thailand via Burma in 3 BC. The town Nakhon Pathom was settled in the 6th–11th centuries by the Dvaravati empire, a Mon civilisation whose culture flourished in Burma and Thailand. In the early 11th century the Khmers invaded from Angkor, overrunning the city and replacing the original *chedi* with a Brahman-style *prang*.

Then in 1057, King Anawrahta of Burma besieged the town, leaving the religious edifice in ruins. When King Mongkut (Rama IV) visited the old *chedi* in 1853, he was so impressed by its historical significance that he ordered the restoration of the temple. A new *chedi* was built, covering the older one; the present structure was completed by King Chulalongkorn (Rama V).

Set in a huge square park, the massive *chedi* rests upon a circular terrace and is accented with trees associated with the Buddha's life. In November each year, a huge fair in the temple grounds attracts crowds from all over Thailand.

In former times, a visit to Nakhon Pathom was more than a day's journey, so it's not surprising that a number of palaces and residences were built for visiting royalty. One of them, **Sanam Chan Palace**, 2 km (1 mile) west of Phra Pathom Chedi along Thanon Rajamankha Nai comprises several buildings, includ-

ing a Thai-style pavilion that is now used as government offices, and a building in the English Tudor style. The palace was commissioned by King Vajiravudh (Rama VI) in 1907. You should try to visit the **Yaleh Monument**, which honours Yaleh, the pet dog of Vajiravudh. The fierce dog, unpopular with the court, was poisoned by the king's attendants. Even as a statue, Yaleh looks insufferable. Although the grounds are open to the public, most of the palace buildings are off limits apart for one, which serves as a small museum and contains memorabilia of King Vajiravudh.

Samut Sakhon

A good way to approach the coastal port of **Samut Sakhon** ❸ (Ocean City), 28 km (17 miles) from Bangkok, is by the railway line that connects to Thonburi in Bangkok. Called the Mae Khlong Railway, the line carries passengers on the 40-minute journey through the capital's suburbs, then through thriving vegetable gardens, groves of coconut and areca palms, and rice fields. A busy fishing port, Samut Sakhon (also called Mahachai) lies at the meeting of the Tachin River, the Mahachai Canal and the Gulf of Thailand. The main landing stage on the riverbank has a clock tower and a seafood restaurant. At the fish market pier, it's possible to hire a boat for a round-trip to Samut Sakhon's principal temple, **Wat Chong Lom** at the mouth of the Tachin River.

Most of the temple structures are modern, except for an old *viharn* (sermon hall) immediately to the right of the temple's river landing. The *viharn* dates back about a century. The extensive grounds overlooking the water are nicely laid out with shrubs and flowering trees. There is also a bronze statue of King Chulalongkorn commemorating his visit to the temple.

Samut Songkhram

From Samut Sakhon, cross the river to the railway station on the opposite side. Here, board a second train for another 40-minute trip to the province of **Samut Songkhram** ❹, 74 km (46 miles) southwest from

Map on page 164

Close-up of gold leaf offerings covering a Buddha image at Phra Pathom Chedi.

LEFT AND BELOW: the towering Phra Pathom Chedi, and schoolchildren at the temple grounds.

*Rose apples
harvested in the
orchards of Samut
Songkhram.
Indigenous to
Southeast Asia, rose
apples have a lovely
tart flavour.*

Bangkok, on the banks of the Mae Khlong River. The journey goes through broad salt flats, with their picturesque windmills slowly being turned by the sea breezes. Thailand's smallest province, Samut Songkhram has abundant fruit orchards. Pomelo, jackfruit, rose apple, lychee, mango, as well as the more ubiquitous banana and coconuts, are harvested here before being loaded onto the ice-packed vending carts that trundle the streets of Bangkok.

Samut Songkhram itself is just another fishing town; wandering in its wharf is an olfactory and visual experience. Teak barges can be hired for private dinner cruises up the river (ask at riverside restaurants), and the area is known for swarms of fireflies that magically illuminate the shoreline of *lamphu* trees in the evenings.

King Buddhalertla Naphalai Memorial Park

From Samut Songkhram, you can make a fairly short detour to the Amphawa District to visit **King Buddhalertla Naphalai Memorial Park**, also known as Rama II His-

torical Park (park daily 9am–6pm; museum Wed–Sun 9am–4pm; admission charge), situated at the birthplace of Rama II. This small museum houses displays of art and crafts from the early Rattanakosin period in four beautifully reconstructed teakwood stilted houses, illustrating how Thai people lived during the rule of King Rama II. In the well-maintained gardens around the museum are rare species of trees, some of which are mentioned in classical Thai literature. A special exhibition is held every February to celebrate the birthday of Rama II.

Also found in Amphawa is the **Amphawa Floating Market**, which anchors in front of the old Wat Amphawa each morning from 6–8am. It's located about a 10-minute walk from the historical park. The market is smaller and more authentic compared to Damnoen Saduak (see page 171).

Don Hoi Lot

Another option, accessible by both car or longtail boat from Samut Songkhram is **Don Hoi Lot**, at the

mouth of the Mae Khlong River. Don Hoi Lot is in fact a bank of fossilised shells that has become a popular attraction with locals. It's a great place to enjoy fresh seafood and tube-like clams (*hoi lot* in Thai means straw clams). In the late afternoon when the tide is low, villagers enthusiastically search the muddy estuary for clam burrows. They spread a little bit of lime powder at the entrance of the holes, and when the clams become agitated and come out from the ground, they are eagerly fished out.

Damnoen Saduak

From Samut Songkhram, hire a longtail boat for a trip up the Mae Khlong River to **Damnoen Saduak Floating Market** ❺ (daily 7am–1pm). An early morning departure is necessary if you want to beat the tour buses from Bangkok, 65 km (40 miles) away, that flock to this famous floating market in Ratchaburi province by 10am.

While it is possible to walk along the bankside lined with souvenir stands, it's better to hire a longtail boat to get a better sense of the water-bound commercial bustle. Be prepared though for the worst: this 100-year-old market is little more than a sideshow today, with tourists clambering to snap pictures of the colourful fruit- and vegetable-laden wooden vessels, oared by smiling sun-beaten women wearing wide-rimmed straw hats.

If you've hired your own longtail boat, it might be worthwhile asking the boatman to take you deeper into the canals where you can get a glimpse of the canal communities.

Kanchanaburi

Located around 130 km (75 miles) west of Bangkok, the sleepy provincial town of **Kanchanaburi** ❻ is well worth the two-hour drive it takes to get there. It can be done as a busy day trip but better yet, plan for a more relaxing overnight, with an evening spent on the banks of the Kwae Yai River.

Kanchanaburi received widespread publicity in the last half century for its infamous railway, which was built during World War II by Allied POWs and Asian labourers, under the watch of the Japanese occupying army. Thousands of lives were lost as the ill-equipped prisoners struggled in appalling conditions to complete over 400 km (249 miles) of railway track, called the "Death Railway", linking Thailand with Burma. Despite its association with the war and the railway, Kanchanaburi remains a laid-back provincial town. Situated close to the Burmese border, it has several interesting temples, as well as nearby caves, waterfalls, forests and the remnants of a 13th-century Khmer palace.

River Kwai Bridge

Spanning the Kwae Yai River (also known as Kwai Yai), the latticed steel **Bridge over the River Kwai** (which takes its name from a movie

 TIP

Instead of staying at a land-based hotel in Kanchanaburi, opt for a floating guesthouse moored by the riverbank instead. Be warned though; while these are atmospheric, they can also get very noisy during weekends, thanks to discos and karaoke boats packed with drunken young Thais on a night of revelry.

BELOW:
outdoor tour "office" in Kanchanaburi.

Only the eight curved sections of the "Bridge over the River Kwai" are original; the rest of it was rebuilt after World War II.

BELOW: the famous bridge spanning the Kwai River.

of the same name) has become a memorial for the fallen. It can be reached by boat or rickshaw from Kanchanaburi town. The bridge has lost some of its significance to tourist commercialisation, but walking across it is a sobering experience. A steam locomotive used shortly after the war is displayed beside the tiny Kanchanaburi station platform, along with an ingenious Japanese supply truck that could run on both road and rail. Floating restaurants and hotels line both banks of the river.

The bridge itself was the second of two bridges, built side by side, crossing the river; the earlier wooden structure was completed in 1942, with the sturdier steel bridge erected by May 1943. Both bridges became a constant target for Allied bombers and were eventually bombed out of action in 1945. Only the eight curved segments on each side of the current structure are original; the rest was rebuilt after the war as part of Japan's war reparations.

The tragic saga of the bridge was represented on celluloid in the 1957 Film *Bridge over the River Kwai* directed by David Lean and starring the late Sir Alec Guinness. Winner of seven Academy Awards, this version contains several historic inaccuracies, most blatant of which was that the bridge was destroyed by commandos, when in fact it was bombed by allied planes.

Today, most of the old railway tracks have been removed, except for a section that runs from Kanchanaburi to the terminus at Nam Tok. The 50-km (30-mile) journey takes about 90 minutes to complete and the train passes over the reconstructed bridge, the old wooden tracks creaking beneath.

World War II Museum

Located beside the bridge is the rather garish **WWII & JEATH War Museum** (daily 9am–6pm; admission charge). Capitalising on the name JEATH, the name of another and infinitely better museum located in Kanchanaburi town *(see page 173)*, this one contains an odd mixture of exhibits, most of which have nothing to do at all with the war. But

f you are into kitsch, however, there's plenty to interest you. Around the building's exterior are life-size sculptures of significant figures involved in the war; the likes of Hitler, Churchill, Einstein and Hirohito are among those given an almost comic treatment of artistry. One of the more unusual displays is a wall dedicated to the Miss Thailand pageant – now you see what we mean – with life size murals of some of the more notable winners. The rooftop offers great views of the bridge and surrounding panorama.

JEATH War Museum

The small but informative **JEATH War Museum** (daily 8.30am–6pm; admission charge), tucked away in the grounds of Wat Chaichumpol on Thanon Pak Phraek in the southern end of Kanchanaburi town will give you a better appreciation of the enormous obstacles the prisoners faced. Its peaceful locale on the banks of the Mae Khlong River (the larger river which splits into the two tributaries of Kwae Yai and Kwae Noi), shadowed by a 500-year-old

samrong tree, provide for a quiet moment of poignant reflection.

The acronym jeath comes from the first letter of some of the principal countries that were involved in this regional conflict during World War II, namely Japan, England, America, Thailand and Holland. The museum is split into two buildings, the larger of which is a long bamboo hut similar to those that housed the pows during their construction of the Siam-Burma railway. Inside is a collection of poignant photographs, sketches, paintings, newspaper clippings and other war memorabilia, giving you an idea of the harsh conditions pows endured during their period of enforced labour and incarceration.

Allied War Cemetery

At the **Kanchanaburi Allied War Cemetery** (daily 7am–6pm; free) opposite the museum are the graves of 6,982 Allied soldiers, representing less than half of the 16,000 soliders who lost their lives. Immaculate green lawns planted with colourful flowers add a sense of serenity to the graves of the British,

Bomb display at JEATH War Museum.

Map on page 164

BELOW:
Kanchanaburi Allied War Cemetery.

Death Railway

The Japanese began work on a railway between Thailand and Burma in 1942. For most of its 400-km (260-mile) length, the railway followed the river valley because this allowed its construction simultaneously in different areas. In the end, nearly 15 km (9 miles) of bridges were completed. The Japanese forced some 250,000 Asian labourers and 61,000 Allied POWs to construct 260 km (160 miles) of rail on the Thai side, leading to the Three Pagodas Pass on the Thai-Burmese border. An estimated 100,000 Asian labourers and 16,000 Allied POWs lost their lives between 1942–5 from beatings, starvation and disease.

American, Australian, Dutch and other Allied soldiers that are lined up row upon row. Look at the grave markers and you'll notice that most of the young men who died for their countries were under the age of 30. Its location, however, beside noisy Thanon Saengchuto detracts from the solemnity of the place.

Located in a more tranquil setting is the **Chung Kai Allied War Cemetery**, found at the edge of Kanchanaburi town across the river (daily 7am–6pm; free). Another 1,750 POWs are buried at this site.

Around Kanchanaburi

For those who opt to stay overnight in Kanchanaburi, the surrounding countryside holds plenty of surprises. There are a couple of cave temples found within limestone crags on the southern outskirts of Kanchanaburi, some requiring nimble legwork in order to navigate the claustrophobic passageways that lead to eerily-lit meditation cells filled with Buddha images. While generally safe don't venture into the more remote caves unaccompanied;

in 1996 a British female tourist was murdered by a drug-crazed monk at Wat Tham Kao Pun.

One of the frequently visited cave temples is that of **Wat Tham Mangkhon Thong**, primarily known for its "floating nun" (daily 8am–5pm; admission charge). An old nun, who has since passed away, used to float on her back in a pool of water while in a state of meditation. Today, a young disciple gives her own interpretation of the ritual – in return for a fee – for busloads of gaping Asian tourists.

Prasart Muang Singh

Located 43km (27 miles) west of Kanchanaburi, the Khmer ruins of **Prasart Muang Singh** ❼ (daily 8am–5pm; admission charge) are situated in a manicured park. The site makes for a great picnic as it is beside the picturesque Kwae Noi River (a smaller tributary of the Kwae Yai). The central sanctuary of this 13th-century temple complex points east, and is in direct alignment with its more grandiose sister, the Angkor Wat in Cambodia.

Over the years, trees and vegetation have grown and embedded their roots into the ruins of Prasart Muang Singh.

BELOW: Wat Tham Mangkhon Thong.
RIGHT: Khmer ruins at Prasart Muang Singh.

Although nowhere near as impressive or intricate as the Angkor Wat, Prasart Muang Singh is still a fascinating testament to just how far west the Khmer empire stretched at the height of its power. On the same site is a small exhibition hall containing duplicates of Khmer sculptures, while near the river is a Neolithic burial site displaying partially uncovered skeletons.

Erawan National Park

Other alternative trips in the vicinity include the spectacular seven-tiered **Erawan Waterfall**, found in **Erawan National Park** ❽ (daily 8am–6pm; admission charge). The falls are best visited during and just after the rainy season (May–Nov), when the water is at full flow. Situated some 70 km (40 miles) north of Kanchanaburi, Erawan Falls can become quite congested with locals who visit the national park at weekends and on public holidays.

The route to the waterfall starts from the national park office. The climb up to level five of the waterfall is manageble; getting up to the slippery sixth and seventh levels is not recommended unless you are fit and have enough derring-do. You can cool off at the inviting natural pools (don't forget your swimsuit) at the base of each of the tiers. The thundering water flow from the highest level is said to take on the shape of the three-headed elephant Erawan, hence its name.

There are several hiking trails in the park, which covers some 550 sq km (212 sq miles) and comprises mainly deciduous forests with limestone hills rising up to 1,000 metres (3,281 ft). One of the more popular hiking trails is the 90-minute Khannak-Mookling trail; the 1,400-metre (4,593-ft) long circular trail starts from the national park office. Also taking 90 minutes, the Wang-badan Cave trail takes you through bamboo and evergreen forest along a 1,350-metre (4,429-ft) long route.

Sai Yok National Park

Less visited is **Sai Yok Waterfall** in **Sai Yok National Park** ❾ (daily 6am–6pm; admission charge). Sai Yok's waterfall is a little more remote at 100 km (62 miles) northwest of Kanchanaburi and best undertaken on an overnight tour. The national park itself covers over 500 sq km (193 sq miles) of mainly teak forests, with one side of it bordering Burma. Apart from the stunning cascade (again best seen in the rainy season, or just after), the park is known as the habitat of the smallest known mammal in the world – the bumblebee bat. Found in Sai Yok's limestone caves in 1974, the creature, which weighs a mere 2 grams (and hardly larger than a bumblebee), has been declared an endangered species.

More adventurous travellers should enquire in lodges and hotels in these national park areas about organised kayaking, rafting and mountain biking trips. ❑

Map on page 164

TIP

There are some 140 gazetted national parks in Thailand, a number of which are easily accessed from Bangkok, like Erawan, Sai Yok, Kaeng Krachan and Khao Sam Roi Yot. For more information on Thai national parks, look up www.thaiparks123.com or www.trekthailand.net.

BELOW: base of a giant buttress tree at Sai Yok National Park.

SOUTH OF BANGKOK

This culturally distinct region is home to exclusive weekend beach retreats and a nascent spa industry. Large mammals find sanctuary in Kaeng Krachan National Park, the largest in Thailand, with terrain comprising rainforest, savanna and mountain ranges

Map on page 164

Wedged between the Gulf of Thailand and the Andaman Sea, Southern Thailand geographically resembles an elephant's trunk, narrowly snaking down from below the Central Plains to the tip of the Malay Peninsula. The inhabitants have their own distinct dialect and the further south one travels, the more noticeable Malay influences are, evident in the number of mosques dotted between the spread of lush rubber plantations. Southern cuisine is rich and spicy with plenty of coconut-based curries, usually centred around seafood freshly caught from the surrounding seas.

Petchaburi

Historically rich **Petchaburi** , some 120 km (75 miles) south of Bangkok, is one of Thailand's oldest towns and has been an important trade and cultural centre since the 11th century. Lying on the Petchaburi River, the town has come under the influence of the Mon, Khmers and Thais at various times, and has over 30 temples that reflect the different cultures and architectural styles of its past invaders. Some of the more important religious sites include the laterite Khmer *prang* of **Wat Kamphaeng Laeng**, and the 17th-century Ayutthayan **Wat Yai Suwannaram**, with its significant temple murals. Both the temples and town are easily navigable on foot.

Just west of town is a 92-metre (302-ft) high hill, locally known as **Khao Wang**, topped by the summer palace of King Mongkut (Rama IV). Commissioned in 1860, the complex is also known as the **Phra Nakhon Historical Park** and contains a mélange of Eastern and Western architectural styles; many of its buildings offer fabulous panoramas of the vicinity, especially at sunset.

LEFT: tourists making the trek up to Khao Wang. **BELOW:** the distinctive Khmer structures of Wat Kamphaeng Laeng.

BELOW AND RIGHT:
rope swing and
suspension bridge
spanning the river at
Kaeng Krachan
National Park.

The hilltop buildings include three throne halls, a neo-classical observatory (the king was a keen astronomer), a large white *chedi* and the **Wat Maha Samanaram** (daily 8am–4pm; free). The steep trail to the summit winds through woods populated by inquisitive monkeys, though the easier option is to take the cable tram to the top.

An interesting excursion only 5 km (3 miles) from town is the **Khao Luang** cave. Adorned with stalactites, small *chedi* and Buddha images, shafts of sunlight filter down from holes in the cave roof, creating a splendid visual. Beside the cave's mouth is **Wat Bunthawi**, a temple with wonderfully carved wooden door panels.

As the railway line south brought greater access to this part of Thailand, a number of palaces were erected for the royal family in times past. Situated beside the Petchaburi River, **Ban Puen Palace** (daily 8am–4pm; admission charge) would look more at home in Germany's Black Forest than the coastal flats of Petchaburi. Built in 1910 for King Chula-longkorn (the same year he died), this stately Germanic home was modelled after the summer palace of Kaiser Wilhelm, and designed by a German architect. The grandiose palace has a luxurious interior and is surrounded by a manicured garden.

Kaeng Krachan Park

Located some 60 km (37 miles) southwest of Petchaburi town is the vast 3,000-sq km (1,158-sq mile) **Kaeng Krachan National Park** ⑪ (daily 6am–6pm; admission charge). The park – the largest in Thailand – covers almost half of Petchaburi province and is a haven for numerous species of large mammals, including tigers, elephants, leopards, bears, deer, gibbons and monkeys. The topography varies between rainforest and savanna grasslands, and includes a freshwater lake and rugged mountain ranges.

At over 1,207 metres (3,960 ft), it is possible to ascend the park's tallest peak, **Phanoen Tung**, for superb views of the lush countryside, or marvel at the 18-tier **Tho Thip** waterfall. Another of the park's attractions is

he man-made **Kaeng Krachan Dam**, which has created a vast reservoir for irrigation. Visitors can hire boats and go sightseeing on the lake.

Considering Kaeng Krachan's proximity to Bangkok, surprisingly few tourists venture here. Trekking is the main activity here, with forestry officials for hire as guides at the park's headquarters at the end of the road beyond Kaeng Krachan Dam. Accommodation consists of basic park lodgings, but the easiest way to visit the park is on a tour organised by many hotels in nearby Hua Hin.

Cha-am

The weekend getaway of **Cha-am** ⑫ is a long stretch of beach that has become popular with groups of young Bangkokians. Around 40 km (25 miles) south of Petchaburi, the resort is very peaceful during weekdays, with plenty of delicious seafood restaurants to choose from. Outside of Thailand's university breaks, the resort is very quiet, so if a little more nightlife suits you, then Hua Hin is better geared up.

Roughly 10 km (6 miles) south of Cha-am heading towards Hua Hin, is the seaside palace of **Phra Ratchaniwet Marukhathayawan** (daily 8am–5pm; admission charge). Built in 1923 from golden teakwood, the airy stilted structures are European in style and have been beautifully renovated and painted in summery pastel shades. Interconnected by raised covered walkways, the palace buildings were a retreat for King Vajiravudh (Rama VI) for the last two years before he died.

Hua Hin

Prachuap Kiri Khan is Thailand's narrowest province and its coast is ringed with mountains and lovely quiet beaches, the most popular of which is the 5-km (3-mile) long sandy beach at **Hua Hin** ⑬. Located 203 km (126 miles) from Bangkok

and taking less than four hours by road or rail, the former fishing village of Hua Hin has long had an air of exclusivity, thanks to its residences maintained by the Thai royalty and Bangkok's wealthy elite. Partly because of this it retains more of a family ambience than most other beach destinations in Thailand.

The royal connection can be seen at the seafront teak wood summer abode called **Klai Kangwon Palace**, which means "far from worries". Built in 1926 at the northern end of Hua Hin beach under the command of King Rama VII, the Spanish-style villa is still regularly used by the royal family and is not open to the public.

One of the country's first rail lines linked Bangkok to Hua Hin at the start of the 20th century, transporting the capital's wealthy to the southern shores. Hua Hin thus had the aura of a European spa town, with the royals coming here for the clean air. Today, the coastal town is beginning to reclaim that mantle as several exclusive spa retreats – like the award-winning Chiva Som –

Map on page 164

Horseriding along the flat sands of Cha-am beach.

BELOW: makeshift stalls at Cha-am beach.

Hua Hin is blessed with bountiful seafood and fine restaurants that serve dishes like this grilled squid salad.

BELOW: interior of the Hotel Sofitel Central.

cater to the holistic needs of international jetsetters. A string of brand-name resorts, like Hilton, Hyatt and Marriott, have opened in the past decade, along with local (and equally expensive) concerns like Dusit and Anantara.

Just across from the quaint **Hua Hin Railway Station** is another historic landmark, the colonial-style former Railway Hotel. Constructed in 1922, the Victorian-looking hotel masqueraded as the Phnom Penh Hotel in the 1984 movie *Killing Fields* before being restored to its original wood-panelled glory as the **Hotel Sofitel Central**.

Today, the wide, sweeping run of Hua Hin beach is backed by opulent summer homes along with a slew of faceless condo development. Hua Hin is fast gaining an international reputation as a place to retire, and more and more condos and beach houses are being built to accommodate the upsurge in interest. The beach lacks the character of Thailand's palm-fringed island bays, but is great for long undisturbed strolls. Pony rides set off from near the main drag. The beaches south of town, **Suan Son** and **Khao Tao**, are rather nicer and more secluded.

Hua Hin activities

These days, as tourism with all its associated trappings increases its grip, the image of the resort as a low-key family getaway may become a thing of the past. The town's nightlife has picked up in the last few years as more beer bars (but no go-go bars as yet) open with more professional girls recruited to draw customers, providing… ahem, additional services if requested. It's a familiar pattern in Bangkok and Thailand's other resorts; once single male tourists descend en masse, working girls also begin their migration. However, Hua Hin still has a long way to go before it resembles the likes of Pattaya.

Along with this upsurge in nightlife, a number of new restaurants have appeared too. While Hua Hin has always been known as a place for fresh seafood, the diversity of culinary options has expanded beyond just Thai, with Japanese, Korean, Scandinavian, German, French and Italian, reflecting the nationality of tourist arrivals. The restaurants and bars are all clustered into a small area around Thanon Naresdamri and behind on the parallel Thanon Phun suk. Soi Bintabaht has the highest concentration of beer bars, and the pier area along Naresdamri grills up some of the best seafood in town.

Hua Hin sees a lot of activities and events, usually organised at weekends so that the Bangkok crowds can join in. These include the annual **Hua Hin Jazz Festival** and the popular **King's Cup Elephant Polo Tournament**, usually held in September. The entertaining tournament raises money for elephant preservation. Around 15 teams from around the world compete according to rules set by the World Elephant Polo

ssociation – yes such an associa-
on exists! With three elephants per
:am on a pitch measuring 100 by
)0 metres (328 by197 ft), a game
omprises two 10-minute chukkas,
ith a 15-minute interval.

uside Hua Hin

isible a few kilometres south of
wn is **Khao Takiab** (Chopstick
ill). This rocky outcrop has a steep
limb to its summit but the views of
e surrounding coast are worth the
weat. There's an unremarkable
:mple at the top with a large Bud-
ha statue standing facing the sea,
round which are resident troops of
oisterous macaques.

The Prachuap Kiri Khan area has
:veral waterfalls, most spectacular
f which is **Pala-U**, some 60 km (37
iiles) west of Hua Hin, towards the
nountain range that forms a barrier
etween Thailand and Burma. Best
:en during rainy season, the falls
ave 11-tiers and are surrounded by
ense forest that is home to swarms
f butterflies and other creatures.

The beaches further south of Hua
lin down towards **Pranburi** are

also starting to see a number of
tastefully designed boutique resorts,
like the Evason and Aleenta, making for a stylish, if expensive, escape
from Bangkok.

Located around 50 km (31 miles)
south of Hua Hin, **Khao Sam Roi
Yot National Park** ⓮ translates as
"Three Hundred Mountain Peaks"
and refers to the limestone pinnacles
jutting up from the park's mangrove
swamps to heights above 600 m
(1,968 ft). Carved from the rugged
coastline and a haven for kayakers,
the park has superb beaches, marshes,
forest walks and caves. Wildlife
includes a multitude of birdlife, crab-
eating macaques, and the rare serow
– a mountain goat-antelope.

Tham Phraya Nakhon is the
most famous attraction here; the huge
cave has a large sinkhole that allows
shafts of light to shine down and illuminate the grand Thai-style pavilion
(*sala*) built in the 1890s for a visit by
King Chulalongkorn. Other noteworthy caves are **Tham Sai** and **Tham
Kaeo**, the latter meaning "Jewel
Cave" and named after its glistening
stalactite and rock formations. ❏

Map
on page
164

*In 1868, King
Mongkut, an astute
astronomer, visited
Khao Sam Roi Yot
National Park to
view a total eclipse
of the sun, which he
had foretold. The
king's prediction, to
the astonishment of
local astrologers,
was only four
minutes off the mark.
Sadly, Mongkut
contracted malaria
from this trip and
died a week after his
return to Bangkok.*

BELOW:
the Hilton Hua Hin at
dusk, one of several
luxury properties that
line Hua Hin beach.

EASTERN SEABOARD

Southeast from Bangkok are diverse attractions that will appeal to many. Take your pick from cultural and wildlife parks, the touristy anything-goes beach town of Pattaya, or choose from unspoilt palm-fringed islands such as Ko Samet and Ko Chang

Map on page 164

amut Prakan Province, near the river-mouth town of Pak-nam, is 30 km (20 miles) or about half an hour's drive southeast of Bangkok. Although not on every tourist's itinerary, a day trip here from Bangkok makes for an interesting alternative. Otherwise, it can be visited while on the way to one of the beaches along Thailand's east coast. The province is home to two local attractions – the world's largest open-air museum in Muang Boran, and the world's largest crocodile farm. Samut Prakan is set to undergo a transformation when the new **Suvarnabhumi Airport** replaces the congested Bangkok International Airport in Don Muang. Scheduled to open in late 2006, it will bring an anticipated influx of hotels, housing for staff, and other peripheral facilities.

Beyond Samut Prakan is Thailand's Eastern Seaboard, stretching from Chonburi province all the way to Trat province and the Cambodian border, and lined with a string of pretty beaches and scenic islands.

Ancient City

One of Bangkok's best-value tourist, and surprisingly under-visited, attractions, **Ancient City ⑮** or Muang Boran, is the brainchild of a Bangkok millionaire with a passion for Thai

art and history (daily 8am–5pm; admission charge; tel: 0-2323 9253; www.ancientcity.com). In what used to be 80 hectares (200 acres) of rice fields, designers sketched an area roughly the shape of Thailand and placed the individual attractions as close to their real sites as possible.

There are replicas – some full-size, most one-third the size of the originals – of famous monuments and temples from all parts of the kingdom. Some are reconstructions of buildings that no longer exist, such

LEFT: lounging at Ao Thian (Candlelight Beach) in Koh Samet.
BELOW: Ancient City.

as the Grand Palace of Ayutthaya, others are copies of buildings such as the temple of Khao Phra Viharn on the Thai-Cambodian border, while a few are salvaged antiquities. Experts from the National Museum worked as consultants to ensure historical accuracy of the reproductions.

At present, there are over 100 monuments, covering 15 centuries of Thai history. There is a lot to see here and you could spend a whole day looking around. The grounds are pleasantly landscaped with small waterfalls, creeks, ponds, rock gardens and lush greenery, while deer graze freely among the interesting sculptures representing figures from Thai literature and Hindu mythology. With the monuments spread over such a large area, the best way to get around and soak up the ambience is on rented bicycles. Finish your tour at the Old Market Town, a street of shops disguised as traditional wooden houses, with local handicrafts and sculptures for sale. Here you can watch craftsmen carve puppets from buffalo hide and woodcarvers sculpt Khmer idols.

In 2002, a grisly spectacle took place at Samut Prakan's Crocodile Farm & Zoo when a Thai woman intent on commiting suicide jumped into the crocodile pool and swam towards the ferocious reptiles. Needless to say she was dead meat within minutes.

BELOW: wrestling a reptile at Samut Prakan's Crocodile Farm & Zoo.

Crocodile Farm & Zoo

Samut Prakan's **Crocodile Farm** **Zoo** ⓰ (daily 7am–6pm; admissio charge; tel: 0-2387 0020) is locate a short distance from the Ancie City on the old Sukhumvit Highwa (Route 3). Seeing the reptiles u close is a fascinating experience even though you know that a goo number of the crocodiles will end u as leather for handbags and wallet and the meat on restaurant tables.

Started in the 1950s with a paltr initial investment, the owner no has three farms (two in the northeas worth millions of dollars. The Samu Prakan farm has over 60,000 fresh water and saltwater local crocodile (making it the largest crocodile far in the world), as well as some Sou American caimans and Nile Rive crocodiles. It also has the world largest captive crocodile (listed the *Guinness Book of Worl Records*) – the 6-metre (20-ft) lon and 1,114-kg (2,456-lb) heavy Cha Yai. The irony of the farm is tha though the beasts are thriving in cap tivity, almost all wild Siamese an Asian species of crocodiles hav been hunted to extinction.

A highlight of the farm is the eigh daily shows (hourly 9am–4pm, rep tile feeding 4–5pm) in which han dlers enter a pond teeming wit crocodiles to wrestle them, includin placing their heads in the beasts mouths. The farm's shops sell hand bags, belts and shoes made from the skins, as well as stewed crocodi meat. Used as an ingredient in trad tional Chinese medicine, the meat purportedly a tonic and aphrodisiac

The farm also has a zoo featurin exotic birds, tigers, chimpanzee ostriches, camels and elephants, well as a Dinosaur Museum and a amusement park with rides.

Chonburi

The sprawling town of **Chonburi**, 8 km (50 miles) from Bangkok, is th

gateway to the Eastern Seaboard, and is often a brief stop for most visitors on the way to Pattaya and beyond. However, Chonburi has its fair share of attractions. Just outside of town is **Wat Buddhabat Sam Yot** (daily 8am–6pm; free). Built by an Ayutthayan king and renovated during the reign of King Chulalongkorn, this hilltop monastery holds a cast of what is supposedly the Buddha's footprint. The climb to the top of the hill is rewarded with coastal panoramas.

Near the centre of Chonburi, a gold-mosaic image of Buddha dominates the Chinese **Wat Dhamma Nimitr** (daily 8am–6pm; free). The largest image along this coastline, and the only one in the country depicting the Buddha in a boat, the 40-metre (135-ft) high statue recalls the story of the Buddha's journey to the cholera-ridden town of Pai Salee.

Bang Saen

Continuing south from Chonburi past the town of Ang Sila, the 2-km (1-mile) long beach at **Bang Saen** ⑰ springs to life each weekend as hordes of middle-class

Bangkok residents descend in cars and buses. The nearest stretch of beach from the capital, it's literally covered with a profusion of beach umbrellas and inflatable inner tubes, the surf filled with bobbing bodies dressed head-to-toe in clothes to avoid getting a tan (Thais associate tanned skin with poor manual labourers who toil in the sun).

Tucked inland near the Bang Phra Reservoir is the **Khao Khieo Open Zoo** (daily 8am–8pm; admission charge; tel: 0-3829 8187-8). Operated by Bangkok's Dusit Zoo, it exhibits deer, elephants and other animals in their natural setting. Cashing in on the current interest for nocturnal zoo observation, it also operates a Night Safari (daily 6–8pm; admission charge).

Si Racha

The next point of interest is the coastal town of **Si Racha** ⑱, home of the famous hot sauce – *nam prik si racha*. At Si Racha's waterfront restaurants fresh shrimp, crab, oyster and mussel are dipped into the thick, tangy red sauce.

If you have time to kill at Si Racha, visit the offshore rock of Ko Loi. It is connected by a bridge and supports a picturesque temple with Thai and Chinese elements. The footprint of the Buddha, cast in bronze, graces the temple, as do pictures of the Goddess of Mercy, Kuan Yin, and the Monkey God.

LEFT: *nam prik si racha*, a flaming hot sauce, comes from the town of Si Racha.
BELOW: tigers at play at the Sriracha Tiger Zoo.

TIP

The most popular beach in Koh Si Chang is Hat Tham Phang (or Collapsed Cave Beach) on the western part of the island. The privately run website www.ko-sichang.com has more info on where to stay and eat, and tips on what to do on this tiny island.

BELOW: family fun on the beach at Ko Si Chang.

The **Sriracha Tiger Zoo**, 9 km (6 miles) to the south, claims to be the largest tiger zoo in the world (daily 8am–6pm; admission charge; tel: 0-3829 6556-8; www.tigerzoo.com). The zoo has over 100 Bengal tigers in captivity – visitors can visit the nursery to hold and feed the young cubs – in addition to a menagerie of other animals, like crocodiles, elephants, ostriches and chimps. While the tigers are the star attraction in the daily circus shows, there is crocodile wrestling, an elephant show and, curiously, even pig racing.

Ko Si Chang

A short boat ride from Si Racha's shore is the small island of **Ko Si Chang** ⓳, known primarily as a coastal retreat for King Chulalongkorn (Rama V). The king built his summer palace here in the 1890s only to abandon it later on. Little remains of the palace grounds – the palace itself was dismantled and rebuilt in Bangkok as the Vimanmek Mansion (*see page 115*) – but the gardens and ponds are still recognisable. The king used to meditate in the now dilapidated Wat Atsadang.

Once a transfer point for cargo ships unloading onto smaller vessels to sail up the Chao Phraya River, the surrounding sea is always crowded with large freighters. Busy at weekends with Thai day-trippers, the island has a couple of reasonably good beaches, though certainly not Thailand's best or cleanest.

Pattaya

Pattaya ⓴ has a reputation that precedes itself, with most people having formed their opinion of this resort town even before they step foot here. Few areas in Asia have undergone such a precipitous rise to fame and subsequent plummet in popularity. This notoriety dates back to the Vietnam War when boatloads of American GIs flocked to the then quiet beaches and bars for a spot of R&R. Today, with the Thai Navy still operating from the nearby port at Satthahip, occasional battalions of visiting US marines still descend on the resort – to the delight of Pattaya's entertainment establishments. The beaches are nowhere near as

pristine as those in the southern islands, but what Pattaya lacks, it more than compensates for in other areas. There is a plethora of good-value accommodation, plenty of international restaurants, a wide range of outdoor and indoor activities, as well as several cultural attractions. Beyond that, the magnitude of Pattaya's buzzing, if salacious, nightlife is something to be experienced, or avoided, depending on your sensibility.

While still retaining a provincial Thai character, Pattaya tries very hard to invoke the ambience of a cosmopolitan playground, with glitzy malls and hotels, a pedestrianised shopping street and tree-lined beach paths. These are just a few of the pluses that have led Pattaya to proclaim itself as "The Rivieria of the Eastern Seaboard".

Located 147 km (91 miles) from Bangkok, or just over two hours by road, the seaside town has long been popular with Thai youth and families. In recent years, apart from Europeans, visitors from China, Hong Kong and Taiwan are Pattaya's most visible foreign tourists, along with sigificant numbers of Russians.

Pattaya is also a popular spot for condos and beach homes, mainly used as weekend getaways for Bangkok expats, and as winter homes for retirees from Europe. Property is being built at an astonishing rate, and improvements to infrastructure, especially international schools, is drawing in more respectable residents. But Pattaya's seedy reputation also attracts a strong criminal element, and a browse through the English-language newspaper *Pattaya Mail* reads like a police alert for Thailand's most wanted. This underworld is rarely visible to the average tourist though and Pattaya feels as safe as anywhere else in Thailand.

On the beachfront, there is the crescent-shaped **Pattaya Bay**, which is the least attractive beach, followed by the nicer 6-km (4-mile) long **Jomtien**, and, lastly, **Nakula**, with its fishing village ambience but no decent beach to speak of. Although Pattaya's aquatic respectability has been tarnished in recent years over the hygiene of its coastal waters, there has been some effort by the local municipality to improve water and sewage treatment.

Pattaya and Jomtien are good locations for watersports fans, with equipment for windsurfing, sailing, snorkelling and diving available for rent, along with jet skis, water scooters and water-skiing equipment. The brave may try parasailing, strapped into a parachute harness and towed aloft by a speedboat.

Map on page 164

Buyer beware: parasailing is a popular activity at Pattaya, but it has been plagued by several mishaps in the past.

Pattaya's land attractions

Pattaya's land-based attractions include everything from golf courses and paintball parks to go-karting, bungy jumping and parachuting. In addition, there are several sights that may be worth seeing.

At the Royal Garden Plaza is a branch of **Ripley's Believe It or**

BELOW:
Pattaya sea front.

TIP

PETA, the People for the Ethical Treatment of Animals, is up in arms over what it perceives as elephant abuse in Thailand. It estimates that 3,800 of the country's some 5,000 endangered Asian elephants are owned privately and made to perform circus tricks and give rides daily at elephant camps. See www.peta.org.

BELOW:
elephant show at Nong Nooch Village.
RIGHT:
gender-challenged performer at one of Pattaya's unsubtle cabaret shows.

Not! with its collection of bizzare oddities (daily 11am–11pm; admission charge; tel: 0-3871 0294). At Thanon Sukhumvit is the **Pattaya Elephant Village** with its elephant shows and rides (daily 8.30am–7pm; admission charge; tel: 0-3824 9818; www.elephant-village-pattaya.com).

At **Pattaya Park**, the young ones will enjoy the cable car rides as well as the exciting waterslides and whirlpools at this large water amusement facility (daily 9am–6pm; admission charge; tel: 0-3825 1201; www.pattayapark.com).

For a unique perspective on Thai temples, visit the **Sanctuary of Truth** in Nakula Soi 12, which has gradually taken shape over the past two decades (daily 8am–6pm; admission charge; tel: 0 3822 5407; www.sanctuaryoftruth.com). Dramatically perched at the seafront, work on this fantastical wooden recreation of a Khmer temple-palace still continues. The elaborate project is worth visiting even though it hasn't been completed.

About 18 km (11 miles) south of Pattaya is **Nong Nooch Village**, a complex of bungalows situated in parkland around a lake and offering a wide variety of activities, including an elephant show, a mini-zoo and an orchid nursery (daily 8am–6pm admission charge; tel: 0-3870 9360)

Pattaya's nightlife

Pattaya's nightlife clusters along o off Beach Road and the so-called Walking Street in South Pattaya There is a staggering range of bars Irish pubs, German brew houses and nightclubs, as well as an overwhelming saturation of go-go bars and massage parlours (Pattaya heaves with sex workers, both female and male). The international mix here has a definite Russian edge, so much so that at least one of the bars now features Eastern European lap dancers. The strip called Boys' Town (Pattayaland Soi 3) i where the gay crowd gathers. Pattaya also has at least three lip-synching Vegas-style cabaret shows which feature a pageant of stunning lady-boy or *katoey* (transsexuals). Tiffany's (tel 0-3842 1700; www.tiffany-show.th is especially good.

A more recent addition is the

multimedia cultural extravaganza called **Alangkarn Theatre** in Thanon Sukhumvit, which combines traditional Thai dancers and elephants with lasers and pyrotechnics (Tue–Sun 6–10pm; shows 7pm and 8.45pm; admission charge; tel: 0-3825 6007; www.alangkarnthailand.com). It is kitschy but makes for a fun (and clean) evening with dinner thrown in.

Ko Larn

Offshore of Pattaya, **Ko Larn** ㉑ – identified in brochures as Coral Island but whose name translates as Bald Island – used to be known for its coral reefs. These have long since been destroyed by fishermen using dynamite to stun fish. Yet, glass-bottomed boats still ferry visitors from the mainland to its shore, their passengers peering in vain at the dead grey coral in the hope of seeing something alive and moving. Ko Larn, however, has the wide, soft sand beaches that Pattaya lacks and it's a great place to spend a leisurely day. The shore is filled with good seafood restaurants, and there are watersports facilities for those who want to stir from their beach chairs.

Further south the coastline continues all the way through **Rayong** and beyond into **Chanthaburi**, with much of it quite undeveloped or with small hotels aimed solely at the domestic market.

Ko Samet

Located 200 km (124 miles) from Bangkok (or over three hours by road) from the capital and a short boat trip across from the fishing harbour of **Ban Phe**, the postcard perfect island of **Ko Samet** ㉒ has become a popular weekend getaway for Bangkok residents. The island is famous among Thais as the place where Sunthorn Phu (1786–1855), a flamboyantly romantic court poet, retired to compose some of his works. Born in nearby Klaeng on

the mainland, Sunthorn called the island Ko Kaeo Phisadan, or "island with sand like crushed crystal", and it was here that his best-known work *Phra Aphaimani* was set. A tale about a prince and a mermaid, a weathered statue stands as tribute on the rocky point at the end of the main beach of Hat Sai Kaew.

From a quiet poetic retreat, the island has gained popularity as a superb resort, helped by the fine white sand beaches and turquoise blue waters. Most activity here is relaxed – sunbathing, beach strolls, swimming and snorkelling – though jet skis and inflatable banana boats do occasionally interrupt the peace. The island is part of a national marine park (entry fee upon arrival at the pier), so, technically, most of the resort and bungalow operations are illegal. However, development along the coast has progressed despite the law, though as yet it remains fairly unobtrusive with simple single-storey huts and bungalows. But as a sign of things to come, a couple of resorts have upgraded their facilities, and the

Map on page 164

Spectacular undersea life awaits divers in the waters around Ko Samet.

BELOW: picture-perfect Hat Sai Kaew beach in Ko Samet.

TIP

While the regular fishing boat ferries are much cheaper, taking a speedboat across to Ko Samet (around B800) from the mainland is much faster, drops you at the bay of your choice, and usually means you escape paying the National Park entry fee of B200 per foreigner, which is pretty steep compared to the B20 that Thais are charged.

BELOW:
sunset over Ko Chang.

west coast's only beach of **Ao Phrao** has two upmarket resorts nestled into this small scenic bay.

Almost all the island's sandy beaches run down the east coast, starting near the larger northern tip with **Hat Sai Kaew** (Diamond Sand), and gradually getting less isolated as the island narrows to the southern bay of **Ao Karang**. The island is relatively small and can be walked from top-to-bottom in just a few hours, though the coastal track traverses some rocky headlands. The single road turns to bumpy dirt track fairly quickly. Hat Sai Kaew is where Thais prefer to stay, having more air-conditioned rooms and seafood restaurants, whereas foreign visitors like to nest at the bays of **Ao Phai** and **Ao Hin Khok**.

The island is best avoided on public holidays, when visitors outnumber beds, and tents are pitched on any spare patch of land. Evenings are relatively low-key; with restaurants setting up fresh seafood beach barbeques, and the restaurant-bars at small hotels like **Naga** (Ao Hin Khok and **Silver Sand** (Ao Phai) the only spots to focus on music, late night partying and the obligatory fire juggling. The mosquitoes on Ko Samet are known to be monsters, so repellent is a must.

Further down at picturesque **Ao Wong Deuan**, the scene, unfortunately, has become more akin to Pattaya with European males being pampered by their hired female "guides", raucous bars on the land and noisy jet skis on the waters. **Ao Thian** (Candlelight Beach), the next bay, is a quieter spot and the facilities are more basic.

Ko Chang

Thailand's second largest island, at 492 sq km (190 sq miles), after Phuket, **Ko Chang** ㉓ (Elephant Island) is part of a national marine park that includes some 50 islands. Around a five-hour drive from Bangkok (or 45 minutes by plane to Trat town on the mainland, then transfer by boat), the verdant island is a part of Trat province, close to the Cambodian border. The mainland pier of **Laem Ngop** in Trat is the main jumping off point to the island.

The island managed to escape rapid development of the likes of Phuket and Ko Samui, remaining a firm favourite with backpackers until recently, when the Thaksin government decided the island wasn't being exploited enough. For better or for worse, the government is now actively promoting Ko Chang as a playground for the rich. This has meant a rapid increase in hotel construction and infrastructure, including an upgrade of the road that runs along the west coast (eventually looping the island), and the opening of a domestic airport in Trat (20 minutes drive from Laem Ngop pier). Other additions in the pipeline include a large underwater aquarium and a yachting marina.

While the upsurge in middle and upper end resorts may detract from the island's untouched appeal, it does mean that there is quality, and in some instances, stylish accommodation available. This is drawing in a greater number of Thai vacationers, who, with the increase of car ferries from the mainland, seem intent on bringing their cars over to explore the island's one road.

However, don't be put off by the changes that are taking place; the island still has a relatively untouched hilly interior, mangroves and some lovely beaches. The main beaches line up along the west coast, with **Hat Sai Khao** (White Sand Beach) the most developed stretch of sand. The last vestige of Ko Chang's hippie traveller scene, **Hat Thanam** (Lonely Beach), also on the west, is no longer such a haven of solitude with plush resorts edging in.

Popular activities include snorkelling and diving, with dive trips to some of the smaller islands, kayaking, and treks to the island's numerous waterfalls. Visit the southern stilted fishing village of **Ban Bang Bao** to get an idea of how local communities are quickly dwindling away. The island's nightlife activity is still relatively subdued, with each beach having its own preferred watering hole, but Hat Sai Khao is certainly where the main energy is, with the large Sabay bar seeing the most action.

Islands near Ko Chang

If Ko Chang still feels a little too well trodden, the string of islands off the southern tip are much quieter and worth exploring. The tiny island of **Ko Wai** has limited and basic accommodation, but the vibe here is very relaxed, the views of the surrounding islands are spectacular, and there is a lovely coral reef just a short swim from the main beach. An hour by speedboat from the mainland pier of Laem Ngop, the flat island of **Ko Mak** is dense with coconut plantations and has two nice main beaches that are sparse of tourists. The island is about half way between Ko Chang and the second largest island in the archipelago, **Ko Kut**. This latter island attracts a lot of organised tour groups with most of the resorts selling all-inclusive packages. ❑

Map on page 164

Seashells from the beach at Ko Chang.

BELOW: fishing villages, such as Ban Bang Bao near the south of Ko Chang, are quickly becoming a thing of the past.

NORTH OF BANGKOK

The undisputed capital city of the Thai kingdom more than 600 years ago, Ayutthaya is a time capsule that captures the faded grandeur of that violent era. To its west lies Khao Yai National Park, a huge expanse of greenery that's also worth exploring

Map on page 164

LEFT: seated Buddha images at Wat Yai Chai Mongkhon in Ayutthaya.
BELOW: exploring the ruins of Ayutthaya on elephant is a novel option.

Even if one were ignorant of the importance and history of **Ayutthaya** , one would still be impressed by the beauty and grandeur of this city – built by 33 Ayutthayan kings over 400 years. From the ruins, it is easy to appreciate the genius of the kings who built it. Located 85 km (55 miles) north of Bangkok, Ayutthaya was laid out at the junction of three rivers: Chao Phraya, Pa Sak and Lopburi. Engineers had only to cut a canal across the loop of the Chao Phraya River to create an island. A network of canals – few of which exist today – acted as streets, and palaces and temples were erected alongside. The Europeans dubbed this city "Venice of the East", and even today, chartering a longtail boat for a trip around the natural moat is the most ambient way to see many of the riverbank ruins. As a UNESCO World Heritage site, Ayutthaya is a must visit. Several boat operators from Bangkok organise regular trips by river from the capital to the historic city, conveying them in either modern express boats or traditional teak wood barges (see page 209).

Ayutthaya's foundations

Ayutthaya was founded around 1350 by Prince U-Thong (later known as King Ramathibodi I). Thirty years later, the northern kingdom of Sukhothai was placed under Ayutthayan rule, which then spread its control to Angkor in the east, and to Pegu, in Burma, to the west. It was one of the richest and most cosmopolitan cities in Asia by the 1600s – exporting rice, animal skins and ivory – and had a population of one million, greater than that of London at the time. Merchants came from Europe, the Middle East and elsewhere in Asia to trade in its markets, with many eventually settling there.

Known in Thai as "dok bua", the lotus is commonly used as a prayer offering at Thai temples. The flower also represents Buddhism. Even though its roots are embedded in dirty mud, the bloom is never tainted with stains. Likewise, a human can overcome his earthly life filled with sin and attain enlightenment or nirvana.

Today, there is a plaque to mark the former Portuguese settlement and a memorial hall and gate to mark the Japanese settlement. Europeans wrote awed accounts of the fabulous wealth of the courts and of the 2,000 temple spires clad in gold.

Thirty-three kings left their mark on the old capital. Although in ruins, very impressive remnants of Ayutthaya's rich architectural and cultural achievements can still be seen today. As fast as it rose to greatness, it collapsed, suffering destruction so complete that it was never rebuilt. Burmese armies had been pounding on its doors for centuries before occupying it for a period in the 16th century. Siamese kings then expelled them and reasserted independence. In 1767, however, the Burmese triumphed again. In a mad rampage, they burned and looted, destroying most of the city's monuments, and enslaving, killing and scattering the population.

Within a year, Ayutthaya was nearly a ghost town; its population reduced to fewer than 10,000 inhabitants as the royal court resettled south near the mouth of the Chao Phraya River in what today is Bangkok. Even after the Burmese garrison was defeated, Ayutthaya was beyond repair, a fabled city left to crumble into dust. Today, the ruins, collectively known as the **Ayutthaya Historical Park** (daily 8am–6.30pm; admission charge) stand on the western half of the island, with the modern city of Ayutthaya on the eastern side.

By the riverside

Start close to the junction of the Nam Pa Sak and Chao Phraya rivers, passing by the imposing **Wat Phanan Choeng Ⓐ**. Records suggest that the temple was established 26 years prior to Ayutthaya's foundation in 1350. The temple houses the statue of a giant seated bronze Buddha, se

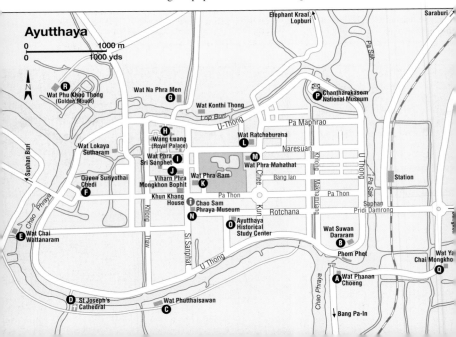

Ayutthaya

0 ____ 1000 m
0 ____ 1000 yds

N

Ⓡ Wat Phu Khao Thong (Golden Mount)

Ⓖ Wat Na Phra Men

Wat Konthi Thong

Lop Buri

U-Thong

Pa Maphrao

Ⓟ Chantharakasem National Museum

Ⓗ Wang Luang (Royal Palace)

Ⓛ Wat Ratchaburana

Naresuan

Wat Lokaya Sutharam

Ⓘ Wat Phra Sri Sanphet

Ⓜ Wat Phra Mahathat

Bang Ian

Station

Ⓙ Viharn Phra Mongkhon Bophit

Ⓚ Wat Phra Ram

Ⓕ Queen Suriyothai Chedi

Khun Khang House

ⓘ Chao Sam Phraya Museum

Pa Thon

Pa Thon

Saphan Pridi Damrong

Rotchana

Ⓝ

Ⓐ Ayutthaya Historical Study Center

Wat Suwan Dararam

Ⓔ Wat Chai Wattanaram

Ⓑ

Phom Phet

Ⓠ Wat Ya Chai Mongkho

Ⓓ St Joseph's Cathedral

Ⓒ Wat Phutthaisawan

Ⓐ Wat Phanan Choeng

Bang Pa-In

Elephant Kraal, Lopburi

Saraburi

Pa Sak

Suphan Buri

Chao Phraya

Suphan Buri

Thaw

S Sanphat

U Thong

Khlong

Khu Chee

Maharat

U Thong

Pa Sak

Chao Phraya

ightly pressed against the roof that the statue appears to be holding it up. With an unmistakably Chinese atmosphere, Wat Phanan Choeng was a favourite with the Chinese traders of the time, who prayed there before setting out on long voyages. The temple also holds the Mae Soi Dok Mak shrine, a tribute to a Chinese princess who supposedly killed herself on this spot after an icy reception from her suitor, an Ayutthayan king.

Ayutthaya was at one time surrounded by fortress walls, only portions of which remain today. One of the best-preserved sections is at **Phom Phet**, across the river from Wat Phanan Choeng. Near Phom Phet is the restored **Wat Suwan Dararam B**, built near the close of the Ayutthaya period. Destroyed by the Burmese in 1767, the temple was rebuilt by Rama I, with the wall murals dating from the reign of Rama II; later, a more unconventional (1925–35) mural depicting King Naruesan's famous battle with the Burmese was added. Still used as a temple, the *wat* is magical in the early evening as the monks chant prayers.

Upstream from Wat Phanan Choeng by the river bank is the restored **Wat Phutthaisawan C**. Seldom visited, it is quiet, and the landing is an excellent place to enjoy the river's tranquillity in the evenings. Further upstream, the **Cathedral of St Joseph D** is a Catholic reminder of the large European population that lived in the city at its prime.

Where the river bends to the north is one of Ayutthaya's most romantic ruins, **Wat Chai Wattanaram E**, erected in 1630. Modelled after the Angkor Wat complex in Cambodia, the dramatically placed temple is a photographer's favourite, especially at sunset. Restored in the 1990s, the temple was built by King Prasat Thong, and has a large central Cambodian-style *prang* fringed by several smaller *chedi*. Perched high on a pedestal in front of the ruins, a Buddha keeps solitary watch. This extraordinary temple with rows of headless Buddhas make a fine contrast to the less impressionable **Queen Suriyothai Chedi F** on the city side of river. The shrine commemorates the life of Ayutthayan

Map on page 194

The foundations of Wat Suwan Dararam's "bot" dip in the centre, in emulation of the graceful deck line of a boat. This typical Ayutthayan decoration is meant to suggest a boat that carries pious Buddhists to salvation.

LEFT: seated bronze Buddha image at Wat Phanan Choeng.
BELOW: *prang* (left) and *chedi* (right) structures at Wat Chai Wattanaram.

BELOW:
the triple *chedi* of
Wat Phra Sri Sanphet.

Queen Suriyothai, who, dressed as a male soldier and riding an elephant into battle, sacrificed herself by intervening in a duel between her husband King Maha Chakraphet and a Burmese prince. The stuff of legend, her passionate act was immortalised in the 2001 film *Suriyothai*, Thailand's most lavish and expensive movie to date.

Across a river bridge from Wang Luang stands the restored temple of **Wat Na Phra Men** . Used as a strategic attack post by the Burmese when they descended on the old city, the temple is one of Ayutthaya's only monasteries not to be ransacked. Here, a large stone Buddha is seated on a throne, a sharp contrast to the yoga position of most seated Buddhas. Found in the ruins of Wat Phra Mahathat *(see page 197)*, the statue is believed to be one of five that originally sat in the recently unearthed Dvaravati-period complex in Nakhon Pathom. The main hall or *bot* contains an Ayutthayan-style seated Buddha in regal attire, which is very unlike the more common monastic dress of Buddha representations.

Palace and surroundings

The palace of **Wang Luang** (Royal Palace) was of substantial size, if the foundations for the stables of some 100 elephants are any indication. Established by King Borommatrailokanat in the 15th century, it was later razed by the Burmese. The bricks were removed to Bangkok to build the city's defensive walls, so only remnants of the foundations survive to mark the site.

A part of the original palace grounds, next door stands the three Ceylonese-style *chedi* of **Wat Phra Sri Sanphet** . The royal temple would have held as much importance as the Temple of Emerald Buddha (Wat Phra Kaew) does in Bangkok today. Two of the *chedi* were built in 1492 by King Borommatrailokanat's son, Ramathibodi II to hold the ashes of his father and brother, while the third was added in 1540 by Ramathibodi II's son to hold the ashes of his late father. The three spires have become the archetypal image of Ayutthaya.

For two centuries after Ayutthaya's fall, a huge bronze Buddha

...at unsheltered near Wat Phra Sri Sanphet. Its flame of knowledge (on the top of its head) and one of its arms had been broken when the roof, set on fire by the Burmese, collapsed. Based on the original, a new building called **Viharn Phra Mongkhon Bophit** was built in 1956 around the restored statue. Dating back to the 15th century and over 12 metres (39 ft) tall, it is one of Thailand's largest bronze images and seems rather cramped in this sanctuary.

Across the road to the east, **Wat Phra Ram** ⓚ is one of Ayutthaya's oldest temples. Founded in 1369 by the son of Ayutthaya's founding king, Prince U-Thong, its buildings dating from the 1400s have been restored twice. Elephant gates punctuate the old walls, and the central terrace is dominated by a crumbling *prang* to which clings a gallery of stucco *naga*, *garuda* and Buddha statues. The reflection of Wat Phra Ram's *prang* shimmers in the pool that surrounds the complex, making it one of Ayutthaya's most tranquil settings.

Ayutthaya's best temples

Two of Ayutthaya's finest temples stand side by side across the lake from Wat Phra Ram. The first is **Wat Ratchaburana** ⓛ, built in 1424 by the seventh king of Ayutthaya, King Borom Rachathirat II (1424–48) as a memorial to his brothers who died as a result of a duel for the throne. Excavations during its restoration in 1957 revealed a crypt below the towering central *prang*, containing a stash of gold jewellery, Buddha images and other art objects, among them a magnificent ceremonial sword and an intricately-decorated elephant statue – all probably the property of the interred brothers. The narrow, claustrophobic and dimly-lit crypt can be accessed through a doorway in the *prang*, leading down steep stairs to some barely visible wall paintings.

The second temple, across the road, is **Wat Phra Mahathat** ⓜ (Temple of the Great Relic), once one of the most beautiful temple complexes in Ayutthaya, and one of its oldest, dating from the 1380s. The site was the focal point for religious ceremonies and reverence, and where King Ramesuan (1388–95) resided. Its glory was its huge laterite *prang*, which originally stood at 46 metres (150 ft) high. The *prang* later collapsed, but its foundations are still there surrounded by restored *chedi*. A much revered symbol here is a stone Buddha head that has been embedded in the gnarled roots of an old banyan tree. Next door, the government built a model of how the royal city may have once looked.

Ayutthaya's museums

While looters quickly made off with a great deal of Ayutthaya's glories, the remaining treasures of what was probably Thailand's greatest archaeological discovery are now kept in the **Chao Sam Phraya Museum** ⓝ to the south (Wed–Sun 9am–4pm; admission charge; tel: 0-3524 1587).

Mural detail on a royal crypt at Wat Ratchaburana.

BELOW: Buddha head overrun with gnarled roots of a banyan tree at Wat Phra Mahathat.

Map on page 194

One of the best ways of exploring the widely spread out ruins of Ayutthaya is on bicycle. These can be rented for about B50 a day at many guesthouses in Ayutthaya. If you can't be bothered to expend your energy, hire a motorised tuk tuk with driver for about B180 an hour.

BELOW: Ayutthayan jewellery on display at the museum.

Nearby is another museum, the **Ayutthaya Historical Study Centre** (Mon–Fri 9am–4.30pm, Sat–Sun 9am–5pm; admission charge; tel: 0-3524 5124). Funded by the Japanese government and on land that was once part of Ayutthaya's Japanese quarter, the modern building houses excellent hi-tech exhibits which guide visitors through 400 years of the development, trade, administration and social changes of the Ayutthayan period. There are also models of the city in its glory days, a Chinese junk and small tableaux of village life.

To the east is **Chantharakasem National Museum** , formerly known as the Chantharakasem Palace (Wed–Sun 9am–4pm; admission charge; tel: 0-3525 5124). It was originally constructed outside the city walls, close to the confluence of the rivers and the canal. King Maha Thammaracha built it for his son Prince Naresuan (later king), and it became the residence for future heirs apparent. In 1767, the Burmese destroyed the palace, but King Mongkut (Rama IV) resurrected it in the 19th century as a royal summer retreat for escaping the lowland heat. Today, it looks out on the noisiest part of modern Ayutthaya. The palace's collection isn't that impressive but it still worthy of a perusal.

To its rear is the European-style four-storey **Pisai Sayalak** tower, built by King Mongkut for stargazing. Across the street from the palace is the boat pier for trips around the island, and the night market with food stalls set up beside the water. It's a good spot to eat cheap local food and unwind at the end of the day.

Ayutthaya's outskirts

Southeast of Ayutthaya is **Wat Yai Chai Mongkhon** , originally established in the mid-1300s. In single-handed combat on an elephant's back, King Naresuan slew the crown prince of Burma in 1592. The immense *chedi*, built to match that of Wat Phu Khao Thong *(see below)*, celebrates the victory. Rows of yellow-sashed Buddha images skirt the inner walls. Also of interest is the statue of a huge white reclining Buddha, which unusually, has its eyes open.

About 2 km (1 mile) northwest of Ayutthaya is the **Wat Phu Khao Thong** , better known as the **Golden Mount**. Its 80-metre (260-ft) high *chedi* rises amidst the rice fields, its upper terraces commanding a panoramic view of the countryside. While the *wat* dates from 1387, the *chedi* was built by the Burmese after their earlier and less destructive conquest in 1569. In 1957, to mark 2,500 years of Buddhism, a 2,500-gram (5.5-lb) gold ball was mounted on top of the *chedi*, only to be stolen almost immediately after.

Bang Pa-In

About 24 km (15 miles) south of Ayutthaya is **Bang Pa-In** **㉕**, an eclectic collection of palaces and pavilions once used as a royal summer retreat (daily 8.30am–4.30pm

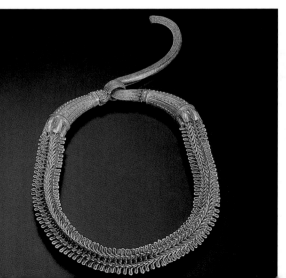

admission charge; tel: 0-3526 1673-82; www.palaces.thai.net).

The palace buildings one sees today at Bang Pa-in date from the late 19th- and early 20th-century reigns of King Chulalongkorn (Rama V) and King Vajiravudh (Rama VI), who came here to escape the mid-year rains in Bangkok. Under the instruction of Chulalongkorn, the manicured grounds contain several buildings that feature Italian baroque, European gothic, Victorian and Chinese architectural styles. Only part of the royal quarters are open to public view, providing a glimpse into Chulalongkorn's penchant for European furniture and decor.

The palace buildings of note at Bang Pa-in include the two-storey Chinese-style **Wehat Chamrun Palace** and the nearby islet with the **Withun Thatsana** observation tower, as well as the Italianate **Warophat Phiman Hall**. The 1876 Thai-style pavilion called the **Aisawan Thipphaya-at**, in the middle of the adjacent lake as one enters the grounds, is regarded as one of the finest examples of Thai architecture.

Across the river and slightly south of the palace, **Wat Niwet Thammaprawat** looks more like a Gothic Christian church than a Buddhist temple, and is topped by a spire. Worthy of an hour's stop on the way to Ayutthaya, the pleasant gardens are embellished with canals, ponds, fountains, bridges and a topiary of large elephant-shaped hedges. Coach tours to Ayutthaya stop off here in the morning, so to avoid the crowds it's better to drop by in the afternoon.

Nakhon Nayok

The most scenic route to the northeast province is Route 305, which branches off Route 1 (Friendship Highway) just north of Rangsit, 30 km (20 miles) north of Bangkok. This wide road runs northeast along a lovely canal, passing rice paddy fields and small rivers to reach the provincial capital of **Nakhon Nayok 26**, some 140 km (90 miles) from the capital. Nakhon Nayok has long been overshadowed by the more famous tourist destinations in Thailand – so much so that it is often

Maps:
Area 164
Site 194

TIP

Most day trips that visit Ayutthaya from Bangkok include Bang Pa-In as a brief stopover either on the way there or back. For more details on tours to Ayutthaya and Bang Pa-In, see page 209 of the Travel Tips section.

BELOW:
Bang Pa-In summer palace, with the Aisawan Thipphaya-at pavilion on the right.

Leech socks are useful for treks through the tropical rainforests of Wang Takrai and Khao Yai national parks.

BELOW: taking in the views at Khao Yai National Park at dawn.

referred to as "Nakhon Nowhere". In fact, nothing could be further from the truth. Thai visitors recognise its abundant attractions – natural forests, craggy gorges and tumbling waterfalls – which offer a respite from the chaos of the city.

Other than a glimpse of a typical rural centre, however, Nakhon Nayok as a town does not have much to offer. From the town centre, Route 33 heads northwest and then, after just a few kilometres, a second road leads off to the right towards two waterfalls, one of which is **Sarika Falls**. Surrounded by dense forest, the nine-tier waterfall is in full force towards the end of the rainy season from September to November. But remember to wear sturdy shoes; the stone paths are slippery.

Wang Takrai National Park

Due north is the **Wang Takrai National Park**, established by Prince Chumbhot (of Suan Pakkad Palace fame in Bangkok) in the 1950s (daily 6am–6pm; admission charge). His wife, Princess Chumbhot, a keen horticulturalist, planted many varieties of flowers and trees, including some imported species. Cultivated gardens sit among tall trees, which line both banks of the main stream flowing through the 2-km (1-mile) stretch of the 80-ha (195-acre) park. For those wishing to stay overnight in the area, bungalows are available for rent.

Just outside the park entrance, the road on the left crosses a river and continues 5 km (3 miles) to **Nang Rong Falls**, an inviting three-tiered cascade located in a steep valley.

Khao Yai National Park

Khao Yai National Park ㉗, one of Bangkok's oldest and most popular nature reserves, lies 200 km (125 miles) north of the capital (daily 6am–6pm; admission charge). It is Thailand's second largest national park at 2,168 sq km (837 sq miles) and cuts across four different provinces.

Most of Khao Yai is located 400 metres (1,312 ft) above sea level, making it a pleasant escape from the hot, humid lowlands of Central Thailand. Most people visit during the dry season from November to Feb-

ruary; be sure to bring warm clothes during this period as temperatures can plummet to as low as 10°C (50°F) at night. The rainy season is one of the best times for animal spotting, but at this time of year remember to cover up bare legs and arms as leeches are common.

Often clad in mist, Khao Yai's highest peaks lie in the east along a landform known as the Korat Plateau. **Khao Laem** (Shadow Mountain) is 1,350 metres (4,430 ft) high while **Khao Khiew** (Green Mountain) rises to a height of 1,020 metres (3,350 ft). Evergreen and deciduous trees, palms and bamboo blanket the park, and unlike much of Thailand, patches of indigenous rainforest can still be seen here. Monkeys, gibbons and langurs are the most commonly spotted wildlife. Wild, but not considered dangerous are the bears, gaurs, boars and deer that roam the reserve. Large mammals including leopards and other big cats have been sighted. Khao Yai is also home to some 200 elephants and a few tigers, but they are rarely seen. In addition, over 300 species of migrant birds have been identified, with regular sightings of great hornbills.

More than 50 km (30 miles) of marked trails criss-cross the park, most of them originally forged and still used by elephants. In several clearings, there are observation towers where you can watch animals feed. After-dark safaris by tour companies claim to spot tigers and elephants; in reality such spotlight-led trucks careering around the park are more likely to yield sightings of deer, deer, and yet more deer.

Other attractions in the park include the 20-metre (66-ft) high **Heaw Suwat** waterfall, east of the the park headquarters, and the larger three-level **Heaw Narok** waterfall, rising to a height of 150 metres (492 ft) and located further south.

Near the entrance to the park are numerous lodges and bungalows, including the recently opened 5-star Kirimaya, a boutique resort in the vein of African safaris with luxury tented villas. Other pursuits include teeing off at internationally designed golf courses and jungle rides on ATVs (All Terrain Vehicles).

Map on page 164

TIP

A common end to a day at Khao Yai National Park is a walk to Khoa Luk Chang Bat Cave at dusk to watch thousands of bats fly out as they head off in search of food.

BELOW: lush greenery at Khao Yai National Park.

Wine Country

Bacchus has discovered Thailand in the past few years, and local vineyards are beginning to grow in popularity and quality. Khao Yai's favourable climate is supposed to be ideal for grape cultivation with vineyards like PB Valley Khao Yai (tel: 0-2562 0858), GranMonte Family Vineyard (tel: 0-2653 1522) and Village Farm & Winery (tel: 0-4422 8407) getting into the act. The word from connoisseurs is that while these wines are eminently palatable, they still need considerable refinement before they will be ready to compete with international wines. Tours, tastings, and in some places, accommodation, can be arranged.

Keep an eye out for the snatch-happy monkeys that run wild around Lopburi's Prang Sam Yot. The macaques are honoured (or pacified) in late November with a feast of fruit, veggies and other foods in a spectacle known as the Monkey Buffet.

BELOW: Phra Narai Ratchanivet ruins.
RIGHT:
prang at Wat Phra Si Rattana Mahathat.

Lopburi

Lopburi lies 150 km (100 miles) north of Bangkok, a 2–3 hour drive through the fertile rice bowl of Thailand. Centuries before Lopburi became the favoured summer residence for Ayutthayan King Narai, the town was known as Lavo and had been a part of the Mon Dvaravati kingdom (6th–10th century). From the 10th–13th century, the strategic town became a Khmer outpost for the Angkor Empire; later it came under the influence of the Sukhothai kingdom to the north. Lopburi had its heyday in the mid-1600s when Ayutthaya flourished as a bustling capital city of more than one million people. It was where King Narai retreated each summer to escape from Ayutthaya's heat. When the Dutch imposed a naval blockade on Ayutthaya from the Gulf of Siam, King Narai decided to install Lopburi as a second capital, running his court from there. It was said that while his throne was in Ayutthaya his heart belonged to Lopburi; indeed after his new palace was completed he began spending more and more time here.

Wat Phra Si Rattana Mahathat

Just across from Lopburi's main train station is **Wat Phra Si Rattana Mahathat** (daily 8am–6pm; admission charge). Originally a Khmer temple with a tall stucco-decorated laterite *prang*, around the 12th-century King Narai added a large *viharn* (sermon hall) that infused elements of European and Persian architecture, the latter influence coming from the strong Persian presence at the Ayutthayan court. On the grounds are several smaller *chedi*.

Phra Narai Ratchanivet

Just northwest, the grounds of **Phra Narai Ratchaniwet** (or Lopburi Palace), built between 1665 and 1677, are enclosed by massive walls, which still dominate the centre of the modern town (daily 8am–6pm, admission charge). Built in a mélange of Thai, Khmer and European styles, the palace grounds have three sections enclosing the complex of official, ceremonial and residential buildings.

The outer grounds contained facilities for utilities and mainte-

nance. The middle section enclosed the **Chanthara Phisan Pavilion**, the first structure built by King Narai, and later restored by King Mongkut. On the south side is the **Dusit Maha Prasat Hall**, built for the audience granted by King Narai in 1685 to the French ambassador of Louis XIV. To the left is the **Phiman Mongkut Pavilion**, a three-storey colonial-style mansion. It was built in the mid-19th century by King Mongkut who wanted to restore the entire palace. The immensely thick walls and high ceilings averted the summer heat in the days before air-conditioning. The mansion, small but full of character, now functions as the **Somdet Phra Narai National Museum** (Wed–Sun 9am–4pm; tel: 0-3641 1458; admission charge). It has a display of bronze statues, Chinese and Sukhothai porcelain, coins, Buddhist fans and shadow play puppets. Some of the pieces, particularly the Ayutthaya bronze heads and Bencharong porcelain, are superb. The inner courtyard housed the private chambers of King Narai; not much is left except for the foundations and the **Suttha Sawan Pavilion**, nestled amid gardens and ponds.

Baan Vichayen

North of Phra Narai Ratchaniwet are the remains of **Baan Vichayen** palace, said to have belonged to Constantine Phaulkon (daily 8am–5pm; admission charge). Phaulkon was a Greek adventurer who arrived in Siam in 1678 to work for the English East India Company. He settled in quickly, becoming fluent in Siamese and gaining favour with King Narai, who promoted him to be his most senior minister. However, he antagonised many of the other foreign settlers in Ayutthaya, as well as Thai nobles who felt threatened by a foreigner wielding so much influence. Phaulkon forged strong ties with the French, but when more

Catholic missionary priests started arriving in Siam, local Buddhists believed the Greek was conspiring with King Louis XIV to covert Siam to Christianity. As King Narai lay on his death bed, his successors had Phaulkon arrested and executed for treason. The period after saw the Siamese court become more xenophobic towards foreign influence.

The palace buildings show strong European influences, with straight-sided walls and decorations over Western-style windows.

Prang Sam Yot

To the east are the three laterite towers of **Prang Sam Yot** (daily 8am–6pm; admission charge). This much photographed sight is of interest as the towers were originally built by the Khmers as a Hindu shrine honouring the gods Brahma, Vishnu and Shiva. It was later converted into a Buddhist shrine, incorporating a hodge-podge fusion of Brahman, Khmer and Buddhist elements that is often dubbed as the Lopburi style. Beware of the annoying monkeys at this site *(see margin picture)*. ❏

Map on page 164

A contentious figure in Thai history, Constantine Phaulkon (1648–88) was done in by a rumour that he had converted King Narai's adopted son to Christianity, and intended to eventually seek succession to the Thai throne. He was arrested and executed in 1688, barely a month after King Narai died.

BELOW: headless Buddha image at Prang Sam Yot.

TRANSPORT

GETTING THERE AND GETTING AROUND

GETTING THERE

By Air

Bangkok is not only a key gateway between Asia and the West, but also a major transportation hub for the rest of Southeast Asia.

Bangkok International Airport (tel: 0-2535 1111; www.airportthai.co.th), known locally as **Don Muang**, is located about 30 km (19 miles) north of the city centre. It takes about 30 to 45 minutes to get to or from the airport, depending on traffic. Serving over 80 airlines and 25 million passengers annually, the airport is running well above capacity, leading to frequent delays at immigration.

Construction of the **New Bangkok International Airport** (NBIA) or **Suvarnabhumi Airport** (www.bangkokairport.org) has been delayed; it is now re-scheduled to open in 2006. The new airport is located on the eastern outskirts of the city in Samut Prakan province, 30 km (19 miles) from the city. No news is yet available on what will happen to the existing airport once the new one opens.

Don Muang has two terminals that serve international carriers, while internal flights are handled by the domestic terminal.

Terminal 1: arrivals, tel: 0-2535 1149 or 2535 1310; departures, tel: 0-2535 1254 or 2535 1123.
Terminal 2: arrivals, tel: 0-2535 1301; departures, tel: 0-2535 1386.
Domestic Terminal: arrivals, tel: 0-2535 1253 or 2535 1305; departures, tel: 0-2535 1192 or 2535 1277.

All the terminals are linked by a free shuttle bus that runs every 15 minutes between 5am to 11pm. Terminals 1 and 2 are also joined by an elevated walkway.

Although nowhere near the standards of other Asian super airports like Changi in Singapore or Chek Lap Kok in Hong Kong, Don Muang airport is still a clean and fairly pleasant place to while away the time before boarding your flight. It has several bars, restaurants, shops, a duty-free shop and a unique golf course located between the runways.

All terminals have an adequate supply of ATMs in addition to currency exchange booths offering similar rates to banks in town. The Tourism Authority of Thailand (TAT) has counters in the Arrival Hall of Terminal 1 and 2 which provide useful information *(see page 236).*

Note: When taking an international flight out of Don Muang, keep B500 for the Passenger Service Charge (airport tax).

Flying from UK and US

Even if you don't plan to spend anytime in Thailand, Bangkok is the most convenient (and sometimes the only) way to transfer to neighbouring countries like Laos, Cambodia and Burma. The recent introduction of low-cost airlines to Thailand means that domestic and regional flights to nearby destinations like Malaysia and Singapore have become incredibly cheap – if booked in advance. These low-cost airlines have also started flights to emerging destinations in Southern China.

Passengers from UK and Europe can fly direct to Bangkok in about 12 hours, though it is considerably cheaper to take an airline that makes a stopover in either Europe, the Middle East or Asia. Airlines that fly non-stop include British Airways, Qantas, THAI and EVA Airways. Many travellers to Australia and New Zealand choose Bangkok as a transit point on their journey.

Travel time from the US is considerably longer. Flying from the West Coast usually takes around 18 hours (not including transit time) and involves a connection in North Asia – Japan, Korea, or Taiwan; the East Coast route via Europe takes about 19 hours in the air. THAI Airways operates the only direct flight from New York to Bangkok.

By Rail

The **State Railway of Thailand** (www.railway.co.th) operates trains that are clean, cheap and reliable. There are two entry points by rail into Thailand, both from Malaysia to the south. The more popular is the daily train that leaves Butterworth near Penang at 2.10pm for Hat Yai (south Thailand) and arrives in Bangkok's Hualamphong Station at 10.05am the next morning. Trains leave Hualamphong Station at 2.45pm for the return journey to Malaysia.

If you like to travel in style and prefer not to fly, then plump for the **Eastern & Oriental Express** (www.orient-express.com). Travelling several times a month between Singapore, Kuala Lumpur and Bangkok, the 22-carriage train is very expensive but very elegant.

By Road

Malaysia provides the main road access into Thailand, with crossings near Betong and Sungai Kolok. From Laos, it is possible to cross from Vientiane into Nong Khai in northeast Thailand by using the Friendship Bridge across the Mekong River. From Cambodia, the most commonly used border crossing is from Poipet which connects to Aranyaprathet, east of Bangkok.

GETTING AROUND

From the Airport

The journey from Bangkok International Airport (Don Muang) to the city centre takes between 30 and 45 minutes, depending on traffic conditions (the worst period is between 4 and 9pm). Negotiating an exit from the Arrival Hall, however, can be more daunting. If you are on a business trip, you'll understand why it is the norm for Bangkok hosts to deploy a personal greeter and escort. Emerging in the Arrival Hall, you may be harangued by touts both inside and outside the barriers. Never volunteer your name or destination to these people. If you already have a reservation at a hotel, a representative will have your name written on a sign, or at least a sign bearing the name of your hotel. If you haven't made prior arrangements, use one of the following modes to get to the city.

By Taxi

Operating 24 hours daily, all taxis officially serving the airport are air-conditioned and metered. The taxi stand is located just outside the Arrival Hall of all terminals. Join the queue and tell the person at the desk where you want to go to. A receipt will be issued, with the licence plate number of the taxi and your destination in Thai written on it. Make sure the driver turns on the meter. At the end of your trip, pay what is on the meter plus a B50 airport surcharge. If the driver uses the expressway to speed up the journey, he will ask for your approval first. If you agree, you have to pay the toll fees of B60 (B20 for the first toll booth and B40 for the second). Depending on traffic, an average fare from the airport to the city centre is around B200–250 (excluding toll fees and airport surcharge).

UNLICENSED TAXIS

Some locals in the know avoid paying the B50 surcharge by going upstairs to the departure area, where taxis drop off passengers on their way to flights. These drivers are not supposed to pick up new fares, but they will be on the lookout and will take a long time to pull away from the curb. However, there has been a couple of incidents where tourists taking unsanctioned taxis have been literally taken for a ride, so this isn't recommended for the sake of saving a few baht.

By Limousine

There are two limousine companies operating at the airport. **Airport Associate Co Ltd** (the counter sign reads Airport Taxi; tel: 0-2982 4900; www.airporttaxi thai.com) in Terminal 1 and 2 operates a limousine service (using Mercedes Benz sedans) to the city for B800, an 8-seater van for B1,100; limousine to Pattaya for B2,400 and 8-seater van for B2,700.
Thai Airways Limos (tel: 0-2535 2801; www.thaiairways.com) in Terminal 1 and 2 has a premium service (using Mercedes Benz E220) to downtown for B1,500, or a regular service (Mercedes Benz 200) for B800.

By Airport Bus

If you don't have much luggage, consider using the Airport Bus, which passes the main hotel locations in downtown Bangkok. Tickets can be bought on the bus or at the booths outside the Arrival Hall of all terminals. Buses depart every 15 minutes from 5.30am to 12.30am, and the fare is B100 per person.
Airport Bus Routes:
   A-1 to Thanon Charoen Krung (New Road) via Pratunam, Thanon Ratchadamri, Thanon Silom and Thanon Surawong.
   A-2 to Sanam Luang (Banglamphu) via Thanon Phayathai and Thanon Lan Luang.
   A-3 to Soi Thonglor (Sukhumvit 55) via Thanon Petchaburi and Thanon Sukhumvit.
   A-4 to Hualamphong Railway Station via Thanon Ploenchit, Thanon Rama, Thanon Phayathai and Thanon Rama IV.

By Train

Another fast and cheap way into the city is to take the train. Don Muang train station is just across the street from the airport (look for the Amari Hotel entrance sign in the Arrival Hall of Terminal 1). It takes roughly 40 minutes to

Hualamphong station, not far from Chinatown. There are trains at 15 to 30 minute intervals from 5am–8pm. The fare is B5 for ordinary trains and B21 for express trains. One drawback: if you have heavy luggage, dragging it over the pedestrian bridge and onto the train may not be easy.

Orientation

Located in the heart of Thailand's fertile Central Plains delta, Bangkok is a flat, low-lying sprawl of a city. Settled near the mouth of the Chao Phraya River (Thailand's longest), Bangkok sits almost in the middle of the country's north-south length. The river runs between Thonburi to its west and Bangkok to its east.

The city spreads out haphazardly across 1,565 sq km (602 sq miles), with the earliest foundations set on the artificial island of Rattanakosin, the city's historic centre. These days it is difficult to pinpoint the city centre; some consider the Lak Muang (City Pillar) as the historic heart, while the younger generation regards the central shopping district around the busy Ratchaprarop intersection as the city's nucleus.

Given the heat and humidity, Bangkok is not a city for walkers, although small sections in Chinatown and Rattanakosin are manageable. To avoid getting stuck in traffic, especially during peak hours, use the elevated Skytrain or the underground metro to get around. Another option is boat travel on the river and canals, a delightful way of commuting and and sightseeing at the same time.

Public Transport

Skytrain (BTS)

BTS Tourist Information Centre: tel: 0-2617 7340; Hotline: tel: 0-2617 6000; www.bts.co.th.

The Bangkok Transit System's (BTS) elevated train service, better known as Skytrain, which started

---

STREET NAME CONFUSION

Note that **Wireless Road** (a street full of embassies and hotels) is more commonly known by its Thai name, **Thanon Withayu**. Similarly, **Sathorn Road**, a main thoroughfare divided into north and south which runs between Lumphini Park and the river, is often referred to as **Sathorn Nua** (north) and **Sathorn Tai** (south). With no standard translated English spellings for the Thai language, it is common to find a street or area spelt with several variants and broken or joined syllables. Skytrain station names often differ from the street sign spelling, so Chidlom district becomes Chit Lom station, Thanon Asoke becomes Asok station, and Soi Thonglor becomes Thong Lo.

---

operations in December 1999, is the perfect way of beating the city's traffic-congested streets.

It consists of two lines. The **Sukhumvit Line** runs from Mo Chit station in the north to On Nut in the southeast. The **Silom Line** runs from National Stadium, near Siam Square, south to Saphan Taksin station near Tha Sathorn (or Central Pier). Both lines intersect at Siam station.

The Skytrain is fast, frequent and clean, but suffers from overcrowding during peak hours. Accessibility too is problem for the disabled and aged as there aren't enough escalators or lifts.

Trains operate from 6am to midnight (3 minutes peak; 5 minutes off-peak). Single-trip fares vary according to distance, starting at B10 and rising to B40. Self-service ticket machines are found at all station concourses. Tourists may find it more useful to buy the unlimited ride 1-Day Pass (B100) or the 30-Day Adult Pass (which comes in three types: B250, 10 rides, B300, 15 rides and 540, 30 rides) – all available at station counters.

BTS Tourist Information Centres are found on the concourse levels of Siam, Nana, and Saphan Taksin stations (daily 8am–8pm).

Metro (MRT or Subway)

Customer Relations Centre: tel: 0-2624 5200; www.mrta.co.th or www.bangkokmetro.co.th.

Bangkok's metro line was launched in July 2004 by the Mass Rapid Transit Authority (MRTA). The line has 18 stations, stretching 20 km (12 miles) between Bang Sue in the northern suburbs of Bangkok and the city's main railway station, Hualamphong, at the edge of Chinatown. The line hasn't secured a popular name among the city's commuters yet, and is variously referred to as the MRT, metro or subway.

Three of its stations – Silom, Sukhumvit and Chatuchak Park – are interchanges, and passengers can transfer to the Skytrain network at these points. More lines and extensions to both rail networks are planned.

Operating from 6am to midnight, the air-conditioned trains are frequent with never more than a few minutes wait (2–4 minutes peak, 4–6 minutes off-peak). Fares start at B14, increasing B2 every station, with a maximum fare of B36.

Unlike the Skytrain, coin-sized plastic tokens are used instead of cards, with self-service ticket machines at all stations. Also available at station counters are the unlimited ride 1-Day Pass (B150), 3-Day Pass (B300) and the stored-value Adult Card (B200 – includes B50 deposit).

Taxis

Taxis are abundant in Bangkok. They are metered, air-conditioned, inexpensive, and comfortably seat 3 to 4 persons.

Taxis can be hailed anywhere along the streets; there are no taxi stands on the streets but you can expect to find them outside hotels and the shopping centres. Metered taxis are recognisable y the sign on their roofs with an luminated red light above the ashboard indicating whether it's ree or not. Taxis mostly come in old colour combinations of red nd blue, or green and yellow, /ith some newer ones completely bright orange or green.

The flag fall charge is B35; fter the first 2 km (1 mile), the eter goes up by B4–B5.50 every ilometre, depending on distance avelled. If stuck in traffic a small er minute surcharge kicks in. If our journey crosses town, ask ne driver to take the expressway. he network of elevated two-lane oads can cut the journey by half. he toll fare of B20 to B50 is ven to the driver at the payment ooth, not at the end of the trip.

Seatbelts must be worn in the ont seat. A 10 percent tip is uggested; it's not a must.

Before starting any journey, neck whether the meter has een reset and turned on; many rivers conveniently "forget" to o so and charge a lump sum at ne end of the journey. On seeing foreign face, some drivers may uote a flat fee instead of using ne meter. Unless you're desper-te, don't use these. Fares, how-ver, can be negotiated for longer stances outside Bangkok: for stance, Pattaya (B1,200), Koh amet (B1,500) or Hua Hin 1,500–2,000).

Drivers don't speak much nglish, but all know the loca-ons of major hotels. Foreigners equently mangle Thai pronunci-ion, so it's a good idea to have destination written on a piece paper. Thai drivers can usually nderstand street addresses ritten in capital Roman letters. else, get someone to write the estination in Thai.

These taxi companies will pick for a B20 surcharge.

am Taxi
l: 1661 (hotline)

lie Taxi
l: 01 846 2014
w.julietaxi.com

ghtly more expensive than etered taxis, Julie's drivers

are polite and speak some English. It has a range of car and minivan options.

Tuk-Tuk

Tuk-tuk are the brightly coloured three-wheeled taxis whose name comes from the incessant noise their two-stroke engines make. Although synonymous with Bangkok, tuk-tuks have been increasingly losing favour with both locals and visitors. The heat, pollution and noise have become too overwhelming for most passengers. Few tuk-tuk drivers speak English, so make sure your destination is written down in Thai. Unless you bargain hard, tuk-tuk fares are rarely lower than metered taxi fares. Some tuk-tuk drivers loitering around hotels will offer a B10 fare "anywhere". The hitch is that you must stop at a tourist shop where the driver will get petrol coupons in exchange for bringing you in.

Expect to pay B30 to B50 for short journeys of a few blocks or around 15 minutes or less, and B50 to B100 for longer journeys. A B100 ride should get you a half hour ride across most parts of downtown. Be sure to negotiate the fare beforehand.

TRANSPORT ETIQUETTE

While it is quite normal to let an elderly person stand up on a crowded bus or train, legions of locals are quick to vacate their seats if a young child steps aboard. On buses, the two seats nearest the door must be vacated for monks; female passengers should not sit next to a monk on any kind of transport. Queuing is still a novel concept to most Thais, so don't expect any orderly behaviour at bus stops or boat piers. At rush hours on the Skytrain and metro, you often see commuters standing in front of train doors blocking passengers from getting off while squeezing to get in.

Motorcycle Taxis

Motorcycle taxi stands (with young men in fluorescent orange vests) are clustered at the mouth of most *soi* (small sidestreets) and beside any busy intersection or building entrance. The drivers are experts at weaving through Bangkok's heavy traffic and may cut travel time in half, but do so at your own peril.

Hire only a driver who provides a passenger helmet. Fares mut be negotiated beforehand, and they are rarely lower than taxi fares for the same distance travelled. Hold on tight and keep your knees tucked in as drivers tend to weave precariously in and out of traffic. Their goal is to get you there as quickly, not as safely, as possible. If the driver is going too fast, ask him to slow down in Thai: *cha-cha*. Females wearing skirts must also cope with sitting side-saddle.

A short distance, like the length of a street, will cost B10 to B20, with longer rides at B50 to B100. During rush hour (8–10am and 4–6pm), prices are higher. A B80 to B100 ride should get you a half-hour trip across most parts of downtown.

Buses

Bus transport in Bangkok is very cheap but can also be equally arduous, time-consuming and confusing. Municipal and private operators all come under the charge of the **Bangkok Mass Transit Authority** (tel: 0-2246 0973; www.bmta.co.th).

With little English signage and few conductors or drivers speaking English, boarding the right bus is an exercise in frustration. Public buses come in four varieties: microbus, Euro II bus, air-conditioned and non-air-conditioned "ordinary". In theory, the routes of both air-conditioned and ordinary buses appear on standard bus maps. In practice, however, routes change and many air-con bus routes have been added in recent years, rendering bus maps out of date.

Boats

The most common waterborne transport is the **Chao Phraya River Express Boat** (tel: 0-2623 6001), which travels from Tha Nonthaburi pier in the north and ends at Tha Wat Rachasingkhon near Krungthep Bridge in the south. Boats run every 15 minutes from 6am to 6.40pm, and stop at different piers according to the coloured flag on top of the boat. Yellow flag boats are fastest and do not stop at many piers, while the orange flag and no flag boats stop at most of the marked river piers. If unsure check before boarding. Fares cost B6 to B15 and are purchased from the conductor on board or at some pier counters.

The **Chao Phraya Tourist Boat** (www.chaophrayaboat.co.th) operates daily from 9.30am to 3.30pm and costs B75. After 3.30pm, you can use the ticket on the regular express boats. A useful commentary is provided on board, along with a small guidebook and a bottle of water. The route begins at Tha Sathorn (Central Pier) and travels upriver to Tha Phra Arthit, stopping at 10 major piers along the way. Boats leave every 30 minutes and you can get off at any pier and pick up another boat later on this hop-on-and-off service.

The **cross-river ferries** are used for getting from one side of the river to the other. They can be boarded at the jetties that also service the Chao Phraya River Express. Costing B2 per journey, cross-river ferries operate from 5am to 10pm or later.

The **longtail boat taxi** plies the narrow inner canals and are used for carrying passengers from the centre of town to the outlying districts. Many of the piers are located near traffic bridges; remember to stand back from the pier's edge to avoid being splashed by foul-smelling water. Choose a seat away from the spray, and be sure to tell the conductor your destination as boats do not stop otherwise. Tickets cost B5 to B10, depending on distance, with services operating roughly every 10 minutes until 6 to 7pm. While there are routes serving Thonburi's canals and Bangkok's outskirts, tourists will probably only use the main downtown artery of Khlong Saen Saep, which starts from from Tha Saphan Phanfah near Wat Saket, into the heart of downtown and beyond to Bang Kapi. It's useful if going to Jim Thompson's House, Siam Centre and the Thanon Ploenchit malls to Thanon Withayu all the way to Thonglor and Ekamai.

If you wish to explore the canals of Thonburi or Nonthaburi, private **longtail boat rentals** can be negotiated from most of the river's main piers. A 90-minute to 2-hour tour will take you into the quieter canal communities. Ask which route the boat will take and what will be seen along the way, trying to avoid major tourist attractions that can be visited independently later. Ask to pull up and get out if anything interests you. Negotiate rates beforehand; an hour-long trip will cost B400 to B500, rising to B900 for 2 hours. The price is for the entire boat, which seats up to 16 people, not per person.

Rental Cars

Driving in Bangkok is not recommended. Road surfaces can be appalling, signs are confusing and, apart from the main roads, most side streets (*soi*) are very narrow and difficult to negotiate. While Thais drive on the left side, traffic flow on main arteries often changes direction at certain times of the day, with little indication as to when. Local drivers can be inconsiderate and aggressive, and drink driving is on the rise. Unless guided to a specific mall or tourist attraction, parking can be a real headache, and in the evenings gangs patrol popular parking streets extorting money to make sure your car is safely watched. If still intent on hiring a car, then an international driver's licence is necessary. A small car can be hired for around B1,500 a day including insurance.

Avis, 2/12 Thanon Withayu, tel: 0-2255 5300-4; and Bangkok International Airport Bldg 2, tel: 0-2535 4031-2, 2535 3004-5.
Hertz, Soi 71, Thanon Sukhumvit, tel: 0-2711 0574-8.

By Road

Thailand has a good road system with over 50,000 km (31,000 miles) of motorways and more being built every year. Road signs are in both Thai and English and you should have no difficulty following a map. An international driver's licence is required.

Unfortunately, driving on a narrow but busy road can be a terrifying experience with right-of-way determined by size. It is not unusual for a bus to overtake a truck despite the fact that the oncoming lane is filled with vehicles. A safer option is to hire a car or a van with driver for trips outside of Bangkok. The rates probably won't be more than B1,500 per day. Try **J&J Car Rent**, tel: 0-2531 2262, or **Krungthai Car Rent**, tel: 0-2291 8888; www.krungthai.co.th.

You can get to several places outside the city, like Pattaya and Hua Hin, by simply flagging a taxi along a Bangkok street or booking one beforehand. Be sure to negotiate a flat rate before boarding; don't use the meter.

By Air

Thai Airways International (THAI) services a domestic network, with as many as 14 daily services to the more popular destination like Chiang Mai and Phuket. **Bangkok Airways** is the second largest domestic operator. In recent years, a slew of low-cost airlines have entered the market flying to the main tourism centres in Thailand.

Air Andaman: 16th Floor, Sirirat Building, Thanon Rama IV, tel: 0-229 9555; www.airandaman.com.

Air Asia: Bangkok International Airport, tel: 0-2215 9999; www.airasia.com.

Bangkok Airways: 99 Thanon Vibhavadi Rangsit, tel: 0-2265 5555; www.bangkokair.com.

Nok Air: Bangkok International Airport, tel: 1318 (Call Centre); www.nokair.com.

Orient Thai Airlines: 919/298 Thanon Silom, tel: 0-2267 3210-9; www.orient-thai.com.

PB Air: 16th Floor, UBC II Building, 591 Thanon Sukhumvit, Soi 33, tel: 0-2261 0220; www.pbair.com.

Phuket Air: Lumpihni Tower, 1168 Thanon Rama IV, tel: 0-2679 8999; www.phuketairlines.com.

Thai Airways International: 89 Thanon Vibhavadi Rangsit, tel: 0-2628 2000; www.thaiairways.com.

By Bus

Air-conditioned buses service many destinations in Thailand. VIP coaches with extra leg room are the best for overnight journeys. All buses are operated by the **Transport Company Ltd** (www.transport.co.th), with terminals at the following locations:

Eastern (Ekamai) Bus Terminal: Thanon Sukhumvit opposite Soi 63, tel: 0-2391 8907.

Northern and Northeastern Bus Terminal: Thanon Khampaeng-phet 2, Northern: tel: 0-2936 2841-8 ext. 311; Northeastern: tel: 0-2936 2841-8 ext. 601.

Southern Bus Terminal: Thanon Boromrat Chonnani, Thonburi, tel: 0-2435 1200.

By Train

State Railway of Thailand (tel: 1690; www.railway.co.th) operates three principal routes – north, northeast and south – from **Hualamphong Railway Station** at Thanon Rama 4, tel: 0-2233 0341-8. Express and rapid services on the main lines offer first-class air-conditioned or second-class fan-cooled carriages

with sleeping cabins or berths. In addition, some trains depart from **Bangkok Noi Station**, tel: 0-2411 3102, in Thonburi.

West
Kanchanaburi

By Train: Take the Southern line from Bangkok Noi Station to Kanchanaburi or to the Kwai River Bridge (via Nakhon Pathom). Two departures daily (7.45am and 1.45pm) for the 2½-hour journey.

By Bus: Although Kanchanaburi is west of Bangkok, buses leave from the Southern Bus Terminal every 20 minutes from 5am to 10.30pm. Journey time: 2½ hours.

South
Hua Hin

By Taxi: A taxi ride from Bangkok to Hua Hin, taking 3 hours, can be negotiated for a flat rate of B1,500–2,000.

By Train: There are 12 daily departures between 7.45am to 10.50pm for Petchaburi and Hua Hin from Hualamphong Station. The journey takes around 4 hours.

By Bus: Buses leave from the Southern Bus Terminal every 30 minutes between 6.30am and 5.30pm, stopping at Petchaburi and Cha-am before Hua Hin. The journey takes around 3½ hours.

Eastern Seaboard
Pattaya

By Taxi: A taxi ride from Bangkok to Pattaya can be negotiated for a flat rate of B1,200. The ride will take 90 minutes.

By Bus: Buses leave every 40 minutes from 5am to 11pm from the Eastern Bus Terminal. The journey takes around 2 hours.

Ko Samet

By Taxi: A Bangkok taxi will make the 3-hour ride to Ban Phe pier in Rayong province for a flat rate of B1,500.

By Bus: Buses leave every hour from 5am to 9pm from Eastern Bus Terminal to Ban Phe pier. Travel time is 3½ hours.

By Boat: Once in Ban Phe pier,

fishing boats leave every 30 minutes to an hour (or when there are enough passengers) for the short ride to Na Dan pier on Ko Samet. If there are a few of you, hiring a speedboat is much faster (B800–B1,000).

Ko Chang

By Bus: Buses leave from Eastern Bus Terminal to Trat every 90 minutes between 6am to 11.30pm. The journey is around 5 to 6 hours. From Trat bus station take a *songthaew* (van with bench seats) to Laem Ngop pier.

By Air: Bangkok Airways has two flights a day to Trat airport. From the airport take a 20-minute taxi ride to Laem Ngop pier.

By Boat: From Laem Ngop pier, ferries leave nine times a day between 7am and 5pm for Tha Dan Kao pier in Ko Chang.

North
Ayutthaya

By Train: There are 8 daily departures from Hualamphong from 6am to 9.30pm. The journey takes around 2 hours.

By Bus: Buses leave every 30 minutes from the Northern Bus Terminal between 5am and 8pm. The journey takes 90 minutes.

By Boat: Several companies operate cruises to Ayutthaya; some return the same day, while others take a leisurely 2 to 3 days. The **Chao Phraya Express Boat** (tel: 0-2623 6001) operates a day trip every Sunday at 8am. The **River Sun Cruise** travels one way by coach and returns by boat (tel: 2266 9125; www.riversuncruise.com). More expensive is the overnight trip on board a restored teakwood barge by **Manohra Cruises** (tel: 0-2477 0770; www.manohracruises.com).

Lopburi

By Train: 11 daily departures from Hualamphong from 6am to 9.30pm. Journey time: 3 hours.

By Bus: Buses leave every 30 minutes from the Northern Bus Terminal between 5am and 8pm. The journey takes about 3 hours.

A CCOMMODATION

WHAT YOU NEED TO KNOW
BEFORE YOU BOOK THE ROOM

Choosing a Hotel

Hotels in Bangkok, with their first-rate service and complete range of facilities, are among the best in the world. The Oriental hotel has consistently been rated as one of the world's best, but nipping at its heels are the top-class Peninsula, Shangri-La and Sukhothai hotels. Many moderately-priced hotels in Bangkok would be considered first class in Europe, and even budget hotels will invariably have a swimming pool and at least one decent food outlet.

Those on a tight budget will find numerous guesthouses offering decent accommodation. Once of primary interest only to backpackers because of their sparse facilities, many have been upgraded to include air-conditioning and en-suite bathrooms. These are mainly found along Thanon Khao San, Soi Ngam Duphli (off Thanon Rama IV) and Sukhumvit Soi 1–15.

Hotel Areas

Downtown Bangkok has the largest proliferation of hotels and is most convenient for getting around on the Skytrain and underground metro system. The prime shopping and entertainment area around Pathumwan and Pratunam is home to several mid- to upper-end hotels. The area around Chitlom and Ploenchit has some high-end chains, as do Silom and Sathorn, with the latter street featuring a cache of chic designer hotels. Heading east along the Skytrain line, Thanon Sukhumvit has the largest proliferation of mid-range accommodation in the city and is packed with dining, drinking and shopping options.

Further down to the river, near Saphan Taksin Skytrain station (close to Tha Sathorn river ferry pier), is where many of city's most luxurious hotels are located on both sides of the river. Aside from riverside panoramas, the proximity to the river gives access to daytime transportation on the express boats. The area north along the river to Chinatown makes for an interesting cultural experience though hotels tend to be faceless and traffic is horrendous.

Access to the Rattanakosin and the Old City area is easiest from the backpacking enclave of Thanon Khao San and Banglamphu; while accommodation is principally budget guesthouses, new mid-range boutique inns and lodges are starting to appear.

Prices & Bookings

Thailand has plenty of good value accommodation, but as more hotels and guesthouses upgrade to compete with new boutique and design-oriented hotels, prices have begun to creep up.

Advanced booking is advised and it's worth checking rates again before arrival as there are high, low and peak seasons. Many hotels have recently started adding compulsory gala dinners to the room rate at Christmas and New Year, some of which charge exorbitant prices in return for what is little more than a fancy buffet dinner.

Many mid- and top-end hotels charge a standard 7 percent VAT and 10 percent service to the bill, so check to see if the rate includes this or not. Increasingly, Internet bookings are cheaper than the walk-in or call-up rate. Either check the hotel website directly or online hotel sites, like **Thailand Hotels Association** (www.thaihotels.org).

Be sure to book a room in advance during Christmas, New Year and Chinese New Year holidays, and if staying outside Bangkok, during Songkran in mid-April.

PRICE CATEGORIES

Price catagories for a double room without breakfast and taxes:
Luxury = over B8,000
Expensive = B4,000–8,000
Moderate = B2,000–4,000
Budget = under B2,000

TRANSPORT

ACCOMMODATION

ACTIVITIES

A – Z

LANGUAGE

THONBURI

HOTELS

Luxury

Peninsula
33 Thanon Charoennakorn
Tel: 0-2861 2888
www.peninsula.com
Standing proud on the
opposite bank of the
Chao Phraya River, this
distinguished hotel has
the city's nicest river
views. It has earned the
reputation of being one
of the world's best

hotels. Stylishly contem-
porary but still Asian in
character, it has some of
the best dining options in
the city, plus impeccable
service. Free shuttle
boats (6am–midnight)
take you to Tha Sathorn
pier opposite and the
Saphan Taksin Skytrain
station. (370 rooms)

Expensive

**Bangkok Marriott
Resort & Spa**
257 Thanon Charoennakorn
Tel: 0-2476 0022

www.marriotthotels.com
With verdant grounds
and a wonderfully
landscaped pool that
fronts the river, this
resort truly feels like an
escape from the
frenetic city. Located on
the Thonburi side, it is
quite far down the river
almost to the edge of
town, but the free 15-
minute boat shuttle to
Tha Sathorn pier is part
of the novelty of staying
here. Self-contained,
with six restaurants,
three bars, a Mandara

spa and a full-service
business centre, the
hotel is also part of a
shopping complex. Its
Riverside Terrace hosts
nightly Thai dance per-
formances along with
dinner. (413 rooms)

OLD CITY AND DUSIT

HOTELS

Expensive

Chakrabongse Villa
96 Thanon Maharaj
Tel: 0-2225 0139
www.thaivillas.com
This is a wonderfully
unique find in this area,
and indeed the city. A
beautifully ambient
early 20th-century
historic residence with
tropical gardens, a
swimming pool and
superb views of Wat
Arun directly opposite.
There are few places in
the capital where you
can walk to the Grand
Palace. There are only
three atmospheric villas
each decked out in tra-
ditional Thai style;
Garden Suite, Riverview
and Thai House.
(3 rooms)

Moderate

Buddy Lodge
265 Thanon Khao San
Tel: 0-2629 4477
www.buddylodge.com
This is Khao San's best
hotel, with a rooftop
swimming pool and
even a well-run spa. The
original Buddy guest-
house was located
further down the strip
but the owner's busi-
ness has taken off in
recent years and he
now owns half of Khao
San's entertainment.
From the outside, the
brick building resem-
bles a European munici-
pal hall, albeit with a
MacDonalds down-
stairs. (76 rooms)

Budget

D&D Inn
68-70 Thanon Khao San
Tel: 0-2629 0526-8

www.khaosanby.com
Right in the middle of
Khao San, this is more
of a hotel than guest-
house, with a rooftop
swimming pool, bar and
an open *sala* for tradi-
tional massage. Rooms
are well equipped with
bathrooms, air-condi-
tioning, TV, fridge and
IDD phone. (200 rooms)
Khao San Palace
139 Thanon Khao San
Tel: 0-2282 0578
Among the better guest-
houses here, this is just
off Khao San down a
small alley. Stay in the
newer annexe as the
original section looks
far more tatty. Clean
rooms (some have
windows), en-suite
showers, air-con and TV.
(200 rooms)
My House
37 Soi Chanasongkram
Tel: 0-2282 9263-4
The rooms at this guest-

house are fairly basic
but still comfortable.
The main draw is its
location in a quieter
lane away from Khao
San with Wat Chana-
songkram right across.
The restaurant-TV room-
lounge area out front is
a great place to perch
and watch life pass by
in backpacker land. (60
rooms)
Peachy Guest House
10 Thanon Phra Athit
Tel: 0-2281 6471, 2281 6659
A real atmospheric find,
this good-value guest-
house occupies a con-
verted school with more

old world charm than most of Khao San's concrete box digs. The rooms are basic but comfortable with most rooms facing the pleasant garden. A short walk to Khao San, but still removed from all the mayhem. (57 rooms)

Royal Hotel
2 Thanon Ratchadamnoen Klang
Tel: 0-2222 9111-26
Fax: 0-2224 2083
One of Bangkok's oldest hotels, its location just across from Sanam Luang and a short stroll to the Grand Palace make it convenient for sightseeing. But it's

short on character and busy traffic arteries surround on both sides. (300 rooms)

Sawasdee Bangkok Inn
126/2 Thanon Khaosan
Tel: 0-2280 1251
www.sawasdee-hotels.com
Located on a quieter side street of Khao San, this is part of a growing

chain of mid-range guesthouses run by the Sawasdee group. The decor is an attempt on old Siam, and the rooms are clean with most having air-conditioning, hot shower and TV. Restaurant, bar, Internet access and travel agent on site. (90 rooms)

CHINATOWN

HOTELS

Budget

Bangkok Centre
328 Thanon Rama IV
Tel: 0-2238 4848
www.bangkokcentrehotel.com
Bit of an odd location, tucked just back off busy Thanon Rama IV

and on the outskirts of Chinatown, but within walking distance of the city's main rail terminus of Hualamphong. Smartly furnished air-conditioned rooms with TV, plus a swimming pool and three restaurants. (245 rooms)

Riverview Guesthouse
768 Soi Phanurangsi, Thanon Songwad

Tel: 0-2235 8501
Fax: 0-2237 5428
There's not much cheap accommodation in the city that has river views, but this one does. While basic inside, it's the location and ambience of Chinatown that is the draw. The better rooms have air-con, fridge and TV, and there's a top floor

restaurant. Finding this place is an adventure in itself. (45 rooms)

PATHUMWAN AND PRATUNAM

HOTELS

Luxury

Conrad Bangkok
All Seasons Place
87 Thanon Withayu
Tel: 0-2690 9999
www.conradhotels.com
Oozing class, this top-notch hotel is located near embassies and next door to the All Seasons Place shopping centre. Spacious and contemporary rooms are furnished with Thai silk and woods, with data ports for high-speed Internet access and large bathrooms with rainshowers. Excellent choice of eateries, as well as chic Plus 87 nightclub/restaurant

and jazzy Diplomat Bar. The serviced apartments here are a better deal for longer stays. Ploenchit Skytrain station is a 6-minute walk away. (392 rooms)

Four Seasons
155 Thanon Ratchadamri
Tel: 0-2251 6127
www.fourseasons.com/bangkok
From the magnificent lobby decorated with Thai murals by renowned local artists and handpainted silk ceilings to the city's best hotel swimming pool and highest staff-to-guest ratio, the Four Seasons is consistently excellent. And it has won the accolades and awards to prove it. Located right in the heart of downtown, a few minutes' walk from

Ratchadamri Skytrain station. The staff's attention to detail helps set it apart from other luxury establishments. Some of the city's best dining outlets are found here. (256 rooms)

Grand Hyatt Erawan
494 Thanon Ratchadamri
Tel: 0-2254 1234
www.bangkok.grand.hyatt.com
It's all about location, and the Hyatt is smack in the middle of downtown shopping and beside the Erawan Shrine. Refurbished a few years ago to a tasteful contemporary style, and still looking good. The basement restaurant-nightclub Spasso is a favourite nightlife spot. Connected to the Erawan Bangkok mall and a short walk to Chit

Lom Skytrain station. Excellent range of eateries. (387 rooms)

InterContinental Bangkok
973 Thanon Ploenchit
Tel: 0-2656 0444
www.ichotelsgroup.com
In the centre of downtown shopping and linked to Chit Lom Skytrain station and Gaysorn Plaza, this glass-fronted tower has all the standard luxury and business facilities you'd expect from this

otel chain. Spacious
ooms come with
ternet access and
D players. A roof-top
wimming pool has fine
ews of the cityscape.
81 rooms)

Expensive

mari Watergate
7 Thanon Petchaburi
l: 0-2653 9000-19
ww.amari.com/watergate
nother good hotel
nder the Amari man-
gement, this large
wer isn't very ambient
ut has excellent facili-
es, including a great
m, and the basement
mericana pub Henry J.
eans. Located just
cross from Pratunam
arket and the main
hopping district around
entral World Plaza. The
osest Skytrain station
Chit Lom but unfortu-
ately not within walking
stance. (563 rooms)

ai Lert Park Bangkok
Thanon Witthayu
l: 0-2253 0123
ww.swissotel.com
et within a beautiful
arden estate with a
ndscaped pool and
gging track, this hotel
located in Bangkok's
entral business and

diplomatic district.
Recently upgraded as
part of the Raffles International hotel group, it
now sports a more
contemporary edge; the
new hip lounge bar, Syn,
affirms its new look.
The curious should
check out the mass of
phallic totems at Nai
Lert Shrine at the hotel
rear beside the canal.
(338 rooms)

Moderate

Asia
296 Thanon Phayathai
Tel: 0-2215 0808
www.asiahotel.co.th
Joined to Ratchathewi
Skytrain station, this
hotel is not particularly
attractive from the out-
side but is well main-
tained within. Many
facilities on site, possibly to offset the noisy
non-stop traffic at its
doors. (604 rooms)

Baiyoke Sky Hotel
Baiyoke Tower II,
222 Thanon Ratchaparop
Tel: 0-2656 3000
www.baiyokehotel.com
Located in Thailand's
tallest building, the main
draw to the Sky Hotel is
its views and well-priced,
if unspectacular rooms.

A short distance from
the downtown shopping
district, the hotel restaurants aren't particularly
good, but at least the
taxi driver won't have a
problem finding your
hotel. (591 rooms)

Novotel Bangkok
Siam Square Soi 6
Tel: 0-2255 6888
www.accorhotels-asia.com
Tailored toward the
business traveller, this
hotel is tucked among
the maze of shopping
alleys in Siam Square
and is a short walk to
the main Siam Skytrain
station. At least four
cinemas are nearby,
and its massive base-
ment entertainment
complex, Concept CM2,
is a frequently packed
local nightspot.
(429 rooms)

Pathumwan Princess
444 Thanon Phayathai
Tel: 0-2216 3700
www.pprincess.com
This centrally located
hotel is joined to huge
and chaotic MBK mall,
making it convenient for
shopping. With a large
saltwater pool and gym,
plus comfortable
rooms, it is a family-
friendly place. Popular
with Asian tourists, it

offers good value for
money. (446 rooms)

Budget

A-One Inn
13–15 Soi Kasemsan 1
Thanon Rama I
Tel: 0-2215 3029
www.aoneinn.com
Located beside Siam
Square and with easy
access to National Sta-
dium Skytrain station,
the narrow lane it's
located on has become
a downtown bargain
hotel area, with lots of
options nearby. Offers
spacious rooms with all
the mod-cons and
friendly service. With its
many repeat visitors it
can be difficult to get a
room. (20 rooms)

Bangkok Palace
1091 New Thanon Petchaburi
Tel: 0-2253 0510
www.bangkokpalace.com
Located almost on the
expressway leading to
the Bangkok Airport,
this hotel has recently
refurbished rooms.
Within walking distance
of Pratunam Market and
the IT mall of Panthip
Plaza, the rooms are
typical for its class, but
it has a wide range of
facilities. (660 rooms)

BANGRAK AND SILOM

HOTELS

Luxury

anyan Tree Bangkok
/100 Thanon Sathorn Tai
l: 0-2679 1200
ww.banyantree.com
ocated in the precari-
usly narrow Thai Wah
Tower, Bangkok's
econd-tallest hotel

features large and
stylishly appointed
luxury suites with sepa-
rate living and working
areas, plus in-room
faxes and high-speed
Internet connection.
The Vertigo restaurant
on the roof of the tower
and the pampering
Banyan Tree Spa (the
tallest in the city) offer
spectacular views of the
capital. (216 suites)

Dusit Thani
946 Thanon Rama IV
Tel: 0-2236 9999
www.dusit.com
The first high-rise hotel
in Bangkok, this classic
example of fashionably
retro 1950s architecture
is located across
Lumphini Park, near
Silom's many corporate
headquarters and the
nightlife of Patpong, with
both the Skytrain and

metro stations right out-
side its doors. It has lost
out a little to younger
and more stylish hotels,

but recent refurbishments will ensure its place among Bangkok's top digs. Enjoy a pampering masage at its exquisite Devarana Spa and then float on to its top-floor D'Sens restaurant for impeccable French dining. Its Thai and Vietnamese restaurants are highly rated too. (532 rooms)

The Metropolitan
27 Thanon Sathorn Tai
Tel: 0-2625 3333
www.metropolitan.como.bz
Sister to the famous Metropolitan in London, Bangkok's younger twin is set among a row of top-end hotels on Thanon Sathorn. Its drink and dine outlets, Cy'an and Met Bar, are among the city's top nightspots. This designer hotel is cool and contemporary, blending East and West minimalist chic in equal measures. 10-minute walk to Saladaeng Skytrain and Lumphini metro stations. (171 rooms)

The Oriental
48 Oriental Avenue
Tel: 0-2659 9000
www.mandarinoriental.com
Part of the history of East meeting West, the Oriental, established in 1876, is the most famous hotel in Bangkok, and well known for its attention to detail and grand setting along the Chao Phraya River. The Authors' Wing is the only original surviving structure and its lounge is a delight to sit in and enjoy afternoon tea, while Le Normandie French restaurant is the only place in town that requires a tie for dinner. (395 rooms)

The Sukhothai
13/3 Thanon South Sathorn
Tel: 0-2344 8888
www.sukhothai.com
This stunning contemporary Asian hotel draws architectural inspiration from the ancient Thai kingdom of the same name. One of the top five hotels in Bangkok and indeed the world, this class act has well appointed rooms, the excellent La Scala Italian restaurant and chic Zuk Bar, tropical gardens and a reflecting pool. An 8-minute walk to Lumphini metro station. (219 rooms)

Expensive

Meritus Suites State Tower
1055/111 Thanon Silom
Tel: 0-2624 9999
www.meritus-hotels.com
Located on the corner of Thanon Silom and Thanon Charoen Krung, these are deluxe serviced apartments within the gigantic State Tower. Just a 10-minute walk to Saphan Taksin Skytrain station, State Tower has established itself as a Bangkok landmark, with its opulent 64th-floor rooftop dine and drink outlets collectively called The Dome. The contemporary Asian-style apartments have 1-3 bedrooms with kitchenettes. (462 suites)

Montien
54 Thanon Surawong
Tel: 0-2233 7060-69
www.montien.com
This 1960s throwback is one of the city's oldest modern hotels, and located just a stone's throw from the naughty nightlife of Patpong and

Soi Thaniya. A short walk to Saladaeng Skytrain station, this grand airy hotel with three restaurants retains a strong Thai atmosphere. (475 rooms)

Royal Orchid Sheraton
2 Captain Bush Lane
Tel: 0-2266 0123
www.royalorchidsheraton.com
Located along the prime riverfront stretch, this hotel was once considered one of the best but this is no longer the case. Most guests these days are package tourists who are herded onto and off tour buses. Still, the hotel does offer some great views of the Chao Phraya River. (740 rooms)

Shangri-La
89 Soi Wat Suan Plu
Tel: 0-2236 7777
www.shangri-la.com
With recently refurbished guest rooms all facing the river, the Shangri-La is the largest of the five-star hotels located along the river, and consistently ranks among the top five hotels in Asia. Just a 5-minute walk to Saphan Taksin Skytrain station, its restaurants, particularly Angelini's and Maenam Terrace, are top notch. (850 rooms)

Moderate

Holiday Inn Silom
981 Thanon Silom
Tel: 0-2238 4300
www.bangkok-silom.holiday-inn.com
Located right next to the Jewellery Trade Centre towards the river end of Thanon Silom, this large comfortable hotel is of much higher quality than its Holiday Inn branding would suggest.

Only an 8-minute walk to Surasak Skytrain station. (725 rooms)

Sofitel Silom
188 Thanon Silom
Tel: 0-2238 1991
www.accorhotels-asia.com
This 38-storey hotel located in the quieter part of busy Thanon Silom is only a short walk to Chong Nonsi Skytrain station. Stylishly refurbished to a chic modern style, it caters to both business and leisure travellers. Wine bar V9 has stunning city views from its 37th-floor perch while one floor above is the excellent Shanghai 38 Chinese restaurant. (454 rooms)

Tarntawan Place
119/5-10 Thanon Surawong
Tel: 0-2238 2620-39
www.tarntawan.com
While Silom received all the commercial action, Surawong was left behind to some degree making the area less hectic, but still right in the middle of all the nightlife action. Located off a quiet *soi*, this small hotel has only one restaurant and bar, but who cares when in this neck of the woods. Excellent service and multilingual staff. Only 10-minute walk to Saladaeng Skytrain station. (80 rooms)

Budget

La Residence
173/8-9 Thanon Surawong
Tel: 0-2266 5400
e-mail: residence@loxinfo.co.th
A small boutique hotel short distance yet far enough away from the pulse of Patpong, with funky individually decorated rooms of different

TRANSPORT

zes. All the expected
om amenities and a
endly vibe, though
iort on trimmings like
swimming pool.
6 rooms)
alaysia Hotel
Soi Ngam Duphli
anon Rama IV
: 0-2679 7127
w.malaysiahotelbkk.com
is is an old Bangkok

favourite and is known
particularly for its late
night coffee shop that
attracts a bizarre mix of
late night drinkers and
working girls. Whether
this deters a stay
depends on your sensi-
bilities, but the 1970s
hotel is reasonable
value and located
among Ngam Duphli's

backpacking infrastruc-
ture. A 10-minute walk
to Lumphini metro
station. (120 rooms)
Tower Inn
533 Thanon Silom
Tel: 0-2237 8300
www.towerinn.com
Halfway down Thanon
Silom towards the river
and within walking dis-
tance of Chong Nonsi

Skytrain station, this well
located high-rise hotel
has large executive
rooms, a swimming pool
and a great rooftop ter-
race with views. There is
also a business centre
and function rooms, a
lobby bar and restaurant.
Sees a lot of repeat visitors, and offers monthly
rates too. (175 rooms)

ACCOMMODATION

SUKHUMVIT

HOTELS

Luxury

**eraton Grande
ikhumvit**
) Thanon Sukhumvit
0-2653 0333
w.starwood.com/bangkok
eat location on
anon Sukhumvit, not
from Benjakitti Park
d walking distance to
ok Skytrain and
ikhumvit metro sta-
ns. First-rate facilities
d services, with extra
ge rooms containing
the bells and whistles
J expect from a five-
ar property. Beautifully
idscaped swimming
ol and excellent spa,
is three good restau-
its, nightclub and
shly-rated Living Room
e jazz bar. (445 rooms)

xpensive

iari Boulevard
inon Sukhumvit Soi 7
0-2255 2930, 2255 2940
w.amari.com/boulevard
rt of the large Amari
ain, this small but
mfortable hotel has
eresting city panora-
is and a 6th-floor
imming pool. With a
ess centre, several

restaurants, and garden
terraces attached to
some of the deluxe
rooms, this is an oasis
in a raucous tourist
area full of street mar-
kets, noodle shops and
girly bars. A 5-minute
walk to Nana Skytrain
station. (309 rooms)
Davis
88 Thanon Sukhumvit Soi 24
Tel: 0-2260 8000
www.davisbangkok.net
Boutique hotel with a
melange of style influ-
ences. Different theme
rooms all with the latest
mod cons, plus 10 large
villas with their own
swimming pools. There
is a rooftop pool with
bar, Club 88, a live
music joint. Adjoining
Camp Davis is a com-
plex of more bars and
restaurants. Phrom
Pong Skytrain station is
12-minute walk. (164
rooms and 10 villas)
Emporium Suites
622 Thanon Sukhumvit Soi 24
Tel: 0-2664 9999
www.emporiumsuites.com
Conveniently located
above the swish Empo-
rium shopping mall and
connected to Phrom
Phong Skytrain station,
this stylish serviced
apartment complex
offers a range of accom-
modation, from studio

and 1-bedroom suites to
3-bedroom apartments.
Full range of in-house
facilities. Ideal for short
or long-term guests.
Some rooms have nice
views of Benjasiri Park
next door. (378 rooms)
JW Marriott
4 Thanon Sukhumvit Soi 2
Tel: 0-2656 7700
www.marriotthotels.com
This classy five-star
hotel is just around the
corner from Bangkok's
risque Nana Entertain-
ment Plaza, but don't
let that deter you. All
the usual amenities,
plus Bangkok's largest
fitness centre, efficient
business facilities and
spacious well-appointed
rooms make this one of
the best hotels in the
city. It has some of the
city's best dining in the
New York Steakhouse.
Convenient location
between the Nana and
Ploenchit Skytrain
stations. (441 rooms)
**Westin Grande
Sukhumvit**
259 Thanon Sukhumvit Soi 19
Tel: 0-2651 1000
www.westin.com/bangkok
Directly opposite the
Sheraton Grande and
just beside Robinson
department store. This
large modern hotel has
newly refurbished rooms

and several dining out-
lets, while the upper level
Horizons Sky Lounge
offers karaoke crooning
with a view. Short walk to
Asok Skytrain and
Sukhumvit metro
stations. (364 rooms)

Moderate

Landmark
138 Thanon Sukhumvit
Tel: 0-2254 0404
www.landmarkbangkok.com
Good location on
Thanon Sukhumvit, with
easy access to Nana
Skytrain station and the
girly bar enclave of Nana
Entertainment Plaza.
Geared toward the
business traveller with a
busy business centre.
Attached to a plaza with
a few shops and
eateries. (415 rooms)
Novotel Lotus
1 Thanon Sukhumvit Soi 33
Tel: 0-2261 0111
www.accorhotels-asia.com
Very tasteful guest
rooms in yet another

ACTIVITIES

A – Z

LANGUAGE

Accor hotel in Bangkok. The hotel lobby is very Zen-like with its lotus pond. Café plus two restaurants. Close to shopping and Phrom Phong Skytrain station. (213 rooms)

President Park
95 Thanon Sukhumvit Soi 24
Tel: 0-2661 1000
www.presidentpark.com
Great for families or business executives, this large modern apartment complex is tastefully designed. Its spacious studios come with kitchenettes. Three large pools and full leisure facilities in its Capitol Club. Daily, weekly and monthly rates available, with breakfast included. Walking distance to Phrom Phong Skytrain station. (228 rooms)

Rembrandt
19 Thanon Sukhumvit Soi 18
Tel: 0-2261 7100
www.rembrandtbkk.com
Decked out in European

opulence, this good-value hotel is at the end of a lane that has mushroomed with shops, eateries and traditional massage services. A free *tuk-tuk* shuttle to the end of the *soi* and then a short walk to Asok Skytrain and Sukhumvit metro stations. The hotel claims to have the city's best Mexican dining at Senor Pico's and best Indian at Rang Mahal. (407 rooms)

Windsor Suites
8-10 Thanon Sukhumvit Soi 20
Tel: 0-2258 0160-65
www.windsorsuiteshotel.com
This former Embassy Suites property is still an all-suite hotel but without the high price tag. Located on a relatively quiet *soi* off a major artery, the rooms are nice but not exceptional. Situated between Asok and Phrom Phong Skytrain stations. (460 rooms)

Ambassador
171 Thanon Sukhumvit
Tel: 0-2254 0444
www.amtel.co.th
A large hotel tucked back slightly from the main thoroughfare and only a 5-minute walk to Nana Skytrain station. While not particularly attractive, it has a wide range of restaurants on site. (832 rooms)

Atlanta
78 Thanon Sukhumvit Soi 2
Tel: 0-2252 1650
www.theatlantahotel.bizland.com
A Sukhumvit legend, this 1950s throwback is rich in character and is a real treasure among faceless modern structures. The first hotel along Sukhumvit, it has a pool set in landscaped gardens and a great Thai restaurant. Quirky extras include Thai dancing on weekends, and classic roll-top desks in the rooms. Closest Skytrain

station is Ploenchit. Its website alone is worth browsing. (49 rooms)

Miami
2 Thanon Sukhumvit Soi 13
Tel: 0-2253 0369
Fax: 0-2253 1266
Florida this certainly isn't, and this retro hotel has definitely seen better days but there's still an appeal that lingers from the time it was an R&R haven in the 1970s. In the middle of Sukhumvit's main action, the nearest Skytrain station is Nana. (100 rooms)

Sukhumvit 11
1/33 Thanon Sukhumvit Soi 11
Tel: 0-2253 5927
www.suk11.com
Located in the heart of the Sukhumvit area and within walking distance of Nana Skytrain station this personable, family-run Thai-style guesthouse is a gem of a find and often booked out. (67 rooms, ensuite and with shared facilities)

BANGKOK'S SURROUNDING S

HOTELS

Kanchanaburi

Moderate

Comsaed River Kwai Resort
18/9 Moo 5 Ladya
Kanchanaburi Province
Tel: 0-3463 1443-9
www.comsaedriverkwai.com
Many of the area's better hotels lie some way outside the main town in the rolling countryside, which is also true of the Comsaed. With manicured lawns, wooden

bridges and riverine views, it is geared up for outdoor activities with canoeing and biking. (91 rooms)

Budget
River Kwai Jungle Rafts
Office: River Kwae Floatel Co. Ltd., 133/14 Thanon Ratchaprarop, Bangkok
Tel: 0-2642 6361-2
www.riverkwaifloatel.com
For a truly unique Kanchanaburi experience, stay on a floating jungle raft. Eat and drink on the adjoining floating restaurant and bar. Aside from the quaint lodgings, you can also swim or fish in the

river, ride elephants and visit nearby ethnic tribal villages. (100 rooms)

Hua Hin

Luxury

Chiva-Som
73/4 Thanon Petchkasem
Hua Hin
Tel: 0-3253 6536
www.chivasom.com
Meaning "Haven Of Life", Chiva-Som resort harnesses the best of traditional Thai style with a relaxing location beside Hua Hin's sandy beach. Superb range of spa facilities, including a unique flotation tank,

Pilates room and gym, water therapy suites, indoor and outdoor pools and tai-chi pavilion. Diet is an integral part of healthy living here, and the resort's

athumwan & Pratunam

qua
our Seasons Hotel
55 Thanon Ratchadamri
el: 0-2250 1000
ip martinis while enjoying the
ophisticated ambience of this
osy atrium bar. Set within a
alm-lined tropical garden with
sh pond, bridges and fountains.

acchus
0/6-7 Soi Ruam Rudee
el: 0-2650 8986
ocated in the pleasant restau-
ant enclave of Ruam Rudee
illage, this elegant four-storey
ine bar sees a steady flow of
reative and media types.

yn Bar
ai Lert Park Hotel
Thanon Withayu
el: 0-2253 0123
his former hotel lobby bar has
een dramatically transformed
to a retro-chic cocktail lounge
y a New York designer. The stun-
ng all-female bartenders mix up
ome devilishly tasty cocktails
nd flavoured martinis.

ilom & Bangrak

stil
tate Tower, Thanon Silom
el: 0-2624 9555
ww.thedomebkk.com
ising taller than any of the city's
ther nightspots, Distil is part of
e opulent Dome complex on
e 64th floor of State Tower
uilding. Choose your poison
om the 2,000-bottle wine cellar,
back on the outdoor balcony
ofa cushions and enjoy the
pectacular panorama.

u'u
e Ascott, Thanon Sathorn
el: 0-2676 6677
is Singapore import is a class
ct, combining a sophisticated
ocktail lounge, restaurant and
art gallery.

et Bar
etropolitan Hotel
anon Sathorn
el: 0-2625 3399
qualling the panache of
ndon's trendy Met Bar,
angkok's younger sister at the
etropolitan is one of the capi-

NIGHTLIFE LISTINGS

Two good sources of information about what's going on are
the *Bangkok Post* and *The
Nation*, both of which have
daily listing sections and
weekend entertainment sup-
plements. Other sources of
information include magazines
like *BK*, *Metro* and *Bangkok
Dining & Entertainment*.

tal's most exclusive yet friendly
nightspots. The dark, intimate
members-only bar has resident
and visiting international DJs.

V9
Sofitel Silom Hotel, Thanon Silom
Tel: 0-2238 1991
With awesome views from the
37th floor, this stylish wine bar
and restaurant is a fine spot to
sip great-value wines. There's a
wine shop in front, while inside
fusion cuisine is served.

Zuk Bar
The Sukhothai Hotel
Thanon Sathorn
Tel: 0-2287 0222
The chic lobby level lounge bar
induces relaxation from the
moment you recline onto its
plush sofas. Overlooking tranquil
ponds and embellished with
Asian antiques, the DJs here
mixes chilled-out grooves.

Sukhumvit

Bar Baska
82/38 Soi 22 Ekkamai (Soi 63)
Thanon Sukhumvit
Tel: 0-711 4748-9
Balinese-inspired bar and eatery
set among lush tropical gardens
and placid pools. Inside, the
decor is just as atmospheric with
comfy sofas and chairs to sit on
and soak up the chilled dance
beats spun by local DJs.

Bull's Head
Soi 33/1 Thanon Sukhumvit
Tel: 0-2259 4444
www.greatbritishpub.com
Tucked away on a street predomi-
nated by Japanese eateries, this
is as English and authentic as a
pub can be. Attracts a loyal group

---

of regular expats who enjoy
monthly visits by international
comedians at the hugely popular
Punchline Comedy Club.

Chi
H1, Soi Thonglor, Sukhumvit 55
Tel: 0-2381 7587
Nestled in the boutique mall H1,
Chi's interior is an artistic
melange of styles, hardly surprising considering the owner used to
work for Sotheby's auction
house. The bar and restaurant
starts as an eatery and switches
focus later in the night to drinking, with DJs providing a cool mix
of dance music.

Dubliner
Thanon Sukhumvit, cnr of
Washington Square (Soi 22)
Tel: 0-2204 1841-2
Arguably the best of Bangkok's
Irish pubs, this friendly place is
decorated with Gaelic bric-a-brac.
Pool tables, a big TV screen
showing major sporting events,
plus live music at weekends.

Face
Soi 38 Thanon Sukhumvit
Tel: 0-2713 6048-9
www.facebars.com
Part of a small exclusive chain of
restaurants and bars (branches
in Shanghai and Jakarta), Face
Bar is part of a Thai villa complex
housing Indian and Thai restaurants. Expect a mellow vibe in
this beautiful, antique-filled
lounge bar.

Londoner Brew Pub
Soi 33 Thanon Sukhumvit
Tel: 0-2261 0238-40
The main draw at this cavernous
basement pub is the micro-
brewed beer; comes in several
varieties including a slightly dark
English-style creamy bitter. Shows
major sports competitions on TV.

To Die For
H1, Soi Thonglor, Sukhumvit 55
Tel: 0-2381-4714
Designed by local fashion house
Greyhound, this funky voguish
bar is one among a clutch of chi
chi entertainment and shopping
outlets at the boutique H1 mall.
Also operates as a restaurant at
mealtimes serving Modern
European cuisine.

TRANSPORT

ACCOMMODATION

ACTIVITIES

A – Z

LANGUAGE

Live Jazz Venues

Bamboo Bar
Oriental Hotel, 48 Oriental Avenue
Tel: 0-2236 0400
The perfect place to soak up jazz, this cosy, intimate bar with its wicker furnishings evokes a by-gone era. The band is almost on your lap as they play laidback jazz classics and back up distin-guished guest singers.

Brown Sugar
231/20 Thanon Sarasin
Tel: 0-2250 0103
Long established and intimate two-floor jazz bar. The music here is more mod than traditional; expect stellar performances by talented musicians.

Diplomat
Conrad Hotel, 87 Thanon Withayu
Tel: 0-2690 9999
One of the city's best bars, this is a great warm-up spot for the hotel's other hip hang out spot, the 87 Plus club. Sit at the circular bartop in the middle and be mes-merised by seductive jazz singers.

Living Room
Sheraton Grande Sukhumvit
205 Thanon Sukhumvit
Tel: 0-2653 0333
Top-notch jazz has become syn-onymous with this open-plan cir-cular bar. Has a reputation for pulling in respected jazz musi-cians and singers from overseas.

Saxophone Pub & Restaurant
3/8 Thanon Phayathai
Victory Monument
Tel: 0-2246 5472
As much a monument as its neighbouring war memorial, this lively venue has been packing them in for close to two decades. This two-floor bar hosts great res-ident bands (at least two a night), who get the whole place jumping and jiving to excellent jazz as well as R&B, soul and funk.

Other Live Music Venues

Ad Makers
51/51 Soi Langsuan
Thanon Ploenchit
Tel: 0-2652 0168
The faux rustic charm and Thai menu obviously appeal but the two acts playing pop and rock covers are the main draws. One of the city's liveliest nightspots.

Mojos
10/20 Soi 33 Thanon Sukhumvit
Tel: 0-2260 8429
One of the few blues clubs in the capital. Strictly for aficionados.

Senor Pico
Rembrandt Hotel
Soi 18 Thanon Sukhumvit
Tel: 0-2261 7100
This colourful open-plan cantina cooks up some wicked Latin treats, complimented nightly by the energetic Latin band.

Spasso
Grand Hyatt Erawan
Thanon Ratchadamri
Tel: 0-2254 1234
Throbbing with revellers every night, this basement club and Ital-ian eatery is one of the capital's most consistently popular hotel-based nightspots. International bands play mainly pop, soul and R & B covers. Note: lots of working girls cruise the dance floor.

Kathoey Cabaret

For a night of campy fun, see a Vegas-style lip-synching show performed by transsexuals known as ladyboy or *kathoey*.

Calypso
Asia Hotel, Thanon Phayathai
Tel: 0-2216 8937-8
www.calypsocabaret.com
One of the city's best cabarets is staged twice nightly at 8.15pm and 9.45pm. Tickets cost B1,000, including one free drink.

Mambo
Washington Square
Thanon Sukhumvit
Tel: 0-2259 5715
Daily shows at 8.30pm and 10pm; tickets cost B800.

Gay Venues

Babylon
34 Soi Nantha, Sathorn Soi 1
Tel: 0-2679 7984/5
www.babylonbangkok.com
Not quite a nightlife spot but leg-endary as a gay meeting place.
An all-in-one complex housing accommodation, gym, sauna, massage, restaurant and café, plus an ongoing schedule of entertainment and party nights.

Balcony
86-88 Soi 4 Thanon Silom
Tel: 0-2235 5891
www.balconypub.com
Longstanding lively bar with a mixed party crowd who spill out onto the street.

Boy's Bangkok
894/11-13 Soi Pratuchai
Duangthawee Plaza
Tel: 0-2237 2006
One of the better gay go-go bars on a strip of several such places.

DJ Station
8/6-8 Silom Soi 2
Tel: 0-2266 4029
www.dj-station.com
Bangkok's most popular gay club, packed throughout the night. The atmosphere is electric and patrons often dress outra-geously. On theme nights, the crowd wears costumes that would rival Sydney's Mardi Gras.

Dick's Café
894/7-8 Soi Pratuchai
Duangthawee Plaza
Tel: 0-2637 0078
www.dickscafe.com
Taped jazz music and paintings by local artists create a mellow mood. A great place to unwind.

Freemans
60/18-21 Thanon Silom
Tel: 0-2632 8033
www.freemanclub.com
A three-storey club with an indus-trial-like setting where techno-pop rules. A young, trendy crowd arrives by midnight to catch the *kathoey* (transsexual) cabaret, con-sidered one of the best in town.

SHOPPING

General

Shopping has become an obses-sive leisure activity for many Bangkokians. Teenagers, young couples and families love mean-dering through the new mega alls and department stores. These air-conditioned sanitised nvironments provide an escape om the city's heat and smog. At eekends, the human traffic at he most popular places can ecome almost unbearable.

While imported items can be ery expensive, visitors will find ocally and regionally produced roducts incredibly cheap. For ore details on this subject, see hapter on **Shopping** (page 57).

Most malls and department tores open daily from 10am– 0pm. Every Jun–July and ec–Jan, major department tores and malls take part in the hailand Grand Sales, though any also offer a 5 percent tourist scount year round – simply show your passport at the point of purchase. Alternatively, you can claim the 7 percent VAT refund at the airport (see text box below).

Shopping Malls

Central World Plaza
Thanon Ratchadamri
Tel: 0-2255 9400
Mammoth mall with spacious walkways propped either end by Zen and Isetan department stores. Also an ice-skating rink, cineplex and numerous restaurants.

Emporium
622 Thanon Sukhumvit (cnr Soi 24)
Tel: 0-2664 8000-9
Mainly brand-name stores, as well as more practical electronics shops. Exotic Thai section on the 4th floor has a tasteful selection of handicrafts and jewellery, plus an excellent food court.

Erawan Bangkok
494 Thanon Ploenchit
Tel: 0-2250 777
www.erawanbangkok.com
Behind the famous Erawan shrine and connected to the Grand Hyatt Erawan, this new boutique mall has both chic shops and eateries and a wellness/beauty centre.

Gaysorn Plaza
999 Thanon Ploenchit
Tel: 0-2656 1149
Another glitzy mall for high fashion labels, while the 3rd floor has elegant home decor shops.

H1
998 Soi Thonglor, Sukhumvit 55
Tel: 0-2714 9578
A clutch of low-rise trendy shops, restaurants and bars on the road that is becoming Bangkok's home to boutique malls.

Mahboonkrong (MBK)
444 Thanon Phayathai
Tel: 0-2217 9119
This is one of Bangkok's most popular malls, hence the heaving crowds. In general, most goods and services are aimed at Thai youth or bargain-hunting tourists. Great for cheap leather luggage, jewellery and electronics. Bargain hard here. Also has restaurants, a large food court and a multi-screen cinema on the top floor.

Playground
818 Soi Thonglor, Sukhumvit 55
Tel: 0-2714 7888
www.playgroundstore.co.th
Bangkok's newest boutique mall combines art installations with home decor and fashion shops, trendy cafés, and a cooking school.

Siam Centre
989 Thanon Rama I
Tel: 0-2658 1000
Several tailors and numerous clothing stores, a video game arcade for kids and home decor stores. Restaurants and sports zone on the top floor.

Siam Discovery Centre
989 Thanon Rama I
Tel: 0-2658 1000
Packed with imported brands with prices to match. On the 5th floor is Kids World, a whole floor devoted to youngsters. Top floor has the Grand EGV cinema.

Siam Paragon
Thanon Rama I
www.siamparagon.co.th
Massive new mall next to Siam Centre. It's so huge you could get literally lost in here. Mainly hip and upmarket goods.

Shopping Areas

Chinatown: With its maze of crowded streets, Chinatown will give you a taste of old Bangkok without the tacky tourist goods. Open-air markets and small family businesses predominate, selling everything from antiques and jewellery to fresh produce and even car parts.

Thanon Khao San: Young backpackers have been descending on Khao San for years so expect to find shops specialising in tattooing, hair-braiding, funky clothes, used books and silver jewellery plus a good assortment of travel agents and Internet cafés. A unique place.

Pratunam: Around the corner from Central World Plaza is a bargain-hunter's paradise with shops selling cheap clothes, shoes, handicrafts and cosmetics at Nai Lert and Pratunam markets. Nearby Panthip Plaza has computers, and bootleg software, games and DVDs.

Thanon Rama 1 and Thanon Ploenchit area: Gaysorn Plaza and Erawan Bangkok along Thanon Ploenchit are havens for designer labels while adjacent Narayana Phand is a Thai handicrafts paradise. The jewel of the crown is the recently opened Siam Paragon. Along Thanon Rama 1 are Siam Centre, Siam Discovery Centre and teenage hangouts Siam Square and Mahboonkrong, all within striking distance.

Thanon Silom: In the evenings, Silom's street stalls (Soi 2 to 8) sell cheap souvenirs, t-shirts and fake Rolexes. Patpong, notorious for its go-go bars, also has a night market of tourist goods.

Thanon Sukhumvit: Soi 5–11 is a street bazaar for fake designer gear, souvenirs and handicrafts where haggling is the norm. Further east is upmarket Emporium mall. Nearby sidestreets fanning out from the Emporium are good for home decor shops. Soi Tonglor is the city's trendiest street for design-oriented shopping.

Department Stores

Central Chidlom
1027 Thanon Ploenchit
Tel: 0-2655 7777
The best of the chain and one of Bangkok's top department stores. The Loft food court on the top floor is a great place to eat.

Emporium
622 Thanon Sukhumvit (cnr Soi 24)
Tel: 0-2664 8000-9
Emporium is one of the classiest department stores (part of the mall of the same name).

Isetan
Central World Plaza
Thanon Ratchadamri
Tel: 0-2255 9898-9
Japanese department store with high-quality international goods at slightly above average prices.

Robinson
Soi 19 Thanon Sukhumvit
Tel: 0-2252 5121
The chain's biggest and most popular branches are on Thanon

Silom, Thanon Sukhumvit and Thanon Ratchadaphisek and in Seacon Square mall. While not as high quality as Central, the goods are cheaper.

Zen
Central World Plaza
Thanon Ratchadamri
Tel: 0-2255 9667-9
With a similar look and feel as Isetan, Zen has a wide range of international and local products.

Markets

Despite the proliferation of air-conditioned shopping malls in the city, markets (both day and night) and street vendors still cater for the majority of Bangkok's ordinary people with their cheaply-priced goods and basic necessities. They are also colourful places to observe the more visceral aspects of Bangkok. For more details on markets and streetside shopping, see **Bangkok Bazaar** *(page 61)*.

What To Buy

Antiques

O P Place
Soi 38 Thanon Charoen Krung
Tel: 0-2266 0186
Just across from the Oriental hotel this upmarket antiques mall is as expensive as you'd expect for the location. Worth a browse if only to see what you cannot afford.

River City
23 Trok Rongnamkaeng
Tel: 0-2237 0077-8
Bangkok's art and antiques centre, with the 2nd to 4th floors selling art and antiques goods. Antique auctions are held monthly in the Auction House, but beware of pilfered artefacts from historical sites.

Books

Asia Books
4th Floor, Siam Discovery Centre
Thanon Rama 1
Tel: 0-2658-0418-20
www.asiabooks.com
Publisher and distributor with branches all over Bangkok,

EXPORT PERMITS

The Thai **Department of Fine Arts** prohibits the export of all Thai Buddha images, images of other deities and fragments (hands or heads) of images dating before the 18th century. All antiques must be registered with the department. The shop will usually do this for you. If you decide to handle it yourself, take the piece to the office at Thanon Na Prathat (tel: 0-2226 1661) together with two postcard-sized photos of it. The export fee ranges from B50 to B200 depending on the antiquity of the piece. Fake antiques do not require export permits, but airport customs officials are not art experts and may mistake it for a genuine piece. If it looks authentic, clear it at the Department of Fine Arts to avoid problems later.

including Emporium and at 221 Thanon Sukhumvit.

B2S
7th Floor, Central Chidlom Dept Store, Thanon Ploenchit
Tel: 0-2655 6178
Major bookstore retail chain with several outlets in downtown Bangkok.

Basheer Books
H1 Place, Sukhumvit Soi 55
Tel: 0-2391 9815
Ample range on art and design-oriented publications.

Bookazine
286 Thanon Rama I
Tel: 0-2255 3778
Another large bookstore chain with branches all over the city.

Dasa Book Café
710/4 Thanon Sukhumvit (between Soi 24 and 26)
Tel: 0-2661 2993
www.dasabookcafe.com
Second-hand books in a cosy environment with drinks and desserts to fuel your page thumbing.

Kinokuniya
3th Floor, Emporium
Thanon Sukhumvit

el: 0-2664 8554-6
apanese chain store with well-
rganised and comprehensive
election of books on all topics.

Electronics

Panthip Plaza
04/3 Thanon Petchaburi
el: 0-2251 9724-8
he biggest marketplace for com-
uter gear in Thailand, plus virtu-
lly every PC software in existence
although much of it pirated). 150
hops spread over five floors sell-
g hardware and software.

Fashion and Clothes

hais follow fashion trends closely
nd are quick to copy the latest
ollections from foreign design
ouses and flog them at a fraction
f the cost. The only downside is
hey fit the Thai physique, ie small
nd slim. There aren't any interna-
onal Thai fashion houses but **Fly
Now** and **Greyhound** are making
najor inroads. The **Nagara** label is
he Jim Thompson's line of
ontemporary women's clothing.

Anurak (ANR)
nd Floor, Emporium, Soi 24
hanon Sukhumvit
el: 0-2664 8473
Men's and women's clothing with
lean lines, but you have to be
ltra slim in order to fit into them.

Fly Now
nd Floor, Gaysorn Plaza
hanon Ploenchit
el: 0-2656 1359
ww.flynow.co.th
ne of the country's few home
rown fashion labels to grace the
orld's catwalks.

Greyhound
nd Floor, Emporium, Soi 24
hanon Sukhumit
el: 0-2664 8664
ww.greyhound.co.th
his trendy domestic fashion
rand can sometimes be hit or
niss, with branches and great
afés in several malls.

Inspired by Inner Complexity
'35/3 Soi 31 Thanon Sukhumvit
el: 0-2258 4488
 tearoom is found downstairs
hile upstairs is hip streetwear
nd accessories.

It Happened to Be a Closet
266/3 Soi 3 Siam Square
Thanon Rama I
Tel: 0-2658 4696
Stocks mainly vintage female
clothes and accessories.

Jaspal
2nd Floor, Siam Centre
Thanon Rama I
Tel: 0-2251 5918
www.jaspal.com
Local fashion chain with
branches in most shopping malls.
Influenced by British and Euro-
pean style trends. Unlike most
Thai labels, sizes go up to XL.

Tailors

There are nearly as many tailors
as noodle shops in the capital,
and while the craftsmanship isn't
a stitch near to Saville Row,
prices are a bargain. There is a
proliferation of cheap tailors
around Sukhumvit's early soi and
also at Thanon Khao San.

Embassy Fashion House
Thanon Withayu
Tel: 02-251 2620
Most tailors give you the hard
sell, but this place stands out for
its relaxed service. Wide range of
local and imported fabrics.
Nearby embassy staff patronise
this shop, and many big name
hotels recommend it too.

Textiles

Almeta Silk
20/3 Thanon Sukhumvit Soi 23
Tel: 0-2258 4227
Made-to-order handwoven silk
designs in stunning colour combinations that can be turned into
home furnishings.

Jim Thompson Thai Silk
9 Thanon Surawong
Tel: 0-2632 8100-4; and

Jim Thompson Factory Outlet
153 Thanon Sukhumvit Soi 93
www.jimthompson.com
With several branches around the
city, this famous silk company has
had a contemporary makeover in
recent years. Clothing, accessories and home furnishings.

Mae Fah Luang Foundation
4th Floor, Siam Discovery Centre
Thanon Rama I

Tel: 02-658 0424-5
www.doitung.org
This royally initiated craft foundation has been credited for its traditional weaves infused with a
funky sense of the contemporary.

Gems & Jewellery

Bangkok is well known for its
gemstone scams. Buy only from
reputable shops endorsed by the
Tourism Authority of Thailand and
the Thai Gem and Jewellery
Traders Association. These shops
carry the Jewel Fest (www.jewelfest.
com) logo and issue a certificate of
authenticity that comes with a
money-back guarantee.

Ki-Ti's Jewellery
2nd Floor, Playground
Sukhumvit Soi 55 (Soi Thonglor)
Tel: 0-1821 1275
www.kittijewelry.com
Khun Ittipol's stylish take on the
ethnic look has given him a well
deserved following. Apart from
this main outlet, there is also the
KI-TI's Gallery at Baan Silom on
Soi 19 Thanon Silom.

Uthai's Gems
28/7 Soi Ruam Rudi
Tel: 0-2253 8582
Foreign residents like the
personal touch and approach of
this reputable jeweller.

Handicrafts/Home Decor

Apart from Chatuchak Weekend
Market and Suan Lum Night
Bazaar, the shops below are
worth a browse. Expect prices to
be higher though.

Asian Motifs
3rd Floor, Gaysorn Plaza
Thanon Ploenchit
Tel: 0-2656 1093
Unique, elegant, contemporary
spin to traditional celadon,
lacquerware, silks and the like.

Cocoon
3rd Floor, Gaysorn Plaza
Thanon Ploenchit
Tel: 0-2656 1006
Exciting modern twists to Thai and
Asian fabrics and home decor.

Exotique Thai
4th Floor, Emporium, Soi 24
Thanon Sukhumvit
Tel: 0-2664 8000-9 ext. 1554

A well presented open display of handicrafts within the mall.

Narayana Phand

127 Thanon Ratchadamri
Tel: 0-2252 4670
One-stop shop for all things Thai. Spread over several floors, there's everything from traditional musical instruments to ornamental headpieces.

Propaganda

4th Floor, Siam Discovery Centre
Thanon Rama 1
Tel: 0-2658 0430
www.propagandaonline.com
Quirkily designed home decor items (think a Thai version of Alessi) like funky tableware and molar-shaped toothbrush holders. Second outlet at Emporium.

Rasi Sayam

82, Sukhumvit Soi 33
Tel: 0-2262 0729
Sells fine traditional Thai handicrafts and *objet d'art*, with many one-of-a-kind pieces.

SPORTS

Participant Sports

Bowling

RCA Bowl

3rd Floor, RCA Plaza
Tel: 0-2641 5870-3
Teenagers come here to rock 'n' bowl to the modern music and disco-like lights. There are 42 lanes open from 10am to 1am.

SF Strike Bowl

7th Floor MBK Centre
Tel: 0-2611 4555
A 28-lane bowling alley, and a Game Zone with pool, table football and air hockey.

Fitness Centres

Most gyms are located within hotels and sell expensive 1-day passes to non-guests.

California Wow Xperience

Soi 23 Thanon Sukhumvit
Tel: 0-2665 2999; and
Liberty Square, Thanon Silom
Tel: 0-2631 1122
www.californiawowx.com

This big and brash chain of exercise centres exude corporate America branding, with little personal touch. However these trendy workout centres with hi-tech equipment and specialised classes are always packed with Thais. Only a 30-day pass is available.

Golf

Thais are big golfing buffs, going so far as to employ some of the golfing world's stellar architects to design international-class courses. At around B500 to B2,000, green fees are considerably lower than abroad and clubs are not sticky about letting guests play.

Green Valley Country Club

92 Moo 3, Thanon Bangna-Trad
Tel: 0-2316 5883-9
Beautifully landscaped with an opulent clubhouse, this 18-hole course was designed by Robert Trent Jones Jr.

Panya Indra Golf Course

99 Moo 6, Km 9 Kannayao,
Thanon Ramindra
Tel: 0-2943 0000
www.panyagolf.com
About 30 minutes from downtown, this well-kept course has a challenging 27-hole course.

Thana City Golf & Country Club

Thanon Bangna-Trad Km 14
Tel: 0-2336 1971-8
The Greg Norman-designed 18-hole course has played host to numerous competitions.

Go Karting

PTT Speedway Karting Stadium

2nd Floor, RCA Plaza, Royal City Avenue, Thanon Rama IX
Tel: 0-2203 1205
www.kartingstadium.com
One might think of indoor karting as a room full of petrol fumes, but in fact PTT Speedway's 600-metre (1,968-ft) long race circuit is a cool, clean and well-managed place. The karts are extremely fast and light, reaching a top speed of around 60 kph (373 mph). The stadium has a hi-tech computerised time clock, highlighting individual fastest laps and printing it out on a time sheet for you to take away.

Ice Skating

World Ice Skating

8th Floor, Central World Plaza
Thanon Ratchadamri
Tel: 0-2255 9500
A wonderful way to beat the climate is to coast or stumble (according to your ability) around the city's only Olympic-size ice rink. Dress warmly as the drop in temperature can overwhelm.

Racquet Sports

Santisuk Tennis Court

Soi 38 Thanon Sukhumvit
Tel: 0-2391 1830
Five outdoor and three indoor courts that have seen better days but still popular and cheap.

Soi Klang Racquet Club

Soi 49 Thanon Sukhumvit
Tel: 0-2712 8020
Well equipped sports centre has two swimming pools, four tennis courts, three squash courts, 20 badminton courts and a gym.

Waterskiing

Club Taco

Thanon Bangna-Trad Km 13
Tel: 0-2316 7810
Cable-ski (B300 for 2 hours) is the main activity at this large lake found on the eastern edge of Bangkok. A variety of skis and wakeboards to choose from with pulley speeds adjusted to suit different skill levels.

Yoga

Absolute Yoga Bangkok

14th Floor, Unico House Building
Soi Lang Suan
Tel: 0-2652 1333
www.absoluteyogabangkok.com
Part of a world trend for Bikram or hot yoga that is done in a heated room (as if in Bangkok one needs it). The contortionist postures will leave you dripping.

Prana Yoga

Sareerarom Spa
Sukhumvit Soi 55 (Soi Thonglor)
Tel: 0-2391 9919
www.sareerarom.com
One-off yoga classes available for B450. Both Iyengar and Power Vinyasa versions of yoga are taught here.

TRANSPORT

ACCOMMODATION

ACTIVITIES

A – Z

LANGUAGE

Spectator Sports

Takraw

An acrobatic team game of kicking (or heading) a rattan ball over a net, tournaments are held at the **Thai-Japanese Sports Complex** (tel: 0-2465 5325 for dates and times). Otherwise you'll usually find a game being played in **Lumphini Park**.

Muay Thai

Bangkok has two principal places to view Thai boxing, or *muay thai*.
Lumpini Boxing Stadium
Thanon Rama IV
tel: 0-2251 4303
Matches at 6pm on Tues and Fri and Sat. Tickets at B500, B800 and B1,500. Note: this stadium is scheduled to relocate in the near future to Soi Nang Linchi 3.
Ratchadamnoen Boxing Stadium
, Thanon Ratchadamnoen Nok
tel: 0-2281 4205
Matches at 6pm on Mon, Wed and Thur, and 5pm on Sun. Tickets: B500, B800 and B1,500.

THAI BOXING

If you enjoy seeing a punch-out, the frenzied sport of *muay thai*, or Thai kickboxing will keep you on the edge of your seat. Employing not just fists but elbows, feet and knees, in fact almost any part of the body except the head, this highly ritualised sport is accompanied by high-pitched Thai music played by a *phipat* orchestra. Matches are divided into 10 bouts, each session consisting of five 3-minute rounds with a 2-minute rest between each round. Before the match begins, the fighters do a *ram muay*, a stylised dance, which also warms up and stretches the boxers' muscles. The cheers of the audience and the frantic betting at the sidelines almost steals the thunder from the action in the ring.

FESTIVALS

The dates for the traditional festivals listed here change from year to year. Check dates on the Tourism Authority of Thailand's website at www.tourismthailand.org. Also see page 235 for a list of public holidays. In addition to these traditional festivals, the calendar is jam-packed with secular events of all sorts, with many new ones added every year. These range from the high-brow (the International Festival of Music and Dance) to the sporty (Bangkok International Motor Show) and the sexually-liberating (Bangkok Pride Festival).

January/February

Chinese New Year (late Jan/early Feb): Chinatown comes alive as the capital's large Thai-Chinese community celebrates with typical mayhem – with firecrackers, lion and dragon dances, and feasting galore.

February/March

Makha Puja (late Feb/early Mar): The full moon of the third lunar month marks the gathering of 1,250 disciples to hear the Buddha preach before he entered Nirvana. In the evening, Thais gather at temples for a candle-lit procession with offerings of incense and flowers.

April

Chakri Day (6 Apr): Celebrates the founding of the Chakri dynasty (which presently rules Thailand) in 1782. The festivities are confined to the palace. Most Thais celebrate it as a day off from work.
Songkran (13–15 Apr): Thailand's official New Year. In days gone by people would celebrate by visiting temples and sprinkling water on each other's heads. Nowadays it's a different story, as people get wet and wild on the streets with water pistols the size of machine guns. No one is exempt as revellers careen

around the streets in open trucks with barrels of water and drenching everyone in sight. Sanam Luang is one of the best places to witness the festivities. Nearby Thanon Khao San is a relentless party zone where both Thais and Westerners dance and douse each with gallons of water.

May/June

Royal Ploughing Ceremony (early May): Held at Sanam Luang in early May, this Brahman ritual is presided over by King Bhumibol and marks the official start of the rice-planting season. Crimson-clad attendants lead buffaloes drawing a plough over specially consecrated ground.
Visakha Puja (late May/early June): The most important Buddhist day, marking the birth, enlightenment and death of Lord Buddha. Thai people visit temples to listen to sermons by the monks. In the evenings candle-lit processions are held at temples.

July/August

Asanha Puja & Khao Phansa (late July/early Aug): Marks the day when Buddha preached to his first five disciples. It is celebrated on the full moon night in similar manner to Magha Puja and Visakha Puja. Also marks the beginning of the three-month "Buddhist Lent" when Thai monks begin a season of prayers and meditation. Khao Phansa is celebrated immediately after Asanha Puja and marks the start of the annual three-month Rains Retreat. This is when young Buddhist novices are ordained at the temple.
HM The Queen's Birthday (12 Aug): Often dubbed as "Mother's Day" this celebration is in honour of Her Majesty Queen Sirikit's birthday. Thais decorate their houses and public buildings with flags and pictures of the Queen.

October

Ok Phansa: Oct full moon marks the end of the three-month Buddhist Lent, and the beginning

of the *kathin* season when Buddhists visit temples to present monks with new robes.
Chulalongkorn Day (23 Oct): Honours King Rama V (1868–1910), who led Thailand into the modern era.

November

Loy Krathong: On the full moon night of Nov, Thais everywhere launch small floats with candles, incense and flowers into rivers, canals and ponds, asking for blessings from the water spirits.

December

Trooping of the Colour (3 Dec): Presided over by the king and queen, this annual event is a brilliant spectacle. Amid pomp and ceremony, the Royal Guards swear allegiance to the Royal family.
King's Birthday Celebrations (5 Dec): Dubbed Father's Day in honour of King Bhumibol's birthday. Thai people all over the country decorate homes and buildings with flags and lights, and there are firework displays at night.

CHILDREN'S ACTIVITIES

The city's larger shopping malls often have designated kids zones, with playgrounds for kids and video arcades for teenagers, a sign of how Bangkok families like to spend their leisure time. Bangkok may be short on green spaces, but all its major parks, Lumphini, Benjasiri, Benjakitti and Chatuchak, have special children's play areas.

The Places section highlights attractions ideal for familes with children. These include **Dusit Zoo** *(page 117)*, **Snake Farm** *(page 133)*, **Dream World** *(page 160)*, **Safari World** *(page 160)*, **Samphran Elephant Ground & Zoo** *(page 168)*, **Ancient City** *(page 183)*, **Crocodile Farm & Zoo** *(page 184)* and **Rose Garden Country Resort** *(page 167)*. Another option is **Siam Park** at 99 Thanon Serithai (tel: 0-2517 0075), a

water park with two exciting water rides, a waterfall and a large artificial beach with rolling waves.

SIGHTSEEING TOURS

Unfortunately Bangkok has very little in the way of organised sightseeing tours. What little is out there is often directed at the domestic market with guides only speaking Thai. However, all the major hotels have tour desks that can arrange visits (with private guide and car with driver) to the major tourist sites.

The **Chao Phraya Tourist Boat** *(see page 208)* is more of a shuttle service than a tour proper but you do get a running commentary on board of the sights along the Chao Phraya River. For those wishing to explore the canals of Thonburi or Nonthaburi, private **longtail boats** *(see page 208)* can be rented from most of the river's main piers.

Dinner cruises (or evening cocktails) on board an atmospheric teakwood barge is a nice way of spending the evening and soaking up the sights along the river.
Loy Nava Dinner Cruise
Tel: 02-437 4932
www.loynava.com
A teakwood barge was refurbished and converted into the *Tahsaneeya Nava*. Its 2-hour dinner cruise (daily 6pm and 8pm) starts with a traditional welcome by hostesses. Dinner is a Thai set menu accompanied by live traditional music. You also get a map with the main river sites marked out, and an audio commentary on board. Cost: B1,150 per person.
Manohra Cruises
Tel : 0-2477 0770
www.manohracruises.com
This option uses either the *Manohra* or *Manohra Moon*, both rice barges restored for dining and cocktail cruises. Dinner cruises from 7.30pm to 10pm costs B1,500 per person while cocktail cruises (a drink and light snacks) cost B640. Departs daily from the

pier at the Bangkok Marriot Resort but can also pick up from Tha Sathorn or Tha Oriental piers.
Real Asia
Tel: 0-2712 9301/2
www.realasia.net
Offers 1-day cycling tours (including a ride on a longtail boat) into the capital's more scenic and traffic-free countryside (B1,500 per person). Also has walking and canal boat tours plus an interesting train tour into the countryside at Samut Sakhon.
Tamarind Tours
Tel: 0-2238 3227
www.tamarindtours.com
This creative regional tour company offers trips all over Southeast Asia, as well as interesting 1-day trips (like Bangkok X Files for instance) around the city. Informed guides lead unique thematic tours to some of the city's lesser-visited attractions.

COOKING CLASSES

Blue Elephant Cookery School
Blue Elephant Restaurant
233 Thanon Sathorn
Tel: 0-2673 9353
www.blueelephant.com
Located in an old mansion, the school offers half-day classes that begin with a trip to a Thai produce market. Up to four dishes are taught in the hands-on classes.
Oriental Cookery School
Oriental Hotel, 48 Oriental Avenue
Tel: 0-2659 0000
www.mandarinoriental.com
The legendary hotel runs pricey cooking demonstrations rather than hands-on classes, but even this is a fascinating gastronomic experience.
Thai House
Tel: 0-2903 9611, 2997 5161
www.thaihouse.co.th
Combines Thai cookery lessons with a stay in a rustic Thai-style house in the suburbs of Nonthaburi; 1-, 2- and 3-day courses available with meals and lodging included.

TRANSPORT

A–Z

ACCOMMODATION

A HANDY SUMMARY OF PRACTICAL INFORMATION, ARRANGED ALPHABETICALLY

ACTIVITIES

A–Z

A ddresses

ince most of Bangkok developed ith little central planning, finding our way around can be a bit con-using at first, given the size of ie city and its many twisting leyways. The city is mostly laid ut using the *soi* system – maller streets leading off a main ›ad of the same name, with each ›i having a number after the ame. For example, Sukhumvit ›ad (or Thanon Sukhumvit) has umerous streets branching from in sequence such as Sukhumvit ›i 33, Sukhumvit Soi 55, etc. ost hotels provide business

cards with the address written in Thai to show to taxi drivers. Fortunately, taxis are very inexpensive in Bangkok, so if you do get lost, it won't cost you too much to find your destination.

B udgeting your Trip

By Western standards Bangkok is a bargain. Five-star hotels cost half or a third of what they would in New York or London, and at the other end, budget (if a bit dingy) accommodation can be as cheap as B100 per night. Street food can be excellent and you can have a filling and tasty meal for B30 to B40. Transport is cheap

with bus fares priced from B4 to B16, a ride on the Skytrain and metro from B15 to B40. Taxis are inexpensive as well *(see page 206)*. Drinks in bars are from B60 to B100 and in clubs from B180 to B300. If you live frugally, you can get by with B1,000 a day, but the sky is the limit here if you want to live it up at luxury hotels and eat at fine restaurants.

Business Hours

Government offices operate from 8.30am–4.30pm Mon–Fri. Most businesses are open 8am–5.30pm Mon–Fri while some are open 8.30am–noon on Sat.

LANGUAGE

Banks are open 9.30am–3.30pm five days per week. Money-changing kiosks in the city are open until 8pm daily.

Department stores are open 10.30am–9pm daily, though larger stores are open as late as 10pm. Ordinary shops open at 8.30am or 9am and close between 6pm and 8pm, depending on location and type of business.

Small open-air coffee shops and restaurants open at 7am and close at 8.30pm, though some stay open past midnight. Large restaurants generally close by 10pm. Most hotel coffee shops close at midnight; some stay open 24 hours, and the city has several outdoor restaurants that are open as late as 4am for post-bar hopping suppers.

Business Travellers

As Thailand strives to become a regional business hub, the capital hosts an increasing number of business travellers from all over the world. Most hotels have business centres with communications and secretarial services in several languages. Elsewhere in Bangkok, it is possible to lease small offices with shared clerical staff. Interpreter services are also available.

A good starting point for overseas business people wanting to start a company in Thailand is the **Board of Investment** (BOI), tel: 0-2537 8111; www.boi.go.th. The BOI is authorised to grant tax holidays and other incentives to promote certain key industries.

C limate

There are three official seasons in Thailand: hot, rainy and cool. But to the tourist winging in from more temperate regions, Bangkok has only one temperature: hot. There is little wind and the temperature drops only a few degrees during the night, with humidity above 70 percent. Nights, however, during the cool season can be very pleasant.

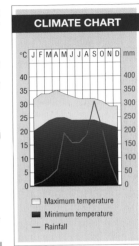

CLIMATE CHART

☐ Maximum temperature
■ Minimum temperature
— Rainfall

Air-conditioning of course makes Bangkok tolerable during the hot season. These temperature ranges give you an idea of what to expect:
● Hot season (Mar to mid-June): 27–35°C (80–95°F)
● Rainy season (June to Oct): 24–32°C (75–90°F)
● Cool season (Nov to Feb): 18–32°C (65–90°F), but with less humidity.

Children

Travelling with children is not especially difficult in Thailand. Thais love kids, and those with blonde hair will receive special attention. It can be a bit overwhelming, but people are just being friendly and it is part of the Thai sense of community.

Footpaths in Bangkok are not pedestrian friendly. They are often in disrepair and inevitably, something or somebody obstructs them: leave the baby stroller at home and bring back- or chest-mounted baby carriers. Children should never approach dogs, monkeys or other small animals; those wandering the streets are more feral than back at home, and rabies is still a risk.

The tropical sun is intense, so sun block and hats are important. Make sure the kids keep their hands clean as well, since kids who suck their fingers or thumbs can easily pick up stomach bugs.

Clothing

Clothes should be light and loose; fabrics made from natural fibres are definitely more comfortable than synthetics. During the height of the rainy season, sandals are preferable to shoes. Sunglasses, hats and sunscreen are recommended for protection from the tropical sun.

Suits are sometimes worn for business but, in general, Thailand does not have the formal dress code of Hong Kong or Tokyo. A shirt and tie is expected for business appointments.

Temple Dress Code

Shorts are taboo for women and men who wish to enter some of the more highly revered temples. Women wearing sleeveless dresses and short skirts may also be barred from certain temples. Improperly dressed and unkempt visitors will be turned away from Wat Phra Kaew and the Grand Palace (though some clothing can be borrowed at the entrance). Dress properly in deference to the religion and to Thai sensitivities.

Crime & Security

Bangkok is a relatively safe city in terms of violent crime. The biggest risk to travellers is from scams and con artists. If you do run into trouble in Bangkok, there are Tourist Police specially assigned to assist travellers, though much of the time there is little they are able to do but record the details of the crime and provide a report for insurance purposes.

Tourist Police: Tourist Service Centre, TAT headquarters, 4 Thanon Rachadamnoen Nok, tel: 0-2281 5051; hotline: 1155.

Most members of the force

speak some English. Tourist police booths can also be found in tourist areas including Lumphini Park (near the intersection of Rama IV and Silom) and Patpong (at the Silom intersection).

Common Scams

● Touts on Patpong offering live sex shows upstairs. Once inside, you are handed an exorbitant bill and threatened if you protest. Pay, take the receipt, and go immediately to the Tourist Police, who will usually take you back and demand a refund.
● Don't take free or very cheap boat rides into the canals. Once you are well into the canal, you are given the choice of paying a high fee or being stranded.
● Don't follow touts who offer to take you to a gem factory for a "special deal". The gems are usually synthetic or of substandard quality and there is no way to get your money back.
● There are no tuk tuk rides for B10. If a driver takes you on one, you will end up stopping at every gem, silver and tailor shop in the city where he will collect commission for wasting your day.

Bear in mind that in Thai culture, strangers rarely approach and engage foreigners in conversation, so if you find yourself on the receiving end, be on guard no matter how polite and innocent they appear to be. Feel free to be rude and walk away, even if it goes against the rules of polite behaviour.

Women Travellers

Thailand is generally safe for women travellers, even those travelling alone. Thais tend to be non-confrontational, so violent and sexual crimes towards foreign women are not common. That said, like anywhere, it isn't a great idea to be walking alone on quiet streets late at night. Also, there is a perception (probably a by-product of Hollywood films) that Western women are "easy", so be careful in your associations with local men, because they

may have the wrong idea about you. Reasonably modest dress will certainly help.

Customs Regulations

The Thai government prohibits the import or export of drugs, dangerous chemicals, pornography, firearms and ammunition. Attempting to smuggle heroin or other hard drugs in or out may be punishable by death. Scores of foreigners are serving very long prison terms for this offence.

Tourists may freely bring in foreign banknotes or other types of foreign exchange. For travellers leaving Thailand, the maximum amount permitted to be taken out in Thai currency without prior authorisation is B50,000. Foreign guests are allowed to bring in without tax 200 cigarettes and one litre of wine or spirits.

Buddha images, antiques and art objects cannot leave Thailand without a Department of Fine Arts permit (see page 224).

For more details check the Thai **Customs Department** website at www.customs.go.th, or call the hotline: 1164.

D isabled Travellers

Thailand falls short on accommodating the disabled, though this is slowly improving. Pavements are often uneven, studded with obstructions and there are no ramps. Few buildings in Bangkok have wheelchair ramps. Traffic is relentless and drivers generally unsympathetic. Some major roads have textured brickwork on the paths for the blind. A few of the Skytrain stations have lifts, but not nearly enough; the metro is better in this regard as there are lifts at every station. Expensive hotels will go a long way to assist disabled travellers, and taxi drivers, if arranged beforehand, are quite cooperative. Still, it would definitely be a challenge for a disabled traveller on his/her own to get around – a companion is essential.

E lectricity

Electrical outlets are rated at 220 volts, 50 cycles and accept flat-pronged or round-pronged plugs. Adaptors can be purchased cheaply at department or hardware stores.

Embassies & Consulates

Australia: 37 Thanon Sathorn Tai, tel: 0-2287 2680. Visas: Mon–Fri 8.15am–12.15pm.
Canada: 15/F, Abdulrahim Place, Thanon Rama IV, tel: 0-2636 0540, 2254 2530.
New Zealand: M Thai Tower, 14th Fl, All Seasons Place, 87 Thanon Withayu, tel: 0-2254 2530.
Singapore: 129 Thanon Sathorn Tai, tel: 0-2286 1434.
United Kingdom: 1031 Thanon Ploenchit, tel: 0-2385 8333. Visas: Mon–Thur 8–11am, Fri 8am–noon.
United States: 120-122 Thanon Withayu, tel: 0-2205 4000. Visas: Mon–Fri 7.30–10am.

Emergency Numbers

Police: 191
Tourist Police: tel: 1155 or tel: 0-2281 5051/2664 0222 For hospitals, see page 233.

Entry Requirements

Visas & Passports

Travellers should check visa regulations at a Thai embassy or consulate before starting their trip as visa rules vary for different nationalities. For an updated list, check the Thai **Ministry of Foreign Affairs** website at www.mfa.go.th.

All foreign nationals entering Thailand must have valid passports with at least six-month validity. At the airport, nationals from most countries will be granted a visa on arrival valid for up to 30 days. Officially you need an air ticket out of Thailand, but this is very rarely checked.

Longer tourist visas, obtained from the Thai consulate of your

TRANSPORT

ACCOMMODATION

ACTIVITIES

A – Z

LANGUAGE

home country prior to arrival, allow for a 60-day stay. People seeking a work permit can apply for a non-immigrant visa which is good for 90 days. A letter of guarantee is needed from the Thai company you intend to work for and this visa can be obtained from a Thai consulate at home.

The on-arrival 30-day visa can be extended by 7–10 days for a fee of B1,900 or you can leave the country (even for half an hour) and return to receive another 30-day visa. The 60-day visa can be extended for another 30 more days for the same price.

Overstaying your visa can carry a daily fine of B200 to a maximum of B20,000. If the police catch you with an expired visa, life can get very complicated, and you can get thrown into the immigration prison.

The Thai **Immigration Bureau** is located at 507 Soi Puan Plu, Thanon Sathorn Tai, tel: 0-2287 3101-10; www.imm.police.go.th; (open Mon–Fri 8.30am–4.30pm).

Etiquette

Thais are remarkably tolerant and forgiving of foreigners' eccentricities, but there are a few things that upset them.

The Royal Family

Thais have a great reverence for the monarchy, and any slight or disrespect directed towards members of the royal family will be taken very personally. At movies the King's Anthem is played before the movie starts and it is the height of bad manners not to stand up when the others do.

Buddhism

A similar degree of respect is accorded to the second pillar of Thai society, Buddhism. Disrespect towards Buddha images, temples or monks is not taken lightly and as with the monarchy, public expressions against the institution are actually illegal.

Monks observe vows of

chastity that prohibit being touched by (or touching) women, even their mothers. When in the vicinity of a monk, a woman should try to stay clear to avoid accidental contact.

When visiting a temple, shorts are unacceptable attire. The scruffy and the underclad are frequently turned away from major temples (see also page 230).

Terms of Address

Thais are addressed by their first rather than their last names. The name is usually preceded by the word *khun*, a term of honour, a bit like Mr or Ms. Following this to its logical conclusion, Silpachai Krishnamra would be addressed as Khun Silpachai.

Thai Greetings

The common greeting and farewell in Thailand is *Sawadee*, (followed by "khrap" when spoken by men and "kha" by women). In more formal settings this is accompanied by a *wai* – raising the hands in a prayer-like gesture, the fingertips touching the nose, and bowing the head slightly. However, don't make the mistake of giving a *wai* to all hotel staff, children or the people at the corner shop – it embarrasses them. In these cases, a nod is sufficient. Almost all Thais understand that this is not a part of Western cultures. In business meetings, the *wai* is often followed by a handshake.

Head and Feet

The Hindu religion, which has had a strong influence on Thai Buddhism, regards the head as the wellspring of wisdom and the feet as unclean. For this reason, it is insulting to touch another person on the head (children are an exception), point one's feet at anything or step over another person. In formal situations, when wishing to pass someone who is seated on the floor, bow slightly while walking and point an arm down to indicate the path to be taken, and a path will be cleared.

Public Behaviour

Two decades ago, Thai couples showed no intimacy in public. That has changed due to modernisation and foreign influence on the young, but even these days, intimacy rarely extends beyond holding hands. As in many traditional societies, displaying open affection in public, such as kissing, is a sign of bad manners.

G ay & Lesbian Travellers

Gays quickly discover that Thailand is one of the most tolerant countries in the world. The gay nightlife scene is a thriving one. See **Bangkok After Dark**, (page 63) and **Gay Venues** (page 222). The city also hosts the annual Bangkok Gay Pride Festival (www.bangkokpride.org/en) in November, with a similar one taking place in Pattaya in December (www.pattayagayfestival.com).

Utopia at 116/1 Soi 23 Sukhumvit; tel: 0-2259 9619; www.utopia–asia.com is Bangkok's centre for gays and lesbians. It's a good place to make contacts and to find out what's going on.

Utopia Tours is an affliated travel agency that caters exclusively for gay travellers. It is located at Tarntawan Place Hotel, 119/5-10 Thanon Surawong, tel: 0-2238 3227, www.utopia–tours.com.

Government

Thailand is a constitutional monarchy with power vested in an elected parliament and a senate appointed by the king from civilian and military officials. The executive branch comprises a coalition of political parties and a prime minister, who in turn rules through a cabinet. There is an independent judiciary.

H ealth & Medical Care

Visitors entering Thailand are not required to show evidence of vaccination for smallpox or cholera. Check that your tetanus boosters are up-to-date. Immunisation against cholera is a good idea as are hepatitis A and B innoculations. Malaria and dengue persist in rural areas but generally not in Bangkok. When in the countryside, especially in the monsoon season, apply mosquito repellent on exposed skin at all times – dengue mosquitoes are at their most active in the day.

Many first-time visitors take awhile to adjust to the heat. It is important to drink plenty of water, especially if you've drunk alcohol. Avoid too much sun when out and about and use sunblock – the sun is far more powerful at this latitude than in temperate regions. Tap water in Bangkok has been certified as potable, but bottled water is still safer and is available widely. Within Bangok, ice is clean and presents no health problems.

Buy travel insurance before travelling to Bangkok. Evacuation insurance is not really necessary since hospitals listed below are of international standard.

Hospitals

The level of medical care can be excellent in Bangkok, particularly at the following hospitals, all of which have specialised clinics as well as standard medical care. In fact, there has been a growing business in "medical tourism" over the past 10 years with people coming to Thailand to have procedures performed (including cosmetic surgery and sex changes) that would cost many times more at home or require waiting in a months-long queue. Equipment is up-to-date and the doctors are usually trained overseas and speak English. By Thai standards, these are considered expensive, but the fees are a fraction of what they are in most Western countries. The hospitals listed also have dental clinics.
Bangkok Christian Hospital: 124 Thanon Silom, tel: 0-2233 6981-9. A medium-sized hospital a bit less luxurious than the others listed here but with high standards.
BNH Hospital: 9/1 Thanon Con-

vent, Silom, tel: 0-2686 2700; www.bnhhospital.com. This squeaky-clean hospital offers comfortable rooms, top-notch equipment and a large team of specialists. Service is efficient and English is widely spoken.
Bumrungrad Hospital: 33 Soi 3, Thanon Sukhumvit, tel: 0-2667 1000; www.bumrungrad.com. This one is the top of the heap, and looks more like a five-star hotel than a hospital. Offers a huge range of specialised clinics, excellent staff, and a selection of rooms from basic four-bed to luxury suites, the latter at only slightly more than the cost of a similar hotel room.

Medical Clinics

For minor problems, the **British Dispensary**, 109 Thanon Sukhumvit (between Soi 3 and 5), tel: 0-2252 8056, has British doctors on its staff. All the major hotels also have an on-premises clinic, or a doctor on call.

Dental Clinics

Apart from the dental clinics at the BNH and Bumrungrad hospitals above, the **Dental Hospital** at 88/88 Soi 49 Thanon Sukhumvit, tel: 0-2260 5000-15, with its long-standing good reputation, is recommended. It looks more like a hotel than a dental hospital and has the latest equipment.

Pharmacies

These are found everywhere in downtown Bangkok. In recent years, official control on prescription drugs have been more strongly applied and require the presence of a licensed pharmacist on the premises. Nonetheless, most antibiotics and many other drugs that would require a prescription in the West are still available without a prescription.

Check the expiry date on all drugs you buy, and wherever possible, purchase them from an air-conditioned pharmacy. There are several branches of **Boots** and **Watson's** pharmacies in central Bangkok.

Internet

Wireless surf zones (WiFi) at the airport, in some hotels, and some branches of Starbucks are a growing phenomenon.

All major hotels offer Internet services, including in the rooms, though these are generally more expensive than the public Internet cafes. The latter usually charge only B30 per hour and the connections are mostly good. Be warned though that as they tend to be full of teenagers playing violent games online, they can be quite noisy. Thanon Khao San has more Internet cafés than any other area in the city, but the Silom and Ploenchit areas have some Internet cafés as well. Ask at your hotel reception for advice.

Left Luggage

There are two left-luggage facilities at Bangkok International Airport. One is on the 1st floor of the Arrival Hall, and the second is on the 3rd floor of the Departure Hall near the currency exchange counter. The fee is B20 per bag per day. All hotels and guesthouses offer a left-luggage service, usually for a small daily fee.

Lost Property

If you lose any valuable property, report it as soon as possible to the **Tourist Police** (see page 230) to get an insurance statement.
Airport: For property lost at the airport, contact 0-2535 1254.
Public Transit: BMTA city bus service, tel: 0-2246 0973; **BTS Skytrain**, tel: 0-2617 6000; **MRTA subway**, tel: 0-2690 8200, **Hualamphong Railway Station**, tel: 1690.
Taxis: Taxi drivers frequently listen to two radio stations that have set up lost property hotlines and it is surprising how often forgetful passengers get their lost items back: **JS100 Radio 100FM** hotline: 1137 and **Community Radio 96FM** hotline: 1677.

TRANSPORT

ACCOMMODATION

ACTIVITIES

N
I
A

LANGUAGE

M aps

Basic maps of Bangkok are available free at the Tourism Authority of Thailand (TAT) offices *(see page 236)* and at big hotels. More detailed ones can be found at bookshops. The *Insight Fleximap* and *Nelles Map* of Bangkok are probably the best. Other more funky insights to Bangkok's attractions can be found in Nancy Chandler's *Map of Bangkok* and Groovy Map's *Bangkok by Day* and *Bangkok by Night*.

Media

Newspapers

Thailand has two longstanding English-language dailies, the *Bangkok Post* and *The Nation*. The *Bangkok Post* is more conservative than *The Nation*, which is more maverick and has had a few run-ins with the current government for their often biting coverage. Many big hotels furnish one or the other for free with the room, or they can be purchased at newsstands for B20.

Magazines

There are several "what's on in Bangkok" type publications in English, covering events, nightlife, art galleries, restaurants, etc, though most of the free ones are advertisement-riddled and out of date. The best two of the paid glossies are *Farang Untamed Travel*, a monthly that provides listings and well-written stories about Thailand, Cambodia and Laos, with a comprehensive Bangkok section. There is also *Metro Magazine*, aimed more at residents than visitors and focusing more exclusively on Bangkok. Both cost B100 each. See page 236 for website addresses.

Radio

AM radio is devoted entirely to Thai-language programmes. FM frequencies include several English-language stations with the latest pop hits. Some frequencies have bilingual DJs and play a mixture of Thai and English songs in the same programme.

● **97 MHz:** Radio Thailand has 4 hours of English-language broadcasts each day.

● **105.5 MHz:** Tourism Authority of Thailand offers useful tips to tourists every hour.

● **Fat FM 104.5:** Has the latest on Thailand's thriving indie music.

● **Eazy FM 105.5FM:** As the name suggests, mostly easy listening middle-of-the road music.

● **FMX 95.5 FM:** Contemporary dance and pop hits.

Television

Bangkok has six Thai-language television channels. ITV or Independent Television specialises in news and documentaries. The rest mainly air soaps, songs and game shows with a sprinkling of mostly domestically-orientated news. There is also UBC, a cable television network that provides subscribers with a choice of about 24 international channels, including BBC, CNN and CNA.

Money Matters

The baht is the principal Thai monetary unit. Though it is divided into 100 units called satang, this is becoming outdated; only 50 and 25 satang pieces are used.

Banknote denominations include 1,000 (light brown), 500 (purple), 100 (red), 50 (blue) and 20 (green). There is a 10-baht coin (brass centre with silver rim), a 5-baht coin (silver with copper edge), a 1-baht coin (silver), and two small coins of 50 and 25 satang (both brass-coloured).

At the time of press US$1 was trading at B39 to B40.

Changing Money

Banking hours are Mon–Fri 9.30am–3.30pm, but nearly every bank maintains money-changing kiosks in tourist areas. Better hotels almost always have exchange kiosks, but generally give poor exchange rates compared to banks.

Credit Cards

American Express, Diner's Club, MasterCard, JCB and Visa are widely accepted throughout Bangkok. Credit cards can be used to draw emergency cash at most banks. If you lose your credit card, call the numbers below:

American Express: tel: 0-2273 0022-44

Diner's Club: tel: 0-2238 3600

Visa: tel: 0-2273 7449

Mastercard: tel: 0-2260 8572

Warning: Credit card fraud is a major problem in Thailand. Don't leave your credit card in safe-deposit boxes. When making a purchase, make sure that you get the carbons and dispose of them.

Travellers' Cheques

Travellers' cheques can be cashed at all exchange kiosks and banks, and generally receive better exchange rates compared to cash. There is nominal charge of B25 for each travellers' cheque cashed.

P hotography

With more than 10 million visitors per year, Thailand gets its photos taken an awful lot. The country and its people are very photogenic, and everything the photographer may need is readily available. Camera shops and photo development outlets are commonly found in the tourist areas, and most now offer digital transfers onto CD and hard copy photos from digital. Prices are cheaper than many other countries at B3–4 per print, with bigger enlargements working out to be a real bargain.

Population

The official population of Bangkok is about 6 million but given the huge migrant population from upcountry (as well as illegals), it's generally acknowledged to be closer to 9 to 10 million.

Postal Services

The Thai postal service is reasonably reliable, though mail seems to go more astray upcountry and at Christmas time. The odds for domestic mail can be improved by registering or sending items by EMS for a fee of B20 for a business-sized letter. EMS is supposed to guarantee that a letter reaches a domestic destination in one day, and it generally does, particularly in Bangkok. If you wish to send valuable parcels or bulky documents overseas, it is better to use a courier service.

The **General Post Office** at Thanon Charoen Krung, tel: 0-2233 1050, is open from Mon to Fri 8am to 8pm, and Sat, Sun and holidays 8am to 1pm.

Post offices elsewhere in Bangkok usually open at 8am and close at 4pm on weekdays. The GPO and many larger offices sell packing boxes and materials.

You can find mini post offices in some office buildings and hotels. Look for a red sign in English. These outlets offer basic mail services and accept small packages, but have no telecommunications services. Kiosks along some of the city's busier streets sell stamps and also ship small parcels.

Courier Services

The usual global courier services are available in Bangkok. You can call direct or book online.
DHL: tel: 0-2345 5000; www.dhl.co.th.
Fedex: tel: 0-2229 8800, or hotline: 1782; www.fedex.com/th.
UPS: tel: 0-2712 3300; www.ups.com/th.

Public Holidays

1 Jan: New Year's Day
Jan/Feb: (full moon) Magha Puja. Note: Chinese New Year, is not an official holiday but many businesses close for several days.
6 Apr: Chakri Day
13–15 Apr: Songkran
1 May: Labour Day

5 May: Coronation Day
May: (full moon) Visakha Puja
July: (full moon) Asanha Puja and Khao Pansa
12 Aug: Queen's Birthday
23 Oct: Chulalongkorn Day
5 Dec: King's Birthday
10 Dec: Constitution Day

Public Toilets

There are few public toilets in Bangkok, though the city is beginning to address this in tourist areas. Restrooms are usually very dirty and often of the squat toilet variety, a tricky experience for the uninitiated. Your best bet is usually to sneak into fast food outlets, which are very easy to find. Shopping malls usually have clean toilets as well, particularly near the food courts. Sometimes a small fee of a few baht applies.

Religious Services

Though it is predominantly Buddhist, Thailand has historically been tolerant of other religions. According to government census, 94 percent are Theravada Buddhists, 3.9 percent are Muslims, 1.7 percent Confucians, and 0.6 percent Christians (mostly hill-tribe people living in the north).

Buddhist people will find no lack of temples to worship at. There are also several mosques, one major Hindu temple, the Maha Uma Devi (see page 144), a handful of Christian churches and at least one synagogue.

Christian

International Church of Bangkok, 67 Soi 19, Thanon Sukhumvit, tel: 0-2258 5821. Services at 8am.
International Christian Assembly, 196 Soi Yasoop 1, Thanon Ekamai, tel: 0-2391 4387. Services at 10.30am and 6pm.

Catholic

Holy Redeemer Church, 123/19 Soi Ruam Rudi, Thanon Withayu, tel: 0-2256 6305. Sunday mass

at 8.30am, 9.45am, 11am and 5.30pm.
St Louis Church, 215/2 Thanon Sathorn Tai, tel: 0-2211 0220. Sunday mass at 6am, 8am, 10am and 5.30pm.

Taxes

Thailand has a Value-Added Tax (VAT) of 7 percent. This is added on to most goods and services (but not goods sold by street vendors and markets). You can get the VAT refunded if you purchase at least B5,000 worth of goods (see page 223).

All major hotels add 10 percent tax plus 8 percent service charge to the room rate. At top-class restaurants, 10 percent service charge is added to the bill.

When leaving the country from Bangkok International Airport, there is an airport departure tax of B500. There is no departure tax for domestic flights.

Telephones

Public Phones

Even though Thais are heavy users of mobile phones, there are still plenty of coin and card operated telephone booths in the city. Public telephones accept B1, B5 and B10 coins. Phone cards for local calls in denominations of B50, B100 and B200 can be purchased at 7-11 convenience shops throughout the city.

Local Calls

In 2002, area codes were merged with phone numbers and in theory do not exist anymore. The prefix 0 must be dialled for all calls made within Thailand, even when calling local numbers in Bangkok. Therefore when in Bangkok, dial 0 first, followed by the 8-digit number. If you need local directory assistance, dial 1133.

International Calls

The country code for Thailand is 66. When calling Thailand from overseas, dial your local international access code, followed by 66 and the 8-digit number (without the preceding 0) in Thailand.

To make an international call from Thailand, dial 001 before the country and area codes followed by the telephone number. If you need international call assistance, dial 100. Peak-hour calls made from 7am–9pm are the highest, so it pays to call during non-peak hours from 5–7am and 9pm–midnight. The lowest call rates are from midnight to 5am.

Prepaid international phone cards (called Thaicard) of B300, B500 and B1,000 value can be used to make international calls. These can be bought at post offices, certain shops that carry the Thaicard sign or the office of the **Communications Authority of Thailand**, tel: 0-2950 3712, www.cat.or.th.

Mobile Phones

Only users of **GSM 900** OR **GSM 1800** mobile phones with international roaming facility can hook up automatically to the local Thai network. Check with your service provider if you're not sure, especially if coming from US, Korea and Japan. Your phone will automatically select a local service provider, and this enables you to make calls within Thailand at local rates. However if someone calls your number, international call rates will apply. Charges will be billed to your account in your home country.

If you're planning to travel in Thailand for any length of time, it's more economical to buy a local SIM card with a stored value from a mobile phone shop. You will be assigned a local number and local calls to and from the phone will be at local rates. International rates will apply to overseas calls.

Time Zones

Thailand is 8 hours ahead of GMT. Since it gets dark between 6 to 7pm uniformly throughout the year, Thailand does not observe daylight savings time.

Tipping

Tipping is not a custom in Thailand, although it is becoming more prevalent. A service charge of 10 percent is included in the more expensive restaurants and is usually, though not always, divided among the staff. Do leave a small tip when service charge has not been included. Do not tip taxi or tuk-tuk drivers unless the traffic has been particularly bad and he has been especially patient. Porters are becoming used to being tipped but will not hover with their hand extended.

Tourist Offices

The **Tourism Authority of Thailand** (TAT) spends billions of baht every year to promote tourism domestically and abroad. They have information outlets in several countries and service kiosks within Thailand that offer maps and other promotional materials as well as advice on things to do and places to see. The main website www.tourismthailand.org has dozens of pages of information.

Bangkok

TAT Call Centre: tel: 1672. Open daily 8am–8pm.
Tourism Authority of Thailand Main Office: 1600 Thanon Phetchaburi, Makkasan, Bangkok 10400, tel: 0-2250 5500. Open daily 8.30am–4.30pm.
TAT Tourist Information Counter (Airport Terminal 1): Arrival Hall, Bangkok International Airport, tel: 0-2504 2701. Open daily 8am–midnight.
TAT Tourist Information Counter (Airport Terminal 2): Arrival Hall, Bangkok International Airport, tel: 0-2504 2703. Open daily 8am–midnight.
TAT Tourist Information Counter (Ratchadamnoen): 4 Thanon Ratchadamnoen Nok. Open daily 8.30am–4.30pm.

Overseas Offices

UK: 3rd Floor, Brook House, 98–99 Jermyn Street, London SW1 6EE, tel: 44-20 7925 2511; fax: 44-20 7925 2512.
USA: 61 Broadway, Suite 2810, New York, NY 10006, tel: 1-212 432 0433 , fax: 1-212 269 2588; and 611 North Larchmont Blvd, 1st Floor, Los Angeles, CA 90004, tel: 1-323 461 9814, fax: 1-323 461 9834.
Australia & New Zealand: Level 2, 75 Pitt Street, Sydney 2000, tel: 61-2 9247 7549, fax: 61-2 9251 2465.

Websites

www.tourismthailand.org
The official website of the Tourism Authority of Thailand.
www.bkkmetro.com
What's on and what's hot in Bangkok, plus nightlife and restaurant listings from one of the city's best lifestyle mags.
www.dininginthailand.com
A guide to the hundreds of restaurants and bars in Bangkok.
www.bangkokpost.com
Daily news from the *Bangkok Post* daily newspaper.
www.nationmultimedia.com
Daily news clips from *The Nation* newspaper.
www.bangkoktourist.com
Information on Bangkok from the Bangkok Tourist Bureau.
www.stickmanbangkok.com
An often humorous and insightful look at Bangkok through the eyes of a somewhat embittered expat.
www.farangonline.com
Website of *Farang Untamed Travel* magazine; articles on Southeast Asia and beyond.
www.circleofasia.com
Reliable hotel and tour bookings with lots of feature stories and guides on activities and culture.
www.EnglishThai.com
Interpreter and translation services in Bangkok.

Weights and Measures

Thailand uses the metric system, except for their traditional system of land measurement (1 rai = 1,600 sq km) and gold (1 baht = 15.2 grammes).

LANGUAGE

UNDERSTANDING THE LANGUAGE

Origins and Intonation

For centuries the Thai language, rather than tripping from foreigners' tongues, has been tripping them up. Its roots go back to the place Thais originated from in the hills of southern China, but these are overlaid by Indian influences. From the original settlers come the five tones that seem designed to frustrate visitors. One sound can have five different ones: high (h), low (l), mid (m), rising (r) and falling (f), and each of these means a different thing from the other (see text box).

Therefore, when you mispronounce a word, you don't simply say a word incorrectly, you say another word entirely. It is not unusual to see a semi-fluent foreigner standing before a Thai and running through the scale of tones until suddenly a light of recognition dawns on his companion's face. There are misinformed visitors who will tell you that tones are not important. These people do not communicate with Thais – they communicate at them in a one-sided exchange that frustrates both parties.

Phonology

The way Thai consonants are written in English often confuses foreigners. An "h" following a letter like "p" and "t" gives the letter a soft sound; without the "h", the sound is more explosive. Thus, "ph" is not pronounced "f" but as a soft "p"; without the "h", the "p" has the sound of a very hard "b". The word thanon (street) is pronounced "tanon" in the same way as "Thailand" is not meant to sound like "Thighland". Similarly, final letters are often not pronounced as they look. A "j" on the end of a word is pronounced "t"; "l" is pronounced as an "n". To complicate matters further, many words end with "se" or "r", which are not pronounced.

Vowels are pronounced as follows: **i** as in sip, **ii** as in seep, **e** as in bet, **a** as in pun, **aa** as in pal, **u** as in pool, **o** as in so, **ai** as in pie, **ow** as in cow, **aw** as in paw, **iw** as in you, **oy** as in toy.

In Thai, the pronouns "I" and "me" are the same word, but it is different for males and females. Men use the word phom when referring to themselves, while women say chan or diichan. Men use khrap at the end of a sentence when addressing either a male or a female to add politeness, or in a similar manner as please (the word for please, karuna, is seldom used directly) ie pai (f) nai, khrap (h) (where are you going sir?). Women add the word kha to their statements, as in pai (f) nai, kha (h).

To ask a question, add a high tone mai to the end of the phrase ie rao pai (we go) or rao pai mai (h) (shall we go?). To negate a statement, insert a falling tone mai between the subject and the verb ie rao pai (we go), rao mai pai (we don't go). "Very" or "much" are indicated by adding maak to the end of a phrase ie ron (hot), ron maak (very hot), or phaeng (expensive), phaeng maak (very expensive), and the opposite mai phaeng (not expensive).

Thai Names

From the languages of India have come polysyllabic names and words, the lexicon of literature.

THE FIVE TONES

Mid tone: Voiced at the speaker's normal, even pitch.
High tone: Pitched slightly higher than the mid tone.
Low tone: Pitched slightly lower than the mid tone.
Rising tone: Sounds like a questioning pitch, starting low and rising.
Falling tone: Sounds like an English speaker suddenly understanding something: "Oh, I see!"

Thai names are among the longest in the world. Every Thai person's first and surname has a meaning. Thus, by learning the meaning of the name of everyone you meet, you would acquire a formal, but quite extensive vocabulary.

There is no universal transliteration system from Thai into English, which is why names and street names can be spelled in three different ways. For example, the surname Chumsai is written Chumsai, Jumsai and Xoomsai depending on the family. This confuses even the Thais. If you ask a Thai how they spell something, they may well reply "how do you want to spell it?" So, Bangkok's thoroughfare of Ratchadamnoen is also spelled Ratchadamnern. Ko Samui can be spelled Koh Samui. The spellings will differ from map to map, and from book to book.

To address a person one has never met, the title *khun* is used for both male and female. Having long and complicated surnames, Thais typically address one another by their first name only and preceded by the title *khun* for formality, ie Hataichanok Phrommayon becomes *Khun Hataichanok*. Thais usually adopt nicknames from birth, often accorded to their physical or behavioural attributes as a baby ie *Lek* (small), *Yai* (big), *Daeng* (red), *Moo* (pig), etc. If the person is familiar – a friend, relative, or close colleague – then according to the senior age relationship between both persons, they are addressed *Pii* (if older), or *Nong* (if younger). So an older friend would be addressed *Pii Lek*, or if younger *Nong Lek*.

Numbers

0 soon (m)
1 nung (m)
2 song (r)
3 sam (r)
4 sii (m)
5 haa (f)
6 hok (m)
7 jet (m)
8 bet (m)
9 kow (f)
10 sip (m)
11 sip et (m, m)
12 sip song (m, r)
13 sip sam (m, r) and so on
20 yii sip (m, m)
30 sam sip (f, m) and so on
100 nung roi (m, m)
1,000 nung phan (m, m)

Useful Words & Phrases

Days of the Week

Monday Wan Jan
Tuesday Wan Angkan
Wednesday Wan Phoot
Thursday Wan Pharuhat
Friday Wan Sook
Saturday Wan Sao
Sunday Wan Athit
Today Wan nii (h)
Yesterday Meua wan nii (h)
Tomorrow Prung nii (h)

Colour sii

White sii kao
Black sii dum
Red sii daeng
Yellow sii leung
Blue sii num ngern
Green sii keeow
Orange sii som
Pink sii chompoo

Short Phrases

Hello, goodbye Sawadee (a man then says khrap; a woman says kha: thus sawadee khrap or sawadee kha)
How are you? Khun sabai dii, mai (h)
Well, thank you Sabai dii, khopkhun
Thank you very much Khopkhun maak
May I take a photo? Thai roop (f) noi, dai (f) mai (h)
Never mind Mai (f) pen rai
I cannot speak Thai Phuut Thai mai (f) dai (f)
I can speak a little Thai Phuut Thai dai (f) nit (h) diew
Where do you live? Khun yoo thii (f) nai (r)
What is this called in Thai? An nii (h), kaw riak aray phasa Thai
How much? Thao (f) rai

Directions and Travel

Go Pai
Come Maa
Where Thii (f) nai (r)
Right Khwaa (r)
Left Sai (h)
Turn Leo
Straight ahead Trong pai
Please slow down Cha cha noi
Stop here Yood thii (f) nii (f)
Fast Raew
Slow Cha
Hotel Rong raem
Street Thanon
Lane Soi
Bridge Saphan
Police Station Sathanii Dtam Ruat
Ferry Reua
Longtail boat Reua haang yao
Train Rot fai
Bus Rot may
Skytrain Rot fai faa
Metro/subway Rot fai tai din
Pier Tha Reua
Bus stop Pai rot may
Station Sathanii (rot may), (rot fai), (rot fai faa)

Other Handy Phrases

Yes Chai (f)
No Mai (f) chai (f)
Do you have...? Mii...mai (h)
Expensive Phaeng
Do you have something cheaper? Mii arai thii thook (l) kwa, mai (h)
Can you lower the price a bit? Kaw lot noi dai (f) mai (h)
Do you have another colour? Mii sii uhn mai (h)
Too big Yai kern pai
Too small Lek kern pai
Do you have any in a bigger size? Mii arai thii yai kwa mai (h)
Do you have any in a smaller size? Mii arai thii lek kwa mai (h)
Do you have a girlfriend/ boyfriend? Mii faen mai (h)
I don't want it Mai ao
Hot (heat hot) Ron (h)
Hot (spicy) Phet
Cold Yen
Sweet Waan (r)
Sour Prio (f)
Delicious Aroy
I do not feel well Mai (f) sabai

FURTHER READING

General

Mai Pen Rai Means Never Mind by Carol Hollinger. Asia Books, 1995. A very personal book that describes hilarious experiences in Thailand half a century ago. Both amusing and informative.
Travellers' Tales Thailand edited by James O'Reilly and Larry Habegger. Travelers' Tales Inc., 2002. A stimulating collection of observations and true stories from around 50 writers.

Fiction

Bangkok 8 by John Burdett. Vintage, 2004. A best-selling story about a half-Thai, half-American policeman who avenges his partner's death.
The Beach by Alex Garland. Riverhead Trade, 1998. The beach read that inspired the movie staring Leonardo Dicaprio about a group of backpackers trying to find their own paradise. Bangkok's Khao San area features prominently.
The Big Mango by Jake Needham. Asia Books, 1999. An action-adventure story about a search for millions of dollars in cash that went missing during the fall of Saigon in 1975.
Evil in the Land Without by Colin Cotterill. Asia Books, 2003. A gripping novel about Detective John Jessel being threatened by a serial killer called "The Paw".
A Killing Smile by Christopher G Moore. Heaven Lake Press, 2004. A gripping thriller set in the capital city of Thailand.
Sleepless in Bangkok by Ian Quartermaine. IQ Inc., 2002. A tough and funny erotic thriller, based on actual events, about an ex-SAS security consultant on a covert assignment to Siam.

History/Society

Thaksin: the Business of Politics in Thailand by Dr Pasuk Phongpaichit and Chris Baker. Silkworm Books, 2004. A carefully researched study of Prime Minister Thaksin Shinawatra and his impact on the nation's economy, society and democracy.
A History of Southeast Asia by D.G.E. Hall. 3rd ed. Macmillan, 1968. The classic history text.
Jim Thompson: The Legendary American by William Warren. Asia Books, 1979. The intriguing story of the American Thai silk magnate, Jim Thompson.
The Revolutionary King: The True-Life Sequel to The King and I by William Stevenson. Robinson, 2001. An intimate portrait of the current King Bhumibol Adulyadej. As monarchy matters are taken very seriously here, the book is unavailable in the kingdom.
Bangkok Then & Now by Steve Van Beek. AB Publications, 2000. A hardcover book with many photos both old and new showing how the city has changed in many ways, but also remained the same as others.
The Balancing Act: A History of Modern Thailand by Joseph Wright. Pacific Rim Press, 1991. Accessible and detailed history of modern Thailand from 1932 to 1991.

Art and Culture

Bangkok Inside Out by Daniel Ziv and Guy Sharett. Equinox Publishing, 2005. A journey of the chaotic city's urban landscape.
Very Thai: Everyday Popular Culture by Philip Cornwel-Smith. River Books, 2005. If you've ever wondered why every compound in Thailand has a spirit house or why insect treats are such a hit, this book is for you. A must-read for tourists and residents.
Flavours: Thai Contemporary Art by Steven Pettifor. Thavibu Gallery, 2005. Brimming with colourful illustrations, this is the only book that offers insights into Thailand's burgeoning contemporary visual arts scene.
The Arts of Thailand by Steve Van Beek and Luca Tettoni. Periplus Editions, 1999. Beautifully illustrated and includes the minor arts.
Things Thai by Tanistha Dansilp and Michael Freeman. Periplus Editions, 2002. Coffeetable book that presents quintessential Thai objects and artefacts.
The Grand Palace by Nngnoi Saksi, Naengnoi Suksri, and Michael Freeman. River Books, 1998. Beautifully illustrated and detailed account of Bangkok's Grand Palace and its surroundings.

Religion

A History of Buddhism in Siam by Prince Dhani Nivat. Bangkok: Siam Society, 1965. Written by one of Thailand's most respected scholars.
What the Buddha Taught by Walpola Rahula. Grove Press, 1974. Comprehensive account of Buddhist doctrine.

Cookery

Green Mangoes and Lemongrass: Southeast Asia's Best Recipes From Bangkok To Bali by Wendy Hutton. Tuttle Publishing, 2003. Presenting the rich diversity of Southeast Asian cuisine, accompanied by striking photographs.

ART & PHOTO CREDITS

Catherine Karnow 50
David Henley/CPA 159M, 166, 191
Devarana Spa 9L, 9RT, 68, 69, 71
Francis Dorai/APA 5B, 7L, 84R, 88M, 92M, 99, 101, 101M, 102L, 102M, 111, 113R, 114, 142R, 143M
Getty Images 19, 20, 26, 27
Jason Lang 7RT/B, 8L, 12/13, 30/31, 51, 52, 59, 60, 61, 63, 65, 76, 120, 185L, 194M
Jack Hollingsworth/APA 125M
Jason Lang/APA 2/3, 6L, 8RB, 25, 32, 33, 34, 35L/R, 62, 66, 74/75, 81, 83L/R, 84L, 87M, 88, 89M, 90M, 91, 93M, 94L, 102R, 103M, 109L/R, 110, 110M, 111M, 113L, 113M, 115M, 123R, 128, 129, 130M, 131, 132R, 134L/R, 140, 141, 145R, 146L/R, 150, 151, 153L/R, 158, 160, 161L/R, 162/163, 168, 169L/R, 169M, 170L, 170M, 171, 172M, 174L/R, 174M, 176, 177, 178L/R, 179, 179M, 180M, 181, 182, 183, 186, 190, 191M, 193, 197, 198M, 202L/R, 202M, 203
Joe Louis Puppet Theatre 46
Jock Montgomery 4T, 10/11, 29,

36, 55, 72/73, 117, 135, 173M, 175, 189, 195L, 200, 200M, 201
Luca Invernizzi Tettoni 17, 18R, 24, 57, 70, 85M, 89R, 90, 98, 192, 195R, 199
Marcus Gortz 8RT, 64
Marcus Wilson Smith/APA all back cover, 1, 3L, 4B, 5T, 6RT/B, 9RB, 14, 16, 28, 37, 38, 39, 40, 41, 44, 45, 48L/R, 54, 56, 58, 67L/R, 80, 84M, 86, 87, 89L, 92, 93L/R, 94R, 95M, 100, 106, 107, 108M, 112, 112M, 115, 116, 117M, 121, 122M, 123L, 124L/R, 124M, 125, 126, 126M, 132L, 132M, 133, 133M, 135M, 144, 144M, 145L, 167, 170R, 172, 173, 180, 184, 187, 187M, 188L/R, 189M, 196
M.C. Piya Rangsit 18L, 21
Oliver Hargreave/CPA 185R
Oriental Hotel 53, 142L, 142M
Patravadi Theatre 47L/R
Photobank 23, 197M, 198
Rainer Krack/CPA 159
Steven Pettifor 49

Pages 42/43: Top row from left to right: Marcus Wilson Smith/APA, Marcus Wilson

Smith/APA. Bottom row from left to right: Marcus Wilson Smith/APA, Marcus Wilson Smith/APA, Francis Dorai/APA, Marcus Wilson Smith/APA, Derrick/APA
Pages 96/97: Top row from left to right: Michael Freeman, Michael Freeman. Bottom row from left to right: Michael Freeman, Michael Freeman, Gerald Cubitt, Michael Freeman.
Pages 104/105: Top row from left to right: Jason Lang/APA, David Henley/CPA. Bottom row from left to right: Francis Dorai, Oriental Hotel, John Brunton, Jock Montgomery.
Pages 138/139: Top row from left to right: Michael Freeman, Michael Freeman, David Henley/CPA. Bottom row from left to right: John Brunton, Michael Freeman, Gerald Cubitt, Michael Freeman.

Map Production: Dave Priestly, Mike Adams, James Macdonald and Stephen Ramsay

BANGKOK STREET ATLAS

The key map shows the area of Bangkok covered by the atlas
section. An index of street names and places of interest
shown on the maps can be found on the following pages. For
each entry there is a page number and grid reference.

Map Legend

Motorway with Junction	⊖ Border Crossing	Motorway	ⓂⓈ MRT/Skytrain
Motorway (under construction)	✈ ✦ Airport	Dual Carriageway	🚌 Bus Station
Dual Carriageway	† ♰ Church (ruins)	Main Roads	❶ Tourist Information
Main Road	† Monastery		✉ Post Office
Secondary Road	🏰 🏚 Castle (ruins)	Minor Roads	🕀 Cathedral/Church
Minor road	∴ Archaeological Site		☾ Mosque
Track	∩ Cave	Footpath	✡ Synagogue
International Boundary	★ Place of Interest	Railway	⚑ Statue/Monument
Province Boundary	🏠 Mansion/Stately Home	Pedestrian Area	⌱ Tower
National Park/Reserve	☀ Viewpoint	Important Building	🗼 Lighthouse
Ferry Route	⚑ Beach	Park	

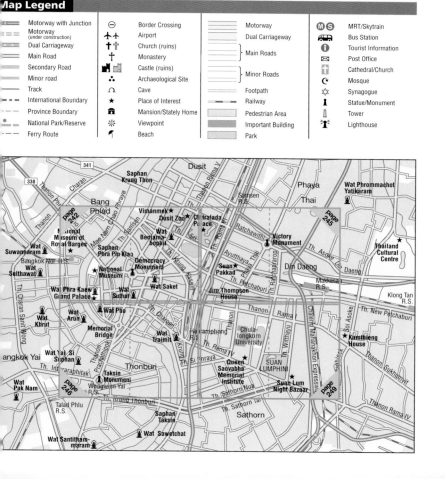

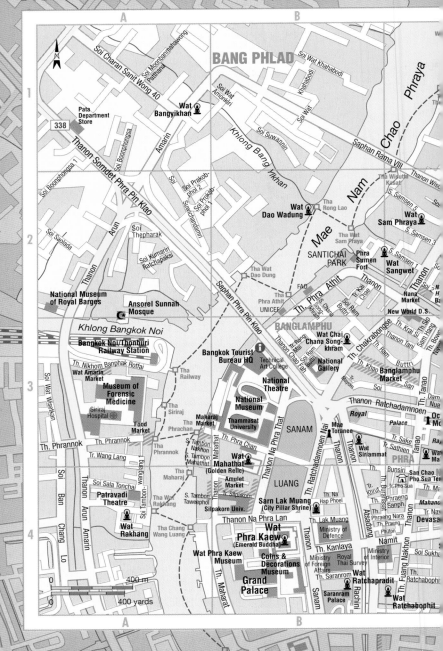

BANG PHLAD

Soi Charan Sanit Wong 40

Soi Moonhaarmnawong Patthana

Pata Department Store

338

Thanon Somdet Phra Pin Klao

Soi Boonphongsa

Soi Boonphongsa

Amarin

Wat Bangyikhan

Soi Wat Amonkiri

Soi Wat Khahabodi

Khlong Bang Yikhan

Khahabodi

Soi Suwannin

Saphan Rama VIII

Mae Nam Chao Phraya

Soi Prakob-phol 1

Soi Prokob-phol

Soi

Suwichandamri

Wat Dao Wadung

Tha Rong Lao

Tha Wisutthi Kasat

Thanon Wisu

S. Samsen 5

Wat Sam Phraya

S. Samsen 3

Tha Wat Sam Praya

SANTICHAI PARK

Phra Sumen Fort

S. Samsen 1

Wat Sangwet

Thanon

Soi Saolada

Thanon

Arun

Soi Thepharak

Soi Kumarin Ratchapaksi

Tha Wat Dao Dung

FAO

Tha Phra Athit

UNICEF

Th. Phra Athit

S. Chana Song Kram

Tr. Kai Chae

Nana Market

New World D.S.

National Museum of Royal Barges

Ansorel Sunnah Mosque

Saphan Phra Pin Klao

Khlong Bangkok Noi

Bangkok Noi/Thonburi Railway Station

Th. Nikhom Banphak Rotfai

Wat Amarin Market

Museum of Forensic Medicine

Siriraj Hospital

Food Market

Tha Railway

Tha Siriraj

Bangkok Tourist Bureau HQ

Technical Art College

National Theatre

National Museum

Thanon Chao Fah

Soi Rani

Soi Ram Buttri

BANGLAMPHU

Wat Chai Chana Song-khram

National Gallery

Th. Chakrabongse

Th. Ram

Thanon Tani

Buttri

Banglamphu Market

Thanon Ratchadamnoen

Royal Palace

Th. Phrannok

Th. Phrannok

Tr. Wang Lang

Maharaj Market

Tha Phrachan

S. Tambon Nakhon

S. Tambon Mahathat

S. Tambon Taweephol

Tha Phrannok

Tha Maharaj

Tha Wat Rakhang

Silpakorn Univ.

Thammasat University

Th. Phra Chan

Wat Mahathat (Golden Relic)

Amulet Market

Tr. Silpakorn

Sarn Lak Muang (City Pillar Shrine)

SANAM

LUANG

Thanon Na Phra That

Mae Toranee

Th. Na Hap Phoel

Th. Lak Muang

Patravadi Theatre

Wat Rakhang

Tha Chang Wang Luang

Thanon Na Phra Lan

Wat Phra Kaew (Emerald Buddha)

Wat Phra Kaew Museum

Coins & Decorations Museum

Grand Palace

Ministry of Foreign Affairs

Ministry of Defence

Royal Thai Survey

Saranrom Palace

Th. Saranrom

Thanon Ratchadamnoen Nai

Thanon

Thanon

Th. Ratchadamnoen Nai

Wat Sir/ammat

Tr. Sake

Tr. Sathien

PHRA

Bunsiri

San Chao Pho Sua

Th. Pho Sua

Th. Burapha

Phraeng Sanph.

Th. Praeng Nara

Tr. Phuton

Th. Kanlaya

Th. Namit

Mahan

Devasa

Tr. Ma

Ra

Wat Ma

Th. Prang Nakhon

Wat Ratchapradit

Th. Ratchabophi

Wat Ratchabophit

Ministry of Interior

Alsadang

Atsadang

Rachini

Sanam

400 m

400 yards

A   **B**

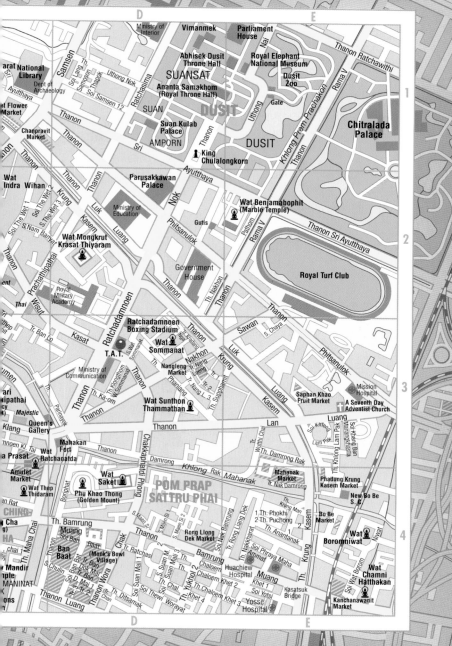

D   E

ral National
Library

Ministry of
Interior

Vimanmek

**Parliament
House**

Thanon Ratchawithi

Dept of
Archaeology
Ayutthaya

Samsen

Th.
Soi
Liang
Samsen
Th. Thanok
Uthong Nok

Ratchasima

**Abhisek Dusit
Throne Hall**

SUANSAT

**Royal Elephant
National Museum**

**Dusit
Zoo**

Rama V

1

t Flower
Market

Soi Samsen 12

**Ananta Samakhom
(Royal Throne Hall)**

DUSIT

Gate

**Chitralada
Palace**

Chanpravit
Market

Thanon

SUAN

**Suan Kulab
Palace**

DUSIT

Uthong

Khlong Prem Prachakon

Sri

AMPORN

**King
Chulalongkorn**

Thanon

Wat
Indra Wihan

Thanon

Krung

Kasem

Luang

**Parusakkawan
Palace**

Nok

Ayutthaya

**Wat Benjamabophit
(Marble Temple)**

Pathom

Rama V

2

Soi The Wet 2
Soi The Wet 3

Ministry of
Education

Gutis

Thanon

Prachathippathai

Wisut

Thanon

Soi S. Nam Banya

Soi The Wet

**Wat Mongkrut
Krasat Thiyaram**

Phitsanulok

Thanon Sri Ayutthaya

ent

Thai

Royal
Military
Academy

**Government
House**

Th. Nakhon

Thanon

Royal Turf Club

Thanon

Tr. Ban Lo

Kasat

Ratchadamnoen

**Ratchadamnoen
Boxing Stadium**

Thanon

Sawan

S. Chaya

Phitsanulok

3

imen

Ministry of
Communication

T.A.T.

Wat
Sommanat

Nakhon

Luk

Krung

Kasem

Luang

Mission
Hospital

Thep
y
4)

Th. Ka-om

Th. Klongthom
Soi Sommanat

Nangleng
Market

Tr. Neng
Neng

Tr. Nang L. 3

Phanjang

**Saphan Khao
Fruit Market**

A Seventh Day
Adventist Church

ari
ipathai
cy

Majestic

Thanon

**Wat Sunthon
Thammathan**

Tr. Suk Sumprait

Lan

Luang

Soi Khlong
Lam Pak

Soi Khong Ban
Manang Kasila

Klang

Queen's
Gallery

Thanon

Th. Witthi Chai

Th. Damrong Rak

Th. Khlong Lam Pak

nnoen Kl. Tai

Mahakan
Fort

Thanon

Damrong

Khlong Rak Mahanak

**Mahanak
Market**

**Phadung Krung
Kasem Market**

a Prasat

Wat
Ratchanatda

Chakkaphatdi Phong

Tr. Nak Damrong

New Bo Be
S. C

Amulet
Market

Wat Thep
Thidaram

Bongphat

**Wat
Saket**

**Phu Khao Thong
(Golden Mount)**

**POM PRAP
SATTRU PHAI**

Soi Nak Bamrung

Soi Khong Man

Kasem

Krung

Bo Be
Market

**Wat
Boromniwat**

4

n Rat

CHING

Cha
g)

HA

chai

Th. Maha Chai

Th. Bamrung

Muang

Ban
Baat

Soi Ban

Baat
(Monk's Bowl
Village)

Tr. Ratchasi

Thanon

Chak

Bamrung

Tr. Rong Liang Dek

**Rong Liong
Dek Market**

Soi Phraya Maha
Aminat

1. Th. Phokhi
2. Th. Puchong

Th. Anantanak

Soi Wat Borom

Nikrat

**Wat
Chamni
Hatthakan**

Mandir
ple

Soi Chulin

Ban Bat
Tr. Dok Mai
Tr. Ban Bat

S. D. Mai 1

Suan M
Suan Mali 3

Suan Mali 2

Th. Chal

Th. Khet 4

Huachiew
Hospital

Muang
Khet 1

Kasatsuk
Bridge

Kanchanawanit
Market

MANINAT

ons

Thanon Luang

Thanon Wora

Soi Thew

Worayat

Th. Ditsamak

Th.Chaloem Khet 2

Th.Chaloem Khet 3

Soi Yotsi

Yosse
Hospital

D   E

A
B

Soi Suandusit
Soi Sukhothai 1
Soi Sukhothai 3
Th. Sukothai
Soi Sukhothai 2
Soi Sukhothai 4
Soi Sukhothai 5
Thanon Sawankhalok
Thanon Rama VI
Soi 4
Soi 5
Soi Bun Chuai

PHAYA THAI

Thanon
Ratchawithi

Thanon

Soi Suan Ngen

Khlong Samsen

S. Phay

1

Chitralada
Palace

Sawankhalok

Prasat Neurological
Hospital

National Cancer
Institute

Ramathibodi
Hospital

Phramongkhut
Medical College

Phramongkhutklao
Hospital

School for
the Blind

Health Hygine
Centre

War Veterans
Organization

Ratchawithi

Mahidol
University

Research
Institute
of Medical
Science

Soi Wat Makog

S. Bandit

Wat Aphai
Thayaram

Anutsa
Chaisamo
(Victory M

Thanon Sri

Mahidol
University

Rama VI

Ministry of Sciences
Technology & Energy

Mineral
Research
Museum

Soi Senarak

Ratchawithi
Hospital

Children's
Hospital

2

Victory
Monument

Thai

Soi Lbet Panya

Soi Vai

Ayutthaya

Buddhist
Monk's
Hospital

Mahidol
University

Provost
Marshal
General Dept

RATCHA THEWI

Yothi

Thanon

Phaya

Soi Lbet Panya

Soi Luet Panya

3

Thanon Sawankhalok

Metropolitan
Police
Headquarters

Thanon

S. Chavarul

Soi Wiraya

Sri

Siam
City

Soi
Polait

Soi Sombun

Suan
Pakkad
Palace

Petchaburi 1

Rama VI

Yommarat
Market

Soi Man Sin 4

Soi Man Sin 3
Soi Man Sin 2
Soi Man Sin 1

Soi Petchaburi 5

Soi Petchaburi 7

Phaya Thai

S.Daeng Bunga

Soi Chamsai

Florida

Decha
Hospital

Soi Kolit

Soi 11

Soi Petchaburi 13

PRATU

S. 2

S. Uru-
phong 1

S. Uruphong 2

S. Uruphong 3

Thanon

Soi 3

Soi 4
Soi 6

S.D. Coliseum
Dept. Store

Petchaburi

Soi 10

S. Aram Si

S. Nom Chit

Darun Aman
Mosque

Soi
Senakit

Petchaburi
Market

Wongwian
Ratchathewi

Soi 9

Opera

Church of
Christ

Juldis
Tower

Center
Point

Wat
Phaya
Yang

Soi Rongrian Sudarak

Thanon Phaya Nak

S. Rongrian
King Phet

Soi 14

Soi 16

S. Phaya Nak

Asia Bldg

Asia

S.Worarit

Soi Petchaburi 12

Soi Petchaburi 18

First

S. 20

Panthip
Plaza

Soi 17

Soi 15

Soi 22

Soi 24

4

Thanon

0   400 m

0   400 yards

Khlong Saen Saep

Student
Christian
Centre

Ratchathewi

Jim Thompson
House Museum

Srapathum
Palace

A
B

Prachakhom Church

Thanon Mit Maitri

Thanon Mit Maitri 3

S. Phen Lae Phuen

inam Pao

hannel 5

Thanon Sa Nam Phao

Veterans General Hospital

Thanon Wiphawadirangsit

Soi Din Daeng

Thanon Mit Maitri 2

Din Daeng Sports Complex & Auditorium

HUAY KHWANG

Thanon Mit Maitri 1

Soi Santisuk

Soi Phra Nang

Soi Athiwimron

Soi Bun Chu Si

Soi Bun Chu

Soi Amnoarumit

Soi Ruamit

Thanon Prachasongkhro

S. Rongrian Chamnong

Uthawon Market

Asoke Din Daeng

Thanon

S. Rongrian Ratprasong

Thanon Asoke Din Daeng

Utai Thip

Ratchanukun Hospital

Phayathai Market

Soi Sutthiphon

Century Park

Soi Taladsawanich

Soi Wat Taphan

Soi Saeng

Soi Utai Thip

Soi Phrasat Saraban

Thanon Din Daeng 1

Takusluk

Soi Sutthiphon 1

Soi Thatsuwan

Soi Sutthiphon 2

Ratchaprarop

S. Attaphanorapha

Si Din Daeng Market

Soi Pracha Santi

Soi Thiamakon

Fatima Church

Soi Hemawong

Soi Mahawong Nua

Soi Khwanphatthana 1

Khwan Patthana Market

S. Bun Trarop

S. Ratchataphan

Bangkok Doll Factory & Museum

Soi Mortang

Soi Mae Phra Fatima

S. Thabsuwan

Soi Mana-wong Tai

kasan Market

Thanon

Khlong Samsen

Wongwian Makkasan

Chalerm

Maranakhon

Makkasan Railway Plant

Bung Makkasan

Soi Watthanawong

Makkasan Market

Makkasan Railway Station

Thanon

Nikhom

Makkasan

Hope of Bangkok Church

Soi 39

Soi 41

Soi Watthanasin

Bangkok Palace

Railway Hospital

Petchaburi

Metro D.S.

31

i Hasadin ermlap arket

Soi Chaurat

Soi 33

Soi Petchaburi 35

Soi 37

Expressway

New

TAT

Soi 36

Soi 29

Soi 27

Soi 25

Soi 23

S. 29

Soi Chitlom

Thanon

Petchaburi Hospital

Khlong Saen Saep

Soi Nana Nua

Petchaburi

Soi 30

Soi 32

Bangkok Nai Lert Park

A B

RATTANA-
KOSIN

SANAM
LUANG

Thanon

Charoen Krung

Thanon Thai Wang

Wat Po
(Wat Phra
Chettuphon)

Long
Krasuang
Market

HiFi

S. Wat
Phiphya
Tham

N

S. Wat Nak Klang

Thanon

Thanon

Th. Phra
Phiphit

Sanam

Th. Phra Phitak
Market

Tha Rong Mo

Th. Chettuphon

Chaeng

Tha
S. Tha
Tian

Alsadang

Ban

Si

Thanon Itsaraphap

42

S. Thanee, Khlong Wat
thaphIsek

Soi

Thanon Arun Amarin

Tha Tien

Tha Phru
Nokyung

Maharat

P

1

Soi 40

Soi Prok Wat Arun 3
S. Pr. Wat Arun 2

Wat Arun
(Temple of Dawn)

S. Setthakan

Chai

Pak Khlong Talad
(Flower Market)

Wat R
buranai
phe

Thanon Itsaraphap

S. Vutha
Sukda

S. Pr. Wat Arun 1
Prok
Wat Arun

Thanon Chakka-

Wang
Doem

Vichaiprasit
(Old Fort)

Tha Rajini

Coffee
Shop

Yot Phimai
Market

Phra
Buddha
Monum

Thanon

S. Wat Hong

Royal Navy
Headquarters

Phak
Khlong
Talad

Thanon Saphan

Phosamton
Market

Soi 38

Wat
Kalayanamit

Tha
Sapan Phut

Saphan Phra Buddha Yotfa
(Memorial Bridge)

Saphan Phra
Pok Klao

Phut

Soi 36

2

Soi 27

Soi 34

S. Wat Kanlaya

Santa Cruz
Church

W
Le

Thanon Itsaraphap 28

Soi 23

Soi 32

Soi 30

Soi Pho

S. Kudi Chin

Santa Cruz
Convent

Th. Thetsaban Sai 1

Wat Prayun-
wongsawat

Khlong Thon
Th. Bpang Mai

Chao Phraya 1

S. Somdet Phaya Mai

S. Somdet Char

Soi Itsaraphap 21

Thanon
Thetsaban
Sai 2

Thanon
Thetsaban Sai 2

Soi 26

Thanon Thetsaban Sai 3

Soi 19

Soi 17/1

Thonburi
Christian
Hall

Thanon

Thanon

Prachathipok

3

Soi Phet Kasem 4

Khlong Bangkok Yai

Soi 15

Thanon Itsaraphap

Soi 24
S. Monti

Soi 20

Soi 18

Soi 16

Soi 14

Soi 12

Soi 10S

Soi 8

Soi Somdet

Taj
Mahal

Soi 13

Soi 22

Soi 11

Thanon

Khlong Bang Sakai

Wat Yai
Si Suphan

Soi 9

Thanon

Soi 1/1

Soi 9

S. Chem Wian Suk 3

Soi Wat Yai S. Suphan

S. Khang Rong Rap
Chamnam

Soi Wiset San

Ra

S. Pongchit

Thanon

Phet Kasem

S. Chem Wian Suk 2

Soi Phet Kasem 2

S. S. Phom

S. Hiramuch

Tr. Saphan Luang

S. Khiai
Cunda

Mittraphab
Hospital

Central
D. S.

Thanon

Lad

Soi 1

S. S. Talad

Thanon Inthraraphitak

Bangyeerua
Market

S. 3

WONGWIAR

S. Saraphi 2

S. Lad

Taksin
Circle
Wongwian Yai
(King Taksin Mon.)

S. Saeng-
muang

S. Soi 2

Charoen
Rat Market

Soi 3

Charoen

Charoen

Thanon Thoet Thai

Soi Khlong
Wat Weluratchin

S. Phithaksin

Soi 3

Thanon

Soi 4

Soi Suthisuk

Soi Ratyinq
Charoen

Soi Talat

Sesaweech

Wongwian Yai
Railway Station

YAI

Soi 3

Soi 1

Tr. Yenchai
Wa

4

0   400 m

Suanphlu
Mosque

Soi 4

Soi 5

Tr.
Ratchawadt

Soi Ratruam
Charoen

0   400 yards

THONBURI

Soi 4/1

Soi 4

Soi T

Soi Saksin

S. Sanchao Arneaw

Soi 1

Tr. Nai
Thongbai

Tr. Manawitthaya

Soi 6

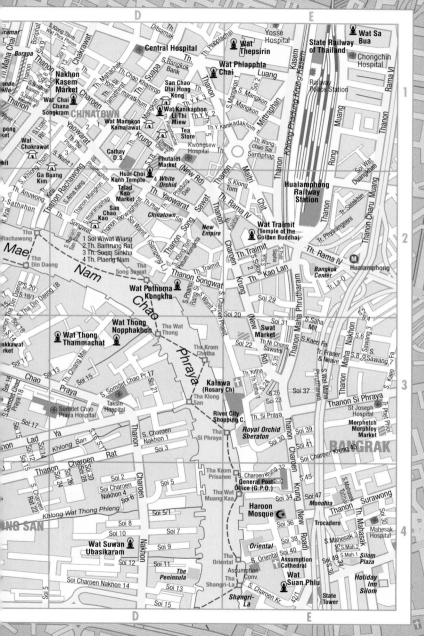

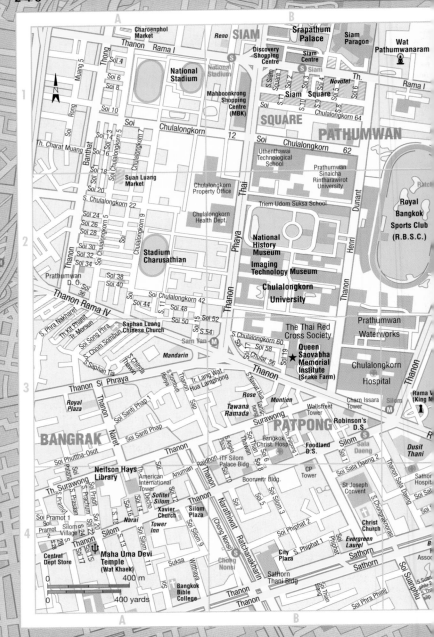

A **B**

Charoenphol Market

Thanon Rama I

SIAM

Reno

Srapathum Palace

Siam Paragon

Wat Pathumwanaram

Thong

Muang

Rong

Soi 4

Soi 6

Soi 8

Soi 10

National Stadium

National Stadium

Discovery Shopping Centre

Siam Centre

Th.

Rama I

Mahboonkrong Shopping Centre (MBK)

S. Siam Square 1

Soi 2

Soi 3

Soi 4

Novotel

Siam Square

Soi 5

Soi 6

Siam

Chulalongkorn 64

SQUARE

PATHUMWAN

Banthat

Th. Charat Muang

Chulalongkorn 5

Soi 14

Soi 16

Soi 18

Soi 20

Soi

Chulalongkorn

Chulalongkorn

12

Soi Chulalongkorn

Thai

Soi Chulalongkorn 62

Uthenthawai Technological School

Prathumwan Sinaicha Rintharawirot University

Suan Luang Market

Chulalongkorn Property Office

Chulalongkorn Health Dept.

Triem Udom Suksa School

S. Chulalongkorn 22

Soi 24

Soi 26

Soi 28

Soi 30

Soi 32

Soi 34

Chulalongkorn 5

Chulalongkorn 9

Phya

Thai

National History Museum

Imaging Technology Museum

Thanon

Prathumwan D.O.

Soi 38

Soi 40

Stadium Charusathian

Soi Chulalongkorn 42

Soi 44

Soi 48

Soi 11

Thanon

Chulalongkorn University

Henri Dunant

Thanon

Royal Bangkok Sports Club (R.B.S.C.)

Thanon Rama IV

Soi 52

Soi 15

Soi 50

S. Phra Nakharet

Th. Kit Phanit

Tr. Morsun

Saphan Luang Chinese Church

S. Song Phra

S. Chom Sombun

S. Saphan Tia

Mandarin

S.54

Sam Yan

S. Chulalongkorn 60

Soi 58

Soi 17

Chula. 56

The Thai Red Cross Society

Queen Saovabha Memorial Institute (Snake Farm)

Prathumwan Waterworks

Chulalongkorn Hospital

Thanon

Royal Plaza

Thanon Si Phraya

Thanon

S. Chinda Thewi

Sap

S. Symbun

Tr. Lang Wat Hua Lamphong

Rose

Tawana Ramada

Montien

Wallstreet Tower

Charn Issara Tower

Silom

Rama V (King M)

M

BANGRAK

Thanon

Naret

Thanon Si Phraya

Soi Santi Phap 1

Soi Santi Phap

Thanon

Surawong

PATPONG

Silom

Robinson's D.S.

Dusit Thani

Sala Daeng

M

Bangkok Christ. Hosp.

Foodland D.S.

Soi Phutta-Osot

Neilson Hays Library

American International Tower

Anuman

Raldhon

ITF Silom Palace Bldg

Soi 10

Boonmitr Bldg.

CP Tower

St Joseph Convent

Thanon Sala Daeng 2

Sathor Hospita

Th. Surawong

Soi Pramol

Soi Prasit

Soi Pradit

Soi 20

Soi Decho

Anuman

Thawan

Soi 6

Soi Pipat

Soi 4

Soi Silom

Thanon Sala Daeng 2

S. Chonnakrorasi

Sofitel Silom

Xavier Church

Narai

Silom Plaza

Thanon

Narathiwat Ratchanakharin

Soi 7

Soi Silom 3

Christ Church

Soi Pramot 1

Soi Pramot

Silom Village

Soi 24

Soi 22

Soi 18

Soi 16

Tower Inn

Silom

Soi Silom 9

Chong Nonsi

Soi Phiphat 2

S. Phiphat 1

Soi Phiphat

Evergreen Laurel

Central Dept Store

Thanon

Soi 15

Soi 17

Maha Uma Devi Temple (Wat Khaek)

Suksa

Withaya

City Plaza

Sathorn

Sathorn

Soi Suanphlu

Assoc

400 m

Chong Nonsi

Bangkok Bible College

Thanon

Sathorn Thani Bldg

Sathorn

Soi Phra Phinit

400 yards

Thanon

A **B**

Robinson D.S.
Thai Daimaru D.S.
Siam Pen House IV
Holiday Inn Bangkok
Intercontinental Bangkok
Maneeya Center D.S.
Soi Chitlom
Bangkok Nai Lert Park
Soi Tonson
Withayu
Loet
31
Bank of America Building
Ploenchit Arcade S.C.
Central D.S.
Thanon Ploenchit
Mahatun Plaza S.C.
Ploen Chit
Plaza Athenee
Soi Nai
Soi Sukhumvit 1
Soi Ruen Rudi 1
Soi Sukhumvit 3
Bamrungrat Hospital
Grace
Soi 5
SUKHUMVIT
Amari Boulevard
Seth Insaf Tower
Soi Sukhumvit 15
Shiva Tower
Ambassador
Soi 13
Thanon
Nana
Soi Sukhumvit
Soi Sukhumvit 11
Landmark Plaza
Shopping
Somerset
Honey
Tourist Shopping Plaza
Rajah
Jai Smarn Church
Thanon Sukhumvit
Area
Westin
All Seasons Place
Conrad
Soi 1
Soi Ruam Rudi
Soi 2
Soi Sukhumvit 4
SNC Tower
Sunstar Complex
Omni Complex
Orchid Tower
Soi 10
Golden Tower
Sheraton Grande Sukhumvit
Soi 12
Wireless Road
Soi Tonson
Suan
Lang 1
Lang 2
Lang 3
Soi Lang Suan 1
Soi Lang Suan 2
Soi Lang Suan 3
Soi Lang Suan 4
Soi Lang Suan 5
Soi Lang Suan 6
Soi Lang Suan 7
Chalerm
Soi 3
Soi 4
Soi Ruam Rudi 2
Calvary Baptist Church
Soi Ulit
Soi Sama Han
Soi Sukhumvit 8
Evangelical Church
Sarasin
S. Ruam Rudi
Soi 5
Holy Redeemer Church
Khlong Phai Singto
SUAN
NI
Withayu
Soi Sanam Khli
S. Phra Chen
Mahanakhon
Thailand
Tobacco
Monopoly
(under
redevelopment)
KHLONG TOEY
LUMPHINI
Thanon
Suan Lum Night Bazaar
Cathay Trust Bldg
Nua
Tai
YCA
JUSMAG
Thai-Belgium Bridge
Thanon
Lumphini
Goethe Institute
Goethegasse
S. Plukchit 2
S. Plukchit
Saphandam Market
31
Expressway
Queen Sirikit National Convention Centre
SOI NGAM
Malaysia
DUPHLI
Soi Nantha
Bhirasri Institute of Modern Art
Soi Atthakan
Prasit
Soi Ngam
Soi Saphankhu
Duphli
Rama IV
Soi Sawansawat
Soi Phyaphiren
Ruam Chitt Church
Khlong Toey
Soi San Chao
Soi Ngam
Soi S. Rong
Thanon Rama IV

STREET INDEX

GENERAL INDEX

Bangkok Skytrain and Metro

Bang Sue

Chatuchak Park

M10 N8 MO CHIT

Kamphaeng Phet

Phahon Yothin

Lat Phrao

Ratchadaphisek

Th. Lat Phrao

Saphan Khwai

N6

Ari **N5**

Sanam Pao **N4**

Sutthisan

Huai Khwang

Thailand Cultural Center

Th. Sutthisan Winitchai

Th. Wiphawadirangsit

Th. Phahon Yothin

Th. Ratchadaphisek

Th. Pracha Uthit

Pradiphat

Thanon Therd Damri

Thanon

Th. Pracharaj

Chao Phraya